ESSAYS & ADDRESSES
ON THE
PHILOSOPHY *of* RELIGION
FIRST SERIES

BY
BARON FRIEDRICH VON HÜGEL,
LL.D., D.D.

LONDON
J. M. DENT & SONS LTD.
NEW YORK: E. P. DUTTON & CO. INC.

All rights reserved
Made in Great Britain
at the
Aldine Press · Letchworth · Herts
for
J. M. DENT & SONS LTD
Aldine House · Bedford Street · London
First published 1921
Last reprinted 1963

TO THE IMMORTAL MEMORY OF

DANTE,

WHO DIED SIX HUNDRED YEARS AGO TO-DAY,
IN LIVELY GRATITUDE FOR INSPIRATION AND SUPPORT
THROUGHOUT SOME SIXTY YEARS OF SPIRITUAL STRESS,
FROM THE WRITER, HIS FELLOW FLORENTINE.

September 14th, 1921.

PREFACE

The following collection of some dozen papers arose in a very simple way. About half of these essays, ever since their several appearances in print, have been a good deal sought after. Hence I have thought it well, pending the re-issue of my *Mystical Element of Religion* and the completion and publication of a new large work on religious fundamentals, to publish in book-form, from amongst my accumulated papers, such studies as appear to possess some abiding interest.

One of the papers given here (as No. 3) has already appeared in a collective volume of essays ; and Nos. 2, 3, 6, 9 have previously been published in magazines. But four papers (Nos. 1, 4, 5, and 10) are quite new to print. Yet all the papers were written, in part also spoken, at the invitation of single persons or of societies ; and all have benefited by questions and criticisms raised on occasion of their first communication. They have thus had some good chances of a certain maturity. There is, assuredly, not a paper here which does not raise more questions than it solves ; nor a piece which could not be improved considerably even by myself. But life is short at sixty-nine, and my remaining strength is required for larger tasks. Also such freshness as these essays may possess would doubtless largely fade away in the process of any considerable re-writing of them. I have, then, restricted myself simply to the formal improvement of my texts, especially in the second Troeltsch article, and to the silent withdrawal or correction of some half-dozen errors of fact. Perhaps the chief formal defect now remaining is a certain repetition. But this I trust may help to drive home one or the other conviction which might otherwise fail to impress the reader.

The Roman Church congregations hold a valuable distinction between the private intention of a writer and the public meaning of his writings. The intention of the writer, what he meant to say, is known in full to God alone and at all adequately only to the writer himself. The meaning of the writings, what as a matter of fact they say, falls outside the jurisdiction of the writer. Not the writer, but the competent and careful students of the writings, decide, in the long run, upon the significance (both as to meaning and as to worth) of any literary production, now become an entity possessed of a life, influence and meaning of its own. Juvenal intended to write poetry, and thought he had written poetry ; mankind has decided that what he wrote is not poetry but splendid rhetoric. Dr. Johnson thought that his tragedy *Irene* was his masterpiece ; the unanimous verdict of some six competent judges settled the question to the contrary, on the very night of the first production of the play, and this also for the heroically docile great doctor himself. And a scholarly parish priest in the Black Forest told me, out there, years ago, how, in the winter-time, he had only one University trained parishioner who could help him a little with his manuscripts— a Government forester. He, the priest, had submitted to this forester an elaborate refutation of von Hartmann's *Philosophy of the Unconscious.* The forester studied the manuscript long and minutely ; and then returned it with the words : " Admirable ! so thorough, so clear ! But on which side of the argument are you yourself, Herr Pfarrer ? " I cannot turn these poor papers into rich and living wisdom, if they are but thin and dead elucubrations. I cannot even mould them into the best that I have written. But I can try and make more clear perhaps here than in the essays themselves—in writings of various dates and very various occasions—what I have mainly intended to transmit and to illustrate. I will, then, first point out certain convictions which constitute the centres of the several sections ; and I will afterwards attempt to mark what it is that specially holds the three sections together—what, I trust, gives a certain definite and stimulating character to the book as a whole.

In Section I., concerning Religion in General and Theism, the twin papers numbered two strive specially to bring out the always double apprehension, feeling, conviction at work in every

specifically religious act and state.   There is the sense of a
Reality not merely human—of a real experience of this Reality;
and there is, at the same time, the sense that this real experience
is imperfect, that it is not co-extensive with the Reality experienced, that it does not exhaust that Reality.   Nowhere, at no   *exist.*
time, does the apprehending soul, if at a stage of fairly full
religious awareness, identify the apprehension, however real
this apprehension may appear to this soul, with the Reality
apprehended.   We have here a strong presumption in favour of
the fundamental sanity and of the evidential worth of the   *all*
religious apprehension in general and we thus ascertain a fact,   *space.*
characteristic of religion in all its stages, which we should
never forget.

    In Paper No. 3 I have striven to make clear how slow and
how difficult at one time, how swift and how spontaneous at
another time, how intermittent and how rarely simply abreast
of the growths in the other insights—artistic, social, even moral
—are the gifts and the growths of the fuller religious insights
and forces of man in his long past ; and how costly will doubtless always remain, in man's earthly future, the maintenance,
and still more the further deepening, of these insights or revelations.   Especially have I striven to discriminate between the
directly religious insights, with the occasions and the pace of
their growth, and the apprehensions primarily ethical and
political, with the circumstances and the rate of their development.   Thus especially the temper, the very idea, of toleration
have developed only tardily : there have existed true Saints of
God, genuine reformers of religion, who were without the temper
or idea of toleration.   Thus King Josiah indeed saved the Old
Testament faith and morals, (the highest then extant upon earth
and the eventual root and *nidus* of Christianity) from irretrievable
dissolution in Canaanitish superstition and impurity, but he did
so by slaughtering, say, a thousand priests of the High Places
and was nerved to so doing by the most complete belief that God
Himself demanded this slaughter from him.   True, Our Lord
rebuked the vindictive zeal of His apostles, based though it was
upon the precedent of the great prophet Elijah who called down
fire from Heaven upon the worshippers of Baal ; and by this
reproof Jesus condemned religious persecution.   And indeed the

*

Christian Church, for well over the first three centuries of her existence, left all the killing to her persecutors and herself persisted and prevailed " not by killing but by dying." Nevertheless, we shall do well, I think, not to deny that even the persecutions tolerated or encouraged by later Church authorities, have contributed, in certain times and places, to the real consolidation of Christendom. And especially we shall be wise if we do not insist upon any sense, innate in all human hearts, of the essential heinousness of all persecution.

And in Paper No. 4 I have attempted to show how the reality of Evil is beyond any direct explanation by anyone—the true state of affairs here is not that believers can explain and that unbelievers cannot explain, still less that Christians cannot explain but that sceptics can. No : but that Christianity does, if something other, yet something more than explain Evil. Christianity has immensely increased the range and depth of our insight as to Evil ; and, at the same time, Christianity alone has given man the motives and the power not only to trust on, unshaken, in the spiritual sun, in God, in spite of these sun spots of Evil, but to transform Evil into an instrument of Good.

In Section II., concerning the Teaching of Jesus and Christianity in General, Paper No. 5 finds that Christ and His Religious Inerrancy occupy a position towards the fact of the belief in the Proximity of His Second Coming (the *Parousia*) strikingly similar to the position occupied by God and His Perfect Goodness towards the fact of Evil present throughout the ages and places of man's earthly existence. Evil is an undeniable reality in the world at large, and the *Parousia* really existed as a primitive Christian belief. The more ancient is a New Testament document, the more clearly does it announce, or the more intimately does it imply, such a keen expectation of a Proximate Second Coming of Christ ; indeed the Synoptic Gospels report words of Our Lord Himself, of a lapidary emphasis, which His hearers evidently took in the same sense. I have ventured here to study this difficult question, because, although, as with the problem of Evil, I do not know any direct and simple solution of it, yet I stoutly believe in the solidity of the delimitations and of the utilisations proposed, and that the full and vivid, operative faith in Jesus Christ, the Way, the Truth and the Life, remain as genuinely grounded in reason and as entirely possible to feeling, after recognition of the facts concerned with the *Parousia*, as does the faith in God, the all powerful and all good, remain well grounded and entirely possible, in full confrontation of the still wider and deeper facts concerning Evil.

Then the Papers Nos. 5–7 insist upon Nature and Super-nature, as two distinct and different kinds of Good, in a manner which may show how much all thoughtful moderns have still to learn from the Golden Middle Age. For myself I do not doubt that a strong and steady revival of a religious mentality amongst cultivated men largely depends upon a renewed grasp of this immensely resourceful outlook.

Again, there is, in Paper No. 7, the discrimination between Perfect and Imperfect Freedom, and the conviction that the possibility of Evil arises, not from Freedom as such, but from the Imperfection of the human kind of freedom—the liberty of Choice. Quite a number of my younger High Anglican friends have on this point, with the best of motives, sacrificed, I believe, the deeper insight to the pressure of popular apologetic. In the long run, however, the more difficult view, if indeed it be the truer, will undoubtedly prevail.

And finally, this same Paper No. 7 insists upon the Abiding Consequences of certain full and persistent self-determinations of the soul—a doctrine, which I am, of course, well aware to be in acute conflict with the trend of thought and feeling now largely represented even, perhaps indeed especially, amongst otherwise Catholic-minded High Anglicans. Yet here again I do not doubt that, not such easier, apologetically inspired views, but the older and sterner, yet also really richer and deeper convictions, spring from religion, especially from Christianity, at the flood-tide of their experiences. In any case it may be of use to some readers to have clearly before them the formidable —I myself believe, the hopeless—task which confronts those who would retain the spiritual teaching of Jesus, as indeed still the standard and ideal of our outlook, and who yet would reject all Abiding Consequences.

And in the Third Section, which concerns the Church and Catholicism, there are three convictions especially dear to me.

There is, chiefly in Paper No. 10, the doctrines of Institutions —that men, at large and upon the whole, attain, in and through the Here and Now of History, to God the Omnipresent and Eternal. Thus Society, Sense, Sacraments, Successiveness are found, in very various degrees and kinds of adequacy, authority and fruitfulness, to accompany the several religions, not as mere accidents, still less as perverse accretions, but, in their substance, as part and parcel of the essence of religion itself, wheresoever this essence is able fully to expand and where men sufficiently unravel the implications and needs of this essence. From the vague or crude semi-magical rites of savage, or at least of still polytheistic, races on to the precisions and elaborations of the Jewish Temple services and then, and above all, to the sober, delicately spiritual sacraments of the Christian and Catholic Church, we find some such sensible occasions and vehicles of spirit. Things these which, at their best, rightly claim great religious personalities as their initiators or transmitters, yet which also correspond to a general human need, especially when and where Supernatural Grace awakens and exalts Nature to needs and achievements beyond its own scope and powers.

Then there is the conviction, specially prominent in Papers Nos. 8 and 10, as to the necessity, for all fruitful human life, and especially for all powerful religious life amongst men here below, of friction, tension, rivalry, mutual help and mutual supplementation, between this religious life and man's other powers, opportunities, needs, tasks, environments ; and, on the other hand, as to the persistent danger (amongst us men so readily exclusive and so easily obsessed by fixed ideas) of working religion in such a way as to remove from its path, as far as ever possible, any and all of these frictions which in reality are essentially necessary to its own force and fruitfulness. I believe this tendency to self-starvation to be the one ultimate difficulty of the Church and to remain as grave an antinomy for the practical life, as truly only capable of limitation, not of sheer removal, as are the antinomies for the intellect of God and Evil and of Christ and the *Parousia*. I know of no other religious difficulties truly comparable, in subtle penetration and in breadth of range, to these three massive facts and seeming deadlocks.

And the third conviction springs readily from the other two.

It sees in the world of human beings more folly and weakness than perverse power and malignity ; and especially does it see there many fragments of truth and goodness and few wholes. *truth*

The fragments of truth and goodness, where they subsist in good faith with regard to fuller truth and goodness, can already, in their degree and way, be of touching beauty and of real worth— of value, also to the opponents of those who hold these frag- ments.   With regard to non-Christian religions and as to how fervent Christians can respect these religions at their best, I love to think of Cardinal de Lavigerie, the zealous Missionary Archbishop—of his alighting from his carriage and proceeding on foot past such Mosques as he happened to pass in his Algerian Diocese.   And with regard to Christians not in communion with the Roman Catholic Church, I gratefully sympathise with Cardinal Manning who spontaneously and persistently com- bined the liveliest possible conviction as to the supreme powers and universal rights of the Catholic Roman Church with a deep and steady recognition of the definitely supernatural faith and virtue of home upon home of Anglicans well known to himself.

If the reader will now take as one whole the three Sections of this book, he will find, I believe, that all are equally penetrated by an ultimate mental and spiritual conviction and habit which the writer has never ceased, now for fifty years, wistfully to find to be somehow rare amongst his fellow-men, even amongst those who are sincerely religious.   There runs here throughout every- thing the sense that Religion, even more than all other convictions *rel* that claim correspondence with the real, begins and proceeds and ends with the Given—with existences, realities, which environ *epists* and penetrate us, and which we have always anew to capture and to combine, to fathom and to apprehend ; all this, how- ever, neither as springing from scepticism nor as leading to it, but, on the contrary, as stimulated and sustained by a tenacious conviction that a real, if dim, " confused " knowledge of reality is with us already prior to all our attempts clearly to analyse or completely to synthesise it.   Now Religion has, for many a century and upon the whole very fruitfully, been discriminated into Natural Religion and Supernatural Religion.   They have both been recognised as two kinds, however distinct, of Religion

—of a habit and conviction of the human soul occasioned or given by but one God in or to this one soul. But the fact that both kinds are, ultimately, Given has tended to be forgotten over the difference in the Givenness. Natural Religion awakes when the human soul, endowed, by its very humanity, with certain religious capacities, comes into conscious contact with the beauties and interdependences of external nature and with the honesties and decencies of human life. The natural religious apprehension and feeling which are thus aroused, and the natural and human happenings which arouse them, are both given; and those interior capacities require the impact of these exterior existences for the two together to render possible an act or habit of religious faith—in this case, of faith of the natural kind. Similarly, Supernatural Religion awakes if and where the human soul has, by Supernatural Grace, been enlarged and raised beyond its natural capacities and natural desires, and if this same soul is presented with facts, actions, realities of a supernatural kind. Here again, both the supernatural religious apprehension and feeling thus aroused, and the supernatural, superhuman events and existences which arouse them, are given; and the two givennesses each require the other, if there is to be, here, the possibility of an act or habit of religious faith, now of the supernatural kind. It is, however, certain that the dispensation under which we men actually live, is not a dispensation of Simple Nature, but a dispensation of Mingled Nature and Supernature, so that the acts and habits specially characteristic of man consist of apprehensions, feelings, convictions, volitions which indeed possess a natural substratum and a natural material, but which have been more or less widened, raised and transformed (or at the soul's worst, have been deflected and perturbed) by supernatural facts, insights and volitions positive or negative. In geological language we have here, not a Sedimentary, nor a Plutonic, but a Metamorphic formation.

There exists unanimity amongst thinkers on religion, as to the appropriate treatment of Supernatural Religion. Such Supernatural Revealed Religion is always described and analysed as an Historical Givenness—as an extant Reality to be studied with the greatest possible sympathy and in the greatest detail. The calling back to life of the Sunnemitess's son by Elishah—

the prophet's eyes upon the lad's eyes, his mouth upon the lad's mouth—is a noble symbol for such patient evocation, in cases where the religion studied has completely disappeared. Yet the greatest of the religions are still alive, in our midst; and here the difficulties of a right apprehension spring in part from this very proximity—from our having to know well the movements of our own, or of our living fellows' minds, hearts and wills. Yet both for the vanished and for the still flourishing historical religions a cautious sympathetic analysis—roughly speaking, an inductive method—is recognised alone to be in place. But the unanimity ceases when we reach Natural Religion. Here the deductive method has reigned long and very widely, and still largely persists amongst those more specially influenced by the Scholastic tradition.

The earlier, Patristic tradition divided these two kinds of religion much less sharply and found in all religion predominantly the Given. The Fathers, upon the whole, attempted to penetrate both realms by much the same methods of experience and analysis. I have, as regards method, largely reverted to the Patristic treatment. Yet as to the conception of the content, the subject-matter of religious philosophy, my attraction is very consciously rather Scholastic than Patristic, Aquinas rather than Augustine. I believe that the Golden Middle Age markedly deepened the apprehension of man as he is, and of man's religion as it ought to be, by putting in the fundamental place, not even Sin and Redemption, but Nature and Supernature. Man is here found, not primarily wicked, but primarily weak; and man here requires, even more than to be ransomed from his sins, to be strengthened in his weakness—indeed to be raised to a new, a supernatural, level and kind of motives, actions, habits, achievements and beatitudes. But here in Aquinas the continuous all-round dependence of the soul upon Grace and upon Prayer is as fully emphasised and required as ever it is by Augustine. We are in Aquinas as little Pelagian as we are in Augustine, whilst with the balanced Norman Italian we entirely escape Gnosticism—that Gnosticism which the vehement African Roman at times dangerously grazes.

The point on which we require more than either Augustine or Aquinas gave or could give mankind is especially History—

the Historic sense. As to this point, I trust that not a line printed within these covers but is steeped in this sense of Conditions, Growth, Contingencies. And yet also that these same writings will reveal a deep apprehension of the Unconditioned, the Abiding, the Absolute—of our need and of our certitude of these ; and especially also of Christianity as the original awakener of the deeper Historic sense, and of our reaching the Superhistoric within it. Nothing indeed is more striking than the perennial affinity between Christianity and History—that History of which indeed Christianity has itself furnished so central a part. Certainly the religion of the Incarnation will be able consistently to despise Happenings, however lowly, and the study of Happenings, however minute, only if and when it does not sufficiently realise its own abiding implications and requirements, its rootedness in the Childhood at Nazareth and in the Cross on Calvary.

Indeed we attain to a great general simplification of these at first sight complicated questions as to Natural and Supernatural Religion and as to the methods of study appropriate to each severally or to both conjointly, when once we have come fully to grasp the two great facts which, in real life, conjointly produce the problem and explain its existence and character. In actual life Natural or Rational Religion or Pure Theism exists as the mirage after the setting, or as the dawn before the rising, of an Historical Religion. And such Historical Religion always claims to be, not Rational but Revelational, and not Natural but Supernatural ; and such a Religion is never purely Theistic, but always clings also to a Prophet or Revealer of God and to a Community which adores God and worships the Revealer. And again in real life Natural Religion exists as a set or as a system of propositions effected by philosophers who, in spite of their frequent disdain of all Sects and Churches, derive both their materials and their understanding of these materials from these despised positive teachings and historical traditions. And beside those rudiments of the positive religions and these abstractions from the positive religions there exists no such thing, in actual life, as a Natural, Philosophical Religion. Thus the three Sections of this book in reality concern, not three levels or constituents of religion which anywhere actually exist, in a stable and flourishing condition, separately the one from the other. Certainly we have here studied God and the Revealer and the Community each in their most perfect and their purest manifestations. Yet here no less than in the lower forms of actual religion, these three facts and the beliefs in them, do not exist and operate separately, but conjointly and with an intimate interpenetration. And this trinity in Unity is a whole given to us for our study which, as with all other Givennesses, cannot but be, at least predominantly, analytic and inductive in its character.

There only remains the pleasant duty of thanks to the several Editors, from whose book or reviews most of the papers have been taken, for kind permission to reproduce these papers here. I have thus to thank Mr. G. S. R. Mead for permission to reprint the two papers from the *Quest* given here as No. 2; Mr. F. S. Marvin and Mr. Humphrey Milford for a similar permission to reprint from *Progress and History* the paper given here as No. 3; Canon Arthur G. Headlam, for a like permission as to Nos. 5 and 7, reprinted from the *Church Quarterly Review*; Mr. Silas McBee, as regards No. 6, reprinted from the *Constructive Quarterly*, of New York; the Rev. W. B. Trevelyan, as to No. 8, reprinted from a *Liddon House Occasional Paper*; Mr. Robert Scott, as to No. 9, reprinted from the *Homiletic Review* of New York; and the Rev. Henry D. A. Major, as to No. 11, reprinted from the *Modern Churchman*. I have also to thank the lady to whom my Paper No. 4 was addressed, for leave to print that letter here; and the Rev. Tissington Tatlow and Bishop Hamilton Baynes for allowing me to announce the occasions on which the Addresses Nos. 1 and 10, and the Address No. 5 were respectively delivered.

And my gratitude is especially due to the helpful support and alert criticism of my two close friends Professors Norman Kemp Smith and Edmund G. Gardner, in matters of the selection of the Papers, the title of the book, and even of the constitution of the text, with several corrections of errors of fact. Yet I remain alone responsible for whatsoever here appears. I have also to thank the same kind friend who helped me with the proofs of my three previous works for similar valuable help on this occasion.

Once again I commend what I have written especially to those who attempt to combine a faithful practice of religion with an historical analysis and a philosophical presentation of it ; and I submit also this collection, the fruit of analogous endeavours, to the judgment of the Catholic Church.

FRIEDRICH von HÜGEL.

KENSINGTON, *September*, 1921.

CONTENTS

I

PAPERS ON RELIGION IN GENERAL AND THEISM

1

RESPONSIBILITY IN RELIGIOUS BELIEF [1]

SOME thirty years ago a saintly French Cleric was telling
me his recent experiences at the death-bed of a Positivist of
European renown. The man was in his seventies, and for a
full half century had organised and systematised the most
aggressively negative of the followers and of the teachings of
Auguste Comte—teachings which reduce all religion to purely
human realities taken for more than human by a sheer mirage *Li três*
of the human mind. The cleric in question was then in his middle
forties, a man of the finest mental gifts and training, and a soul
of the deepest spirituality. He had been sitting, at the express
invitation of the Positivist leader, almost daily for three months
by the sick man, and had kept a most careful diary of all and
everything from day to day. Nothing could be more emphatic
than were this Cleric's convictions that this Positivist had, three
months before he called in this Abbé, been touched by a most
real divine grace. A sudden, intense, persistent pain had then
awakened in this philosopher's heart, without any doing of his
own, a pain which, during the first three months, he had not
succeeded in driving away as morbid, or in explaining away
as an illusion. The pain was a pain for all the Sins—this term
alone was adequate—the Sins of his entire past life. Again
this same cleric had come to know, from the Positivist himself
during the remaining three months of his life, the general
interior history of his long past and the sort of acts which now
so much pained him ; and this Cleric could not but marvel at
the innocence (according to ordinary standards) of a life adulated
from youth upwards and which, until these past three months,
had remained without misgivings as to the truth, the unanswer-

---

[1] A Paper read before the Secretaries of the British branches of the Christian
Student Movement, March, 1920.

ableness, the necessity and the duty, of its intensive, propagandist unbelief. The Positivist died, now explicitly sure of two things —that the pain was no fancy, but, on the contrary, the most genuine of intimations, the most real effect of realities and forces ignored by himself up to now; and again, that he was not going to cease in death, but, on the contrary, would then see the realities and forces of which he was now experiencing this effect. Still worshipped by the few whom he still admitted to his presence, with half a century of intense virile labour and rare moral purity behind him, he was now dying broken-hearted (his own words), prostrate at the foot of that great altar stair of real experiences which was now leading him back to the God from whom they came. On the last day of his life his devotedly Catholic wife, seeing death on his face, asked him whether he would like to be baptised (his militantly unbelieving parents had opposed all such " superstition ") and he answered he would ; he was consequently baptised shortly before he entered upon unconsciousness. But to the end this Positivist, if asked to affirm the Church, or Christ, or even simply God, would answer, " pray do not press me ; not yet, not yet." Apparently, then, a man can be in good faith, at least for many years, in the denial of even the very rudiments of Theism.

Some three years ago I was listening to the account, by a scholarly young High Anglican Cleric, of his recent experiences in an English Officers' hospital during the great war. Many of these officers, young and middle-aged, had met his religious advances, however elementary and tentative—they were all nominally Anglican—with a seemingly prompt, frank and manly repudiation, and with a confident and apparently spontaneous distinction between any and every creed and dogma, as the affairs of a paid clergy and of dreamy bookworms, and a pure life, as what alone mattered. The Chaplain, much as he regretted this refusal of all creed and dogma, still, for something like a year, I think, persisted in thanks to God for this recognition and practice of purity. But at last, one day he came upon one of these very officers, in the act of some grave impurity. Upon the Chaplain upbraiding him, not only for this impurity, but for the long deceit this officer had practised upon him, the officer turned upon the Chaplain, again with that confident and apparently

spontaneous manner, and said : " There now, once more I catch
you out as the artificial paid Cleric, the man who *will* insist
upon the obligation of what is far-fetched and unnatural, and
who *will* be shocked at the like of this. I do nothing but what
nature prompts me to do." Here we cannot but feel that men
can be hardened in bad faith, and this with regard to the most
fundamental facts and principles of the most elementary moral
life.

We all of us, in various degrees and ways, even directly from
the history of our own souls, can readily add further instances to
the two great facts, currents, laws of real life, just illustrated—the
amazing innocences and the no less amazing corruptions of our
poor human minds and wills. But let us now press these great
general facts so as to reach some five large discriminations and
deep maxims, helps towards a right attitude and action in these
very delicate, yet also very important, matters of real life.

I

Our first discrimination is quite preliminary, but none the
less important ; it clears up a confusion very general in our days,
and, with it, a perennial source of indifference. We shrink increasingly—upon the whole rightly, I think,—from attributing
bad faith, or impure life, or selfish motives, to those who differ
from us however largely, short of clear demonstration of the
presence and operation within these persons of such debasing
influences. But this right and proper suspension of judgment
leads with ease to the assumption that we ourselves and others
are, all and always and entirely, in good faith and in the earnest
search and practice of the light. We thus soon come to see around
us a world constituted of countless intelligences and wills, each
as true and strong as, there and then, it is capable of being ; they
are all, so far, equally good—there is no difference either between
the goodness of the one and the goodness of the other, or between
the actual goodness and the possible goodness of any one of
them. But thus we not only fly in the face of, and we rapidly
weaken, the sense of folly, weakness, sin, as very real facts in
our own life and in all human history : we even (and this is my

momentary point) ignore and weaken a still more undeniable set of facts and of awarenesses. I mean that we thus sophisticate our sense of the deep importance of any and every increase of accurate, adequate insight and power, whether or no we be responsible, innocent or guilty, as regards our possession of more or less of these things. Who blames a Hottentot for not knowing Greek ? Yet a full hold of Greek means power for any mind. Who condemns Birkett Foster for not being Turner ? Yet Turner is a genius of the first water, Foster a worthy little stippling talent. So with Milton and Eliza Cook : " I would not burn a man," says Matthew Arnold, " who prefers Eliza Cook to Milton ; nevertheless Milton is greater than Eliza Cook." Much the greater part in the education of a people and in the training of individual souls, and a very large proportion of the immense value of such education and training, is quite independent of any moral blame attaching to such a people or such an individual, or of any moral praise due to their educators. Malaria has ravaged Greece for now some five centuries ; this has been a curse for the country, even if no one was to blame for it. Malaria can now be eradicated there within ten years ; this would be an immense blessing, even if the men who brought this blessing were not more virtuous men than are the malarial Greeks.

If we would keep this preliminary discrimination quite clear and fully active, we must cultivate a vivid sense of the difference between impartiality and neutrality, and we must beware against assuming that God, the one author of any two souls, will have endowed them with an equal depth and range of spiritual insight and of religious call. We do not require to be on our guard against similar errors with regard to the body. I meet two soldiers on my walk, both apparently thoroughly good fellows, and certainly both children of the same God ; the one possesses both his legs, the other retains only one leg. I am here in no danger of declaring the possession of one leg to be equal to the possession of two legs ; and, in frankly recognising this serious inequality, I do not deserve the charge of bigotry or Pharisaicalness. Dr. J. N. Farquhar, in his fine *Crown of Hindooism*, has admirably discriminated throughout against two erroneous extremes in favour of the true mean amongst

the three positions possible for us towards the several religions
of the world. Neither, Dr. Farquhar insists, is any one religion
alone true, in the sense that all the others are merely so much
sheer error ; nor, again, are they all equally true ; but, whilst
all contain *some* truth, they not only differ each from the other
in the points on which they are true, but also in the amount and
importance of the truth and power thus possessed. Not the
neutrality which would stand equally outside and above these
very unequal different religions, and which would level them
down to the constituent common to them all, is what is truly
fair and really sympathetic. A much more difficult, a never
completed task is alone adequate here—the impartiality which
takes sides, not in prejudice and with only imperfect, exterior
knowledge, but which does so according to the respective real
content and objective worth of the several religions, as these
have been ascertained after long, docile study and close sympathetic observation of the devotees of these religions. This
would constitute an attempt to level up,—it would mean an
endeavour gradually to constitute a great ascending scale of
religious values and of their several increasingly adequate
representatives. In such a scheme we can, and ought, clearly
to declare, say, the Sikh religion (in its pristine purity) to stand
higher than unreformed Hindooism, and Christianity to be
fuller and deeper than the Judaism it sprang from ; and all this,
without any reasonable suspicion of partiality and narrow-
mindedness. And the advantages of one religion over another,
and the recognition of these advantages would be well grounded
and of great importance, even if no sin whatsoever were reasonably chargeable against Hindoos and Jews.

II

Passing on now to the question of accountableness, of responsibility in matters of religious belief, we shall do well to
acquire and to maintain reality and richness of insight into the
matter, by a vivid apprehension of the three great fundamental
facts and conditions of man's spiritual life, indeed, of human
existence generally. This will furnish us with our second, third

and fourth discrimination—discriminations, these, in the very
thick of our subject.

Here then, we are first busy with what lies below and up to all
specifically human acts and lives, although this lower range of
life furnishes the prerequisites, materials, occasions, stimulations,
frictions, limitations to these specifically human acts in countless
most subtle ways. We here find man to be a creature with an
existence ranging from the lowliest properties, functions and
impulsions of the animal, indeed of the plant and mineral, up
to lofty mental processes and needs ; and from lowly instinctive
apprehensions of similar existences of the mineral, plant and
animal kind, up to mental and spiritual recognition of, and
fellowship with his fellow-men, even though these men live now
at the Antipodes or have disappeared from this planet three
thousand and more years ago. We here discover that even the
average humanity of man, even man's bread-winning, law-
abiding, tax paying, newspaper-reading, activities all involve,
at every step, a self-discipline, a renunciation of animal impulses,
which it has taken this individual man some twenty years of
physical and mental growth, of psychic check and of moral
docility to acquire, all under the influence of a human civilisation
of some twice twenty centuries at least. And the acquisition
and retention of even a little of such self-discipline involves
responsibility, lapses, sin, for so long as the man lives upon this
earth. No sane mind seriously denies that this is so, with man's
citizen life and with his natural virtues. Why then should we
deny it, with regard to man's supernatural, heroic and spiritual
life ? Is it that self-restraint is necessary, if we would at all
times give twelve genuine coppers for one genuine shilling,
but that self-discipline is not necessary, if we would at all times
wish well to those who wish us ill ? And is a long self-training
necessary for acquiring a steady conviction that " honesty is
the best policy," but no self-discipline necessary for gaining or
retaining the insight that " blessed are the pure of heart, for
they shall see God " ? The fact of the matter is, of course, that
all that is of characteristically human worth in any human life
—all that differentiates the human from the merely animal—
involves (if not for the agent, at least for the human influences
which mould him), a long and costly elaboration, across the

centuries and civilisations right down to the lives of our own parents, teachers, friends. There has occurred here an elaboration of materials and impulsions which, in their raw condition, are, at best, mere possibilities, occasions, and reasons for powers other and greater than themselves. All these materials and impulsions can be, far more readily, turned astray ; if left to themselves they sink downwards. The acquisitive instinct can and should be trained into orderly and moderate support of self and generous help of others ; but it easily degenerates into cruel cunning, callous cheating, and unbounded covetousness. The combative instinct can be disciplined into the career of a soldier, sailor or explorer—into a life devoted to reasonable order and rational service of the pacific activities of the State ; but it easily sinks to a life of unscrupulous adventure. The sex instinct becomes transfigured into a loyal marital companionship and the noble devotion of parenthood, or even becomes transcended altogether, by an heroic celibacy full of the love of God and of men at large. Yet this same instinct readily leads to the utter ruin of body, mind and soul. We are all thus trebly near to the mere animal, to the worse than the animal ; and responsibility, duty, virtue, temptation, sin, are writ large over all man's life and actions right up to, and inclusive of, his spiritual life.

III

At this point I would ask you carefully to distinguish with me between what, I submit, are two really distinct and differing sources or occasions of difficulty in the spiritual life. Hence I pray you to refuse adhesion to the (ultimately single-source) theory of the Rev. Dr. F. R. Tennant, as propounded especially in his suggestive book upon the Origin and Propagation of Sin. Dr. Tennant there draws out in full the position that responsible, deliberately willing man is evolved from the irresponsible, impulsively striving animal, and that this is why man is so persistently tempted to lapse into what now, for man, is Sin—into his, man's, pre-human stage. Sin is thus essentially an *atavism*. Dr. Tennant also very strikingly elucidates how the presence,

within us men, of animal impulses is a necessary condition for
specifically human purity—a purity which is essentially a virtue
within the human body and an orderer of its instincts. All this
may be difficult of harmonisation even with the most moderate
of the Church symbols, *i.e.* the Tridentine definition, concerning Original Sin; but it is in itself, I think, a position of great
psychological interest and of much pædagogic help. The position explains and simplifies many pressing problems. But Dr.
Tennant, very unhappily I believe, extends this his evolutionary
explanation to all sin : sins of Pride and Self-Centredness are
traced here as complications and subtilisations introduced by
the sophisticating mind into the animal instincts. Pride and Self-
centredness thus also depend, in the last resort, as truly upon
the animal descent as do impurity, gluttonness and sloth. Now
this single derivation, I submit, will simply not work ; and indeed
it involves a grave insensibility to the specifically Christian conception of Sin, and of the degrees of its heinousness. I take it
that what specially distinguishes the Christian from the Stoic
and other Philosophical outlooks on to human virtues and vices,
is precisely the Christian sense that Pride and Self-sufficiency is
the central, typical sin. Impurity may indeed be the viler sin,
but even Impurity is instinctively felt here to be less deadly than
Pride. And for this same outlook, whilst Impurity is occasioned
by the body, Pride is not ; the doctrine of the Fall of the Angels
grandly illustrates this deep instinct. Indeed all sensitively
spiritual observation of the human heart bears this out. I take the
occasion to Pride and Self-centredness to spring from the double
characteristic of all intelligent creatures—that they are finite and
dependent upon God, for their very existence and for all their
essentially finite powers ; and yet that God has endowed them
with a certain independence, a certain limited force of initiation,
acceptance or revolt. It is, not the body, but the possession of
this double characteristic, it is this capacity, not only for obedience and dependence, but also for revolt and defiance—it is this
Imperfect Liberty which is the occasion of, at least, Pride and
Self-Sufficiency. And the reason why all creatures, so far as we
know, have been created thus with but imperfect liberty, may
well be that even God cannot create a being possessed of Perfect
Liberty—a being incapable, by his very nature, of falling away

from his best lights—since such a being would no more be finite
and a creature, but infinite and God.

Now this brings us to our third great discrimination and
practical maxim. We thus insist that, as below the level of the
natural human acts—the acts essentially characteristic of a human
being—there are the aberrations of Impurity, Gluttony, Sloth—
so there are aberrations above the level of these first, natural
human acts. Here are Pride, Vanity, Self-sufficiency. I take it
that many minds which see plainly enough the reality of the
lower offences are nowadays in the dark concerning the very
possibility of the higher sins. The root-cause of this blindness
is doubtless the immense, visible and tangible predominance,
and (within its own inexorably limited range) the immense
triumph, of mathematical and mechanical, indeed generally
of Natural, Science; and the inevitable tendency to regard
Arithmetic and Geometry as the sole ultimate type and measure
of all truth and knowledge attainable by man. With this assumption well fixed within our very blood it does certainly appear
supremely ridiculous to blame anyone for denying anything that
cannot, in any place and at any moment, be clearly, demon-
stratively, undeniably proved. How can I blame a man for
sticking exclusively to the lucidity of twice two makes four, if
this knowledge, in its full development, gives him everything he
requires, and if all other supposed knowledge leads him but to
fog and fancy? And yet, nothing is more certain than that the
richer is any reality, the higher in the scale of being, and the
more precious our knowledge of it, the more in part obscure and
inexhaustible, the less immediately transferable, is our knowledge
of that reality. So is the reality and knowledge of a daisy more
difficult and obscure than is that of a quartz crystal, and this
crystal again than " two and two makes four "; so is the sea
anemone beyond the daisy, and my little dog far beyond both.
And so on again to man, to the knowledge of any one human
soul, my own or another, or further to the knowledge of any
great past historical personage or to a great historical event or
period, say, the Great War so recently with us all : the richness
and the value, yet also the complexity and an obscurity which
refuses to be completely banished, are together always on the
increase. True knowledge of God is very certainly not a matter

of great learning or of subtle metaphysics ; yet if God be at all like what all religion proclaims Him to be, man's knowledge of Him must indeed be continuously re-beginning, and all attempts to render this vivid knowledge in terms of a clear science must always leave not a little obscurity.

It may be asked, however, where and how can responsibility and guilt enter here? The evidence for all these realities, from the crystal to God, is what it is : no good will in the world can increase or change it ; no evil inclination can suppress or even diminish it. The answer is, that certain dispositions of the will very certainly enter into all deep and delicate apprehensions, be they of the life-history of a clematis-plant, or of the doings of a spider. A certain rare disoccupation with the petty self is here a *sine qua non* condition of any success ; it is this noble freedom from self which makes the character, *e.g.*, of a Charles Darwin so very great. And the answer is further that, if a certain parental temper, a loving humility which joyfully bends down and contracts itself into the life of creatures lower than man, be necessary for the understanding of the orchid or the earth-worm, so a certain filial temper, a loving humility which joyfully reaches up, and stretches itself out wide towards the life above it, is necessary for our apprehension of God. Indeed the apprehension of the Higher-than-man, of the Highest, the Ultimate, the Perfect,—the Beginner, Sustainer and Consummator of all that is good in us, especially of our very capacity to give ourselves to Him ; this, very certainly, not only attracts our higher and best self, but also tries and tests our lower, our self-centred, our jealous and envious self. It is at this point especially that we ought, I believe, to look for and to find the presence and operation of *Radical Evil* such as Kant traced it in man's jealousy of the higher and highest as that same man sees them, or is capable of seeing them. True, such a life-story as that of the Positivist, sketched above, perhaps also that of John Stuart Mill, should warn us against explaining all and every Atheism by such perverse dispositions. Yet it can do but good if, whilst practising the greatest reserve in our judgment of individuals, we keep alive within us this sense that a certain pang accompanies, in the meanness and jealousy of the human heart, (and any one human heart is liable to more or less of such meanness and jealousy), the full, persistent recognition of a perfection entirely not of our own making, a perfection we can never equal, and yet a perfection, the recognition of our utter dependence upon which constitutes the very centre, the inevitable condition, of our own (even then essentially finite) perfection. I believe that not to be aware of the costliness, to unspiritualised man, of the change from his self-centredness, from *anthropocentrism* to *theocentrism*, means not only a want of awakeness to the central demand of religion, but an ignorance or oblivion of the poorer, the perverse, tendencies of the human heart. This then will be our third great discrimination—the ever possible, and the often actual, faultiness of our attitude to what is above us.

IV

So far we have considered religion as though it demanded only purity with regard to what is below the soul, the body, and humility with regard to what is above the soul, God ; as though, in a word, religion were constituted simply by intercourse of the alone with the Alone—the one soul with the one God. Yet there is a further abiding characteristic of living religion, when taken upon the whole and in the long run, which produces a third great group of responsibilities—occasions of virtue and temptations to various excesses or defects. And this third great group is, of course, in actual life, inter-connected, in the most various ways, with the other two groups. This third group is generated by the great fact, so often and easily overlooked, that though the religion of any one soul is, where fully alive, the most profoundly personal conviction and life within it, and though the religion of any such single soul will always show a certain delicate pitch, temper, application more or less specific to itself : yet religion is a profoundly social force, which operates from one contemporary man to other contemporaries and on from genera-tion to generation, largely by means of groups and organisations, history and institutions. Even the most aggressively individualist of men, provided he be still religious at all, will always reveal, to any at all skilful analysis of the content of his religious belief and spiritual life, large indebtednesses to this social, traditional,

B

institutional element of religion.   This element—this influence
not only of single persons but of Institutions and *things*—is
readily traceable in Our Lord's own life, in that of St. Paul, in
that of St. Francis, in George Fox, in William Law. And this can
only change when man shall walk this planet without a body,
when he shall have nothing to learn from the things of the senses,
and when God has become the God of the individual alone, and
not the God also of human society and of the great human
associations—the Family, the Guild, the State, the Church.
Indeed the paradox is, meanwhile, really true, that the more
utterly independent a man thinks himself of all traditions and
institutions, the more excessively, unwisely dependent he is
usually, in reality, upon some tradition or institution, if only for
the very simple reason that we cannot even begin to discriminate,
and to use instead of being used, where we are unaware of an
influence being present at all.   It is, of course, true that a really
blind obedience to any authority is never equal to enlightened
adhesion, and that it is such adhesion, which should always be
the ideal of all spiritual training ; and, again, that even the most
adequate outlook ceases to have any genuine worth in the soul
concerned, where this outlook is an affair of mere routine.
Nevertheless it is equally true, and far less obvious, that what
any one man can himself directly experience and exhaustively
know at first hand, especially at the first start, is, in all subject
matters and especially also in religion, amazingly limited,
sporadic and intermittent.   Only by a preliminary trust in the
wiser among the teachers and trainers that surround our youth
and adolescence, has any such man any chance of escaping from,
possibly life-long, self-imprisonment.   It is by my not denying
as false what I do not yet see to be true, that I give myself the
chance of growing in insight.   And certainly that man must
be an amazing genius who, at twenty, and even at thirty or
forty, has not very much to learn from even an average representative of any one of the long-tried institutional religions,
in their positive constructive teachings and practices.

Now if all this be so, we have here a third immense field for
wise or unwise docility, for humility, partisanship, generosity,
shrewdness, for meanness, indifference, revolt, and for all possible
shades and combinations of such and similar dispositions.   Three

points appear here to be the most important.¹⁾ There is, first, no such thing *in rerum natura* as a religious institution which can dispense the individual soul from the duty of a wise, discriminating appropriation and detailed application of the teachings and genius of that institution. " A man may cease to be a Christian, and may yet remain a damned fool," is a well known judgment attributed to the late Professor Huxley. Similarly, a man may become a Quaker, or a Presbyterian, or an Anglican, or a Roman Catholic, and may remain almost as unwise as he was before ; he may even add new unwisdoms to the old ones, through an unconscious travesty of even the noblest doctrines he has now more or less mechanically gained. We can even truthfully go further, and can maintain that the richer the creed the greater is the experience and the many-sided aliveness needed by the soul for an at all adequate presentation of this same creed. 2) There is, again, no such thing for man as a complete escape from history and institutions. Thus the Quakers, very wisely, possess the institution of the Meetings of the First Day and of their strict obligation. Indeed the minor religious bodies are generally characterised by the specially emphatic stress laid by them upon some, or all, of the few institutions retained by them. We can thus maintain without undue paradox, that, by appurtenance to a particular religious body, we really keep in touch with the great tradition of mankind at large, and with God's general action in individual souls.3 And there is, finally, no such thing as appurtenance to a particular religious body without cost—cost to the poorer side of human nature and cost even, in some degree and way, to the better side of that same nature. Hence the need of an increasingly wise discrimination—of a generous payment of the cost where it affects the poorer side, and of a careful limitation of the cost, and a resourceful discovery of compensation elsewhere, where the cost affects the better side of our nature. No religious institution, *e.g.*, can, as such, be a society for research into the history and philosophy of religion at large ; no religious institution can, as such, be asked to watch over the laws intrinsic to astronomy or anthropology ; nor can the intellectually finest presentations, even of the particular religious institution, be expected usually to acquire more than a footing of toleration within such institution. Especially will all these limitations be at work in religions of a large popular appeal and following. All this will, however, be bearable, in proportion to the richness in religious history and in present religious life of the institution, and in proportion to the soul's perception and practice of the other divinely willed, fundamental human organisms and lives—the Family, the Guild, the State—science, philosophy and art. Such a soul will have to lead a life of tension and of many levels ; yet the cost of it all will not be found excessive, if only the great central Christian realities and life become more and more the ultimate convictions and the all-pervading final motives of all our doings and aims. The omnipresence of God, His self-revelation in Jesus Christ, the need of all men for all other men, the organic character of the great complexes, especially of the Church, and the love for the occasions of filial, fraternal, paternal habits, also and especially in the spiritual world—these facts and dispositions must become more and more part of our very life. We shall thus be both old and new, derivative and original, supported and supporting—supporting, at the last, in our little measure, not only other individual souls, but the very institution itself.

V

And this brings us out of our three central discriminations—out of, as it were, the three associated clouds constitutive of responsibility in religious belief—into a final serene level, somewhat corresponding to, yet greatly exceeding in richness of content and in positive value, the opening serenity—the preliminary discrimination, which, as yet, was without responsibility for religious belief. For here at last we again come, or seem to come, to no responsibility—to, this time, something beyond responsibility. Nothing is grander, in the development of the human outlook, so long as such development is fully, finely Christian—from Our Lord's own teachings onwards to the general spiritual convictions and the greatest spiritual incorporations of the Golden Middle Age—Aquinas, Dante, St. Francis of Assisi—than the ineradicable implication, and the growing articulation, of the difference between Imperfect and

Perfect Liberty. All through the great movement we can trace the operation of the twin facts that man is by his Nature constituted in Imperfect liberty, but that the same man is called by Grace to the love of, and the indefinite approximation to, the Perfect Liberty of God. St. Augustine tells us " *posse non peccare, magna est libertas ; non posse peccare, maxima est* " (it is already a great liberty to be able to avoid sin ; but the greatest liberty is to be unable to sin at all). This doctrine cannot but be true, unless God, Who cannot sin, is thereby a slave ; and unless human souls which, in proportion to the length and depth of their devotedness, very certainly grow less liable to grave sin, thereby become less free. Thus the <u>Liberty of Choice is an imperfect kind of liberty</u>, and Perfect Liberty consists in willing fully and spontaneously the behests of a perfect nature, and in the incapacity to will otherwise. Hence the more arbitrary an act, the less really free it is. This great insight grew dim soon after Aquinas, amongst the thinkers who successively dominated the later prevalent positions : Duns Scotus and Occham ; Luther; Descartes, Pascal, and many another since, have taught a sheer arbitrary will in God, answered by acts of sheer will in man. Thus religion becomes more and more something which hovers clear outside, which indeed intrinsically contradicts, the rationalities of life and of the world. So with Descartes ; though for him the actual world order is within itself a rationally interconnected system, yet the original choice of just this system is held to have been a purely arbitrary act. So further back with Occham : the Commandments, although interconnected as they stand, might have been established by God quite different, indeed directly contrary, to what they actually are.

When we come to Kant we do indeed, in the doctrine of the Categorical Imperative, attain to something which God Himself could not have willed otherwise—to something expressive of His Nature. But Kant unfortunately, not merely ignores, but explicitly combats, the connection, already so nobly proclaimed by Plato and Aristotle, between Virtue and the Highest Good— between Morality and Happiness ; and in Kant the sense of the Reality of God and of His inviolable Nature (a sense of God which, in all living religion, is, together with man's need of God and prayer to God, always primary and central) is, where not denied altogether, reduced to hypotheses in aid of the moral life. The fact of the matter doubtless is that even Duty, and an entire life spent in Obedience to Duty, these convictions taken alone, are not live religious categories. So little is it true that perfect religion eliminates joy and spontaneity, as unworthy of itself, that only a life penetrated by spontaneity and joy, can be recognised by religion as of supreme religious perfection. The great Pope Benedict XIV., in his standard work on the Beatifica-tion and Canonisation of the Servants of God, points out that, for Canonisation, as distinct from Beatification, the Roman Church requires, not, as is usually supposed, three things, but, in addition, a very important fourth thing. The Roman Church requires for its formal Canonisations a spontaneous popular cultus of one hundred years ; three well-authenticated miracles ; three well-authenticated acts of heroic virtue ; *and* the note of expansive joy in this saintly soul's life and influence, however melancholy may have been its natural temperament. As Matthew Arnold puts it, with delicate perception : what entrances Christendom in St. Teresa is not directly her long years of struggle and of suffering to be faithful to conscience ; it is the rapt joy, the gracious spontaneity, the seeming naturalness of the supernatural, in the last years of her life-long service, a service which has at last become the fullest freedom.

Now if all this be true, the whole question of Responsibility in Religious belief seems utterly to disappear on the heights of the religious life. As well insist to Kepler on the duty care-fully to consider the stars, or to Darwin on his obligation minutely to watch the fertilisation of orchids, or to Monica on her guilt if she does not love Augustine : as to preach responsibility for belief to a soul full of the love and of the joy of God. And yet, even here, indeed here especially, we have to guard against unreality and dangerous simplification. Here below no soul, sufficiently ordinary for us to classify it at all, attains to a love and joy ever unbroken and incapable of increase ; and hence, at some times and in some measure, it has to revert to what were formerly its more ordinary motives. And again, even in the Beyond the perfection of the human soul, still joined to a body however spiritual, and, above all, still a finite creature, will not consist in the elimination of all motives except the most extensive and intensive of them all, but in the full actuation, allocation, super and subordination of all motives variously good in their kind within an immense living system—in an immensely rich harmony, and not in a monotone, however sublime. And thus a chaste fear and filial reverence, a humble trust, a sense of duty, and acts of submission and of self-surrender, homely virtues as well as heroic joys : all will, somehow, not be superseded but included in man's eventual beatitude in God. A holy fear can and will be, even in heaven, the servant and watchman to our love ; and hence there will still remain some place and function, through all eternity, for the sense of responsibility in our religious belief.

2

RELIGION AND ILLUSION

AND

RELIGION AND REALITY[1]

RELIGION AND ILLUSION

IF we know something and care much about man's religious faith, its possibility, reality and depth, and for man's finding or making for this his faith a place within the rest of his many-staged, many-sided life, we can hardly fail to feel the severe strain, the solemn seriousness, of our present situation. True, it is a situation prepared by developments, or driftings, or entanglements, none of which is newer than half-a-century at least. Yet it is a situation which may well provoke specially anxious thought at this particular moment in the history of the world. For here, in the midst of a titanic war, of vast upheavals and of acutest problems, religion seems, at first sight, either to have ceased altogether, or to persist as a feeble ghost rather than as an inspiring, formative energy. Religion appears to be the sleepy sleep-compelling partner of all the institutions and illusions now drifting, under our very eyes, like so much wreckage, before the storm. Look at the wild devastation, the Bolshevik carnival of anarchy and tyranny, now submerging Russia, the land believed by us all to be so full of religious aspiration and of religious faith. Look at Germany. Can religion be accounted a great living power there, where the identification of Government with sheer material force still seems to sterilize all nobler, richer counter-movements? And look at Italy, France, England, America. Is all, is much, in these countries

---

[1] First published in an Italian translation in the *Cœnobium* of Lugano, 1909. Here reprinted from the expanded original published in *The Quest*, April and July, 1918.

in a sound and spiritual state ? And is religion really the central force within what here may, in its degree, be strong and faithful ?

Is not religion, then, a spent power, a played-out thing ? Ought we not to relegate it to the archæological lumber-room —the museum so full already of the curious toys of the babyhood of man ? Indeed, is not religion essentially illusion ? Let us prepare our answer to this poignant question by a glance sufficiently far back and around us to furnish us with a starting point. We shall find that, as soon as we do so at all seriously, we are met by an apparent, or real, contradiction which runs, or seems to run, through the deepest of the things that, though still ever with us, are yet in process of further or new articulation, grouping or fixation.

I want first to describe this contradiction generally, on its affirmative and on its negative side. I shall next draw out roughly the difficulties attaching to the problem at its deepest. And I shall then, with a view to a closer grasp of the problem thus at its deepest, and to securing a fair hearing for the sceptical solution of it, carefully study the leading utterances of probably the best equipped, the ablest and the most thorough of the sceptics. This will suffice for this first paper. Thus fortified in knowledge, I hope to come back to my own general description and questions in a second paper, entitled " Religion and Reality," and there to attempt some final resolution of the whole most delicate, most difficult, most important matter.

I

If we care to look back into human history, we can do so now with a greatly increased refinement of critical method and of sympathetic re-evocation. Workers possessed of these gifts and acquirements are daily increasing and improving our collections of the literary records, the rites and customs, the oral traditions and legends, the psychical concomitants, and the ethical and social conditions and effects of the various beliefs of mankind. And this wide-spreading, very detailed, ever re-tested study, so long as it remains simply busy with the patient collection and sympathetic articulation of the given facts, traces everywhere the following four characteristics of religion.

*B

(margin notes: characteristics of religion; 1) universal; 2) influence for good and evil; 3) many forms; 1)...)

Everywhere this study of the past finds (in various degrees and ways, and in various combinations with other elements of human experience) religion,—the search for religion, or the sense of the want of religion, or evidences of the soul's stuntedness because of the lack of definite religion. Religion, if we take it in this extension of the term, appears to be as universal amongst men as are the ethical sense, the political instinct, æsthetic perception, or the philosophic impulsion,—all of them most certainly characteristic of man in general, yet all as certainly developed only very weakly in this or that individual or family, or even in this or that entire race or period.

Everywhere, again, this study discovers, although here once more in greatly different degrees and ways, the influence, indeed the really central if often indirect importance, for good or for evil, or for both, of all religion, whether good or bad or mixed.

Everywhere, too, such study shows that, as ethics, politics, art, science, philosophy, so also religion manifests itself in what is, at first sight, a bewildering variety of simultaneous forms or successive stages. It shows moreover that for the most part (as indeed is also the case *mutatis mutandis* with those other activities of human life and apprehension) religion remains to this day represented in large part by rude, inchoate beginnings, or by obstinate arrests of growth, or by convictions which, though to some extent more developed and more pure, yet still manifest a considerable admixture of earlier stages of cultus and belief. And this same study shows that religion, in proportion as it gains a fuller consciousness of its own specific character, retains indeed relations with ethics and politics, science, philosophy and art, and even increases or refines such relations, yet in and through all such relations it increasingly differentiates itself from all those other modes and ranges of life and apprehension.

Finally this study discovers the most specific characteristic of all religion to consist in this : That, whereas Ethics and Politics proclaim *oughtnesses,* and seek to produce certain human acts and dispositions, and to organise human society in certain ways ; whereas Science and Philosophy attempt respectively to discover the laws which govern natural phenomena and to lay bare or to divine the unity or harmony of life and the world as one whole ; and whereas Art seeks to create for us beautiful

forms, the incorporations of the ideals which it everywhere
finds indicated, yet nowhere fully achieved, in the actual visible
existence around us;—Religion, on the contrary, affirms a
supreme *Isness*, a Reality or Realities other and greatest in
man, as existent prior to, and independently of, the human
subject's affirmation of It or of Them. Indeed this Reality is
held to occasion such affirmation and to express Itself, however
inadequately, in this human response. Rules, indeed even the
realisations, of moral rightness ; social organisations, even the
deepest and the widest ; discoveries in and utilisations of natural
forces, however stupendous ; laws and ideals of the mind, however essential, however lofty : any and all of these things, in so
far as they are taken apart from any super-human cause, centre
or end, have never been considered, by the specifically religious
sense, to be the concern of religion at all. Religion as such
has ever to do, not with human thoughts, but with Realities
other and higher than man ; not with the production of what
ought to be, but with fear, propitiation, love, adoration of what
already is.

These four characteristics of all religion,—its practical *universality, importance, autonomy*, and *superhumanity*,—now appear
before us in an astonishingly large collection of solid facts,
derived from countless ages, races and stages of mankind.

Yet the opposite, the more or less sceptical, reading of this
same mass of evidence is not uncommon, at least for the moment,
even amongst serious and learned scholars. Indeed, with respect
to the four general conclusions just described, there are certain
apparently ruinous difficulties against the admission of their
conclusiveness. And these difficulties appear to increase with
the degree of significance attaching to them severally.

As to the *universality* of religion, especially if understood as
at least the implicit affirmation of a Reality other and more than
human, we are faced by the following apparent facts. Whole
races, *e.g.* the Chinese and Mongols, seem to be more or less
lacking in such religion. A very ancient, one of the most widely
spread and a still powerfully influential, view and practice
of life and death, which certainly considers itself religious,
viz. Buddhism, seems in its classical, characteristic period,

systematically to look away from all things that are less than man's apprehending powers, yet it apparently does so without thought of, or belief in, any reality or influence other and higher than these powers, existing and operating in itself or elsewhere. A powerful and persistent philosophy, Pantheism, proclaims as its central doctrine the identity of the world, of man and of God ; and this Pantheism, traceable in many a degree and variation throughout more or less all ages, races and countries, can boast of at least one exponent of the first rank, that great soul, Spinoza. And the denial of religion, *i.e.* of religion taken as involving the affirmation of a more than human Reality, can claim so eminent a mathematician as Laplace, so morally fervent and socially constructive a philosopher as Comte, scholars of such æsthetic penetration as Rohde, and so great a critical historian as Theodor Mommsen.

But if we restrict our attention to specifically religious believers, is the *importance*, the effect of this their belief, for or upon their lives and the world at large, so very marked ? Is the difference, in depth, breadth and fruitful force of soul, between the devout Theist Newton and the cold Atheist Laplace readily recognisable ? Is the difference in such effects so very great between Buddhist Tokio, Hindoo Benares, Mohammedan Mecca, and Christian London or Rome ? Or, in so far as cities are frankly materialist, are they very plainly inferior to cities where they are religious ?

As to the *autonomy* of religion, is not this a myth ? Is not every even superficial activity of man bound up with every other ; and is not the whole man dependent, through and through, upon his racial and family heredity, his education and environment ? And cannot religion in particular be shown always to depend upon the moral and intellectual gifts, the general training, indeed upon the political, economic, even upon the psycho-physical, conditions and upon the geographical position of its various votaries ? And if this is so certainly very largely, why should it not be so altogether ?

But especially do the objections against the *superhuman* claim, —the very claim which we hold to run through and to characterise all specifically religious experience,—appear grave, indeed final. Since then even the universality, the importance

and the autonomy of religion can readily be shown to be difficult
of proof, or at least to raise particular difficulties, in proportion
as we insist upon religion as present only where there is a superhuman claim ; and since, according to our conception, this
superhuman claim constitutes the very heart of religion, we can
simplify, and yet deepen, our task by concentrating our attention,
for the rest of these papers, directly upon this, the superhuman
claim of all religion.

II

objection to superhuman claim of rel

The difficulties against the superhuman claim of religion
can conveniently, even though only roughly, be grouped according to the peculiarities in the objects thus presented to and
apprehended by the human mind ; the limitations, real or
apparent, of these our apprehending minds ; and the evils which
result, with seeming necessity, from all such belief in the Superhuman. Thus the first group draws its material specially from
the history of religion, from the examination of still living varieties
of religion, and from the student's analysis of his own religious
experiences. The second group depends upon analytic philosophy—the theory of knowledge in particular. And the third
group once again requires history, and a wide knowledge and
delicate penetration of the operations of religion, as these are
still active around us and within our own soul.

The first group, then, is busy with the objects, be they only
apparent or be they real, presented to the religious human mind
and soul. These seem to inflict a treble, an increasingly final,
denial and refutation upon any and all superhuman claim.

For we can compare these experiences, in the past or even in
the present of religion, simply with each other ; and we shall
then find them to present us with endless variations, and even
grave contradictions. Or we can compare the experiences in
the past of religion with the moral law and with any sensitive
spirituality, precisely in what we now feel sure are their most
certain and most precious constituents ; and we shall then
discover those experiences mostly to fall visibly short of, and
often flagrantly to violate, these constituents. And, finally, we

can compare the religious experiences, in their fuller and more harmonious unfolding and in their completest ethical satisfactoriness, with certain apparently well-grounded conclusions or postulates of natural science or of mental philosophy; and we shall then find ourselves at a loss how to escape from contradiction of those experiences or of these other truths.

Thus, if we take together the question of the variations and contradictions and the question of the violation of the moral and spiritual commands and truths, if we restrict ourselves to the Jewish and Christian Scriptures alone, and if we give these variations and violations the great advantages of taking them in the order of time and according to the tribe or people when and where they occur, we find such well-known facts as the following. We have polygamous and divorcing saints and leaders of God's people, such as Abraham and Jacob; and again such deceivers, as Jacob and Jaël; fiercely vindictive prayers by friends of God, such as are many of the Psalms and certain passages of the Revelation of St. John; and the extermination, by the Chosen People, of entire tribes of the original inhabitants of Canaan. We have also the conception that God Himself both tempts to evil and attracts to good replaced, only after some centuries, by the distinction that God Himself attracts to good alone, and simply permits Satan to tempt the soul to evil; and insistences upon this earthly life as the place of the soul's full consciousness, hence for the deliberate service of God, in contradistinction to Sheol, the grave and the Beyond, where the soul leads a shrunken existence,—insistences which last, practically unbroken by contrary enunciations, right up to the Captivity.

Indeed, even within the limits of the New Testament alone, we get, first, the vivid expectation of Christ's Proximate Second Coming and of the Consummation of the World; and then, gradually, the adjournment, and finally the indefinite postponement, of these cosmical events. Again, certain passages or writings conceive mankind as destined to a happy reign, first or finally, here upon our earth, however rejuvenated; and other passages or writings place the after-life outside of, above, this earth.

And as to the apparent contradictions between the experiences and conceptions of religion and certain facts ascertained elsewhere, there are the three experiences or conceptions which appear to be simply essential to all Theism. We find here the experience of Miracle, which appears to clash with the determinism of natural law ; and two conceptions,—the conception of Creation, which seems to contradict natural science, even in that minimum of evolutionary doctrine which can be taken as reasonably assured, and the conception of Personality in God, which seems to contradict psychology and philosophy in their, surely, well-grounded contention that personality always implies at least some kind of limitation if not actually a physical body.

The second group, which deals with the apprehending mind, contains two main difficulties, and this against precisely the most fundamental of all the evidences and conceptions of religion—Revelation. How can the mind, it is argued, apprehend with certainty anything outside of itself, outside of its own categories and modes ? And, still more, how can the essentially finite and contingent human mind, even if capable of a real knowledge of finite things or of finite minds other than itself, have any real knowledge of, be at all really affected by, an Infinite and Absolute, even if such Infinite and Absolute can reasonably be conceived as Mind and Spirit ? It will be noted that especially these two difficulties are called out to their uttermost by any and every superhuman claim.

And the third group, which dwells upon the effects, *i.e.* the dire evils, accruing from the admission of religion as in any way or degree superhuman, can be taken as containing two main sets of facts. For has not precisely that belief in the superhuman reality of the Infinite, the Absolute, been the cause why religion has so largely ignored other, great and necessary, human activities, —has turned away from science and philosophy, from art and politics, even from society and the family, indeed even from elementary morality itself ? And, again, has not precisely that belief, when it has turned its attention to these other sides of life, attempted to dominate, to mould or to break them by and into the specifically superhuman religious categories, or even by and into whole systems of philosophy or theology deduced logically from those categories ?

Of such turning away from the non-religious activities of life we have instances in the Jewish prophets' antagonism to all statuary; in the Mohammedan Sultan Omar's destruction of the great classical library of Alexandria; and in the huge Christian exodus, in the fourth century, into the Egyptian desert. And as to the domination, was it not precisely some belief in the Superhuman, attached no doubt in these cases to terribly crude and corrupt imaginings of the human heart, that rendered it even possible for Syrian and Canaanitish parents to give their daughters to a life of " sacred " prostitution in the temples of Aphrodite, and to pass their children through the fire as holocausts to the god Moloch? In already morally higher yet still painfully fierce forms, was it not the belief that God Himself was ordering such acts which rendered it possible for the Jews to exterminate without mercy the Canaanite tribes? And, in again less indiscriminate applications and ways, was it not such transcendent claims and beliefs that rendered possible, and indeed terribly actual, the Spanish Inquisition in precisely what constituted its apparently irresistible appeal? Indeed, in all and every attempt at direct regulation or arrest of research, speculation and science by theology, whether the latter be Mussulman or Calvinist or Lutheran or Catholic, is it not in fact the superhuman claim, and the acceptance of the superhuman claim, of religion which render such action possible? Even further, does not the acceptance of any such claim lead *necessarily* to such results? And is not the only sure safeguard against such results, and against their disastrous effects, especially also upon religion itself, the resolute elimination of the superhuman of every kind?

And let us note that, not only the effects we have been thus describing fully explain men's sensitive fear, indeed often their angry hatred, of the very words " metaphysic," " transcendence," " ontology," but that these effects also constitute a serious difficulty against the reasonableness, indeed against the continued possibility, of all and every superhuman belief. For what is the worth of such superhuman affirmations, if we get into troubles and dead-locks of all sorts, as soon as ever we seriously begin to apply them to anything,—as soon as ever we deduce, anticipate or test any scientific method or scientific fact from them? Can affirmations be true, and indeed the deepest of truths, if they have carefully to be kept out of the reach of all tests of their truth ¿ Is a position bearable which forces us either to limit or vitiate our sciences—their results or at the least their methods and intrinsic autonomies—or to emasculate our religion ¿

III

CRITIQUE of FEUERBACH

It is obviously impossible for a couple of papers, indeed it is impracticable for any one man, to enter fully into all the sides and problems of this great matter. But before my second paper attempts some general construction that shall utilise and transcend the objections developed above, I want to take the problem, not according to any formulation of my own, but in the combination of remarkable psychological penetration, of rare knowledge throughout large reaches of the religious consciousness, and of sceptical assumptions and passion presented by Ludwig Feuerbach, in by far his greatest work, *Das Wesen des Christenthums*. [1]

It is true that Feuerbach is considerably dominated by Hegelian positions which have long ceased to be accepted with such exclusiveness by the majority of philosophers or even by the general cultivated reader. It is true also that the very ruthlessness of his logic renders him sometimes unfair to his own general position, and makes him, so far, more easy of refutation than are minds swayed more inconsistently by various, never completely developed or entirely accepted, principles and trains of thought. Certainly much of value has been collected, analysed and speculatively or critically thought out in matters of religion, since Feuerbach died in 1872, an utter materialist, with but little following in his latest development. Nevertheless these earlier positions of Feuerbach, even where they have ceased to be axiomatic for professed philosophers, are still, in secondary forms and in semi-conscious ways, most certainly operative in various sceptical works. The vein of doctrinaire violence that undoubtedly runs through the book does not prevent the work remaining, to this hour, the most probing and thorough account

[1] The book first appeared in 1841 ; the text quoted by me is from the edition of 1849, as carefully reprinted by Quenzel, in Reclam's *Universal Bibliothek*, 1904. I give it in Marian Evans' (George Eliot's) English translation, 1854, as made from the text of the first edition, with such few changes of my own as are rendered necessary by the differences between the editions followed respectively by her and by myself.

of the certain, or even the simply arguable, contributions made by man to religion,—of the resonance of man's mind and heart in response to religion ; and there has not, I think, been since Feuerbach any mind, of a calibre equal to his own, that has argued, with so unflagging a conviction, for the sheer illusion and mischievousness of all religion. And again, in dealing critically with a dead man's work, we escape all personal considerations and subjective complications, so readily awakened by even friendly controversy amongst living writers. And finally, by taking, not this dead man's last, much cruder book, but his fullest and most formidable work, we indicate, by our very self-restriction within the range of the writings of the author chosen by us, that our object is not a complete study of Feuerbach, nor, on the other hand, simply a refutation of Feuerbach at his weakest, but the careful analysis of the leading positions of Feuerbach at his best, to be used as so much vivid enforcement and as so much precise aid towards at least the formulation of the great question here before us. It will be sufficient for our purpose if we restrict our extracts to the two introductory chapters of the whole book.

From the first chapter on " The Essential Nature of Man " let us take the following passages :

" Consciousness, in the strictest sense, is present only in a being to whom his species, his essential nature, is an object of thought. The brute is indeed conscious of himself as an individual —hence he has the feeling of himself as the common centre of successive sensations—but not of himself as a species."— " Science is the cognizance of species. In practical life we have to do with individuals ; in science, with species. But only a being to whom his own species, his own nature, is an object of thought, can make the essential nature of other things or beings an object of thought. Hence the brute has only a simple, man a twofold life ; in the brute the inner life is one with the outer, man has both an inner and an outer life. The inner life of man is the life which has relation to his species, to his general, as distinguished from his individual nature. Man thinks—that is, he converses with himself."

Now " the essential nature of man, in contradistinction from the animal, is not only the *ground*, it is also the *object* of religion.

But religion is consciousness of the infinite ; thus it is, and can
be nothing else than, the consciousness which man has of his
own, not finite and limited, but infinite, nature. . . .   The
consciousness of the infinite is nothing else than the consciousness of the infinity of the consciousness " (pp. 53–55 ; Eng.
Tr. pp. 1, 2).—" Man is nothing without an object. . . . But
the object to which a subject essentially, necessarily relates, is
nothing else than this subject's own, but objective, nature "
(p. 57 ; Eng. Tr. p. 4).—" The *Absolute*, the God of man, is
man's own nature. . . . Since to will, to feel, to think are per-
fections, essences, realities, it is impossible that intellect, feeling,
and will should feel or perceive themselves as limited finite
powers, *i.e.* as worthless, as nothing. For finiteness and nothingness are identical " (pp. 58, 59 ; Eng. Tr. p. 516).

Now on this I would note the following. Feuerbach gives us
here his own description, or rather his own very precise definition,
of what actually occurs within man's consciousness—of what
specifically constitutes the human consciousness. This particular
interpretation has been reached, by some few men, tens of
thousands of years after millions of men have experienced this
specifically human consciousness. And even now, after this
particular interpretation has come and is offered to all thus
conscious mortals, and especially to those who particularly
reflect upon this consciousness, this interpretation is recognised
certainly only by a few, and probably even by a few only for a
time, as a true and complete account of what is taking place
within each one of us. These very certain facts do not prove
that Feuerbach's account is false ; but they do prove that it is
not self-evidently true ; and this point might easily be overlooked, seeing the manner in which the truth of this interpretation is assumed throughout the work as entirely above discussion.

No doubt Feuerbach here proves himself possessed of the
penetration and the courage necessary for drawing the conclusion
of certain assumptions which run, in various degrees and ways,
through much of specifically modern philosophy. Yet it may
well turn out that his main service in so doing is to make us feel,
more strongly than we otherwise should ever have felt, that, if
the older philosophy had its grave faults and limitations, this
newer orientation is still largely infected by the weaknesses and

one sidednesses of every reaction. Hence it will be well, neither simply to attempt a wholesale return to the old philosophy nor blindly to follow the new, but carefully to re-test the great questions as to man's primary knowledge in the light of the great facts of human life and experience—facts which every philosophy worthy of the name has, after all, not to ignore or violently to explain away, but to accept, to elucidate and to harmonise as best it can.

Here then Feuerbach, coming from his radical Hegelism, and writing for a generation still steeped in Hegel, assumes straight away and even angrily emphasises, without any attempt at proof throughout the book, that man essentially consists of mind alone ; that this human mind can penetrate and can be penetrated by, can know at all, nothing but itself ; that it never grows by, or gains a real knowledge of, realities other than man himself. Man's mind is thus affected by but one reality—that of the species man, mankind, the human race, as distinct from what is simply selfishly particularist in an individual man. There is thus, from first to last, in human experience only one object— the subject itself, illusively mistaken, according to Feuerbach, for something different from this subject ; and true philosophy consists in unmasking this inevitable, persistent illusion.

Yet actual life of all sorts and its various special successes, the different sciences with their diverse particular results, and the now truly immense accumulation of historical evidence are all before us to warn us that this is not, that this cannot be, the truth—full and entire. These tell us, as so many elementary facts, as *data* from which philosophy must start, and to which it must ever be willing to grant appeal, that man is not simply mind, but also sense, imagination, feeling, will ; that mind itself is not simply abstractive or discursive, but intuitive as well ; that the human personality, if at all complete and perfect, holds and harmonises all these forces in a generally difficult, always more or less rich, interpenetration ; that these various constituents of the human personality are developed in and by their possessor—they are slowly built up by him into his true manhood—only by, and on occasion of, the contact with, and the action upon them of, other minds, other living beings, other things ; and that, however more or other he be than they, or they be than he, he ever achieves some real knowledge of them, and thus, through his relations with them, he attains some real knowledge of himself. In this way, neither does the mind stand simply by itself in the human personality, nor does this mind merely abstract from itself and then hypostatise these its abstractions, nor does the entire personality stand alone in an empty or simply unknown and unknowable world. But the mind, a live force, finds itself in closest contact with other energisings and impulsions within the human subject. This entire human subject is always in the first instance necessarily related, not to an idea or representation, either of itself or of anything else, but to some, to various, concrete realities distinct from, though not entirely unlike, itself. It is the action of all that objective world upon this human subject, and the manifold reaction of this human subject to that world's action, which is primary; whereas the abstracting activity is secondary and instrumental, and necessarily never fully catches up or exhausts those primary informations. The more real is the subject thus stimulated and thus reacting, and the more real is the object thus stimulating and thus acting, the more " inside " does the subject and the object possess, and the more rich will be such stimulation and such response. This is certainly the case with man when stimulated by a plant, and not by a crystal; by an animal, and not by a plant; by a man, and not by an animal; by Isaiah, Shakespeare or Newton, and not by the man in the street. And thus we are coming again to see that precisely those realms of human experience and knowledge which, like history, politics, ethics, give us the widest and deepest subjective stimulation of the most varied and often the obscurest kind, and where consequently a clarified, harmonious and full conviction is specially difficult for us, are precisely the realms which carry the richest objective content within themselves, and which offer the fullest reward for our attempts to capture this content.

From all this we can readily see that, whether man's consciousness of the Infinite is or is not, as a matter of fact, simply man's consciousness of his own truly infinite consciousness, we cannot decide straight away that " it cannot be anything else." For we certainly, concomitantly with our awaking to a consciousness of ourselves, acquire varying (dim or clear, but very real) experiences of the existence, indeed to some extent of the inner life, of other beings as well. And at this stage of our enquiry it will suffice to point out that the specifically religious consciousness never has been, nor now is, and cannot (even when brought to book) discover itself to be simply the prolongation of the human individual, or of the human species in their own efforts or achievements, even if we take such prolongation as merely potential, or as still actually to be achieved. The religious consciousness is always of Something other than itself; and, in proportion to the spirituality, *i.e.* to the specific religiousness, of this consciousness, does an Infinite *not the soul's own* appear present and operative *here and now* in the world and in the soul —an Infinite different in kind from any simply human prolongation or ideal, since the soul rests upon It, and finds its support in the actual presence and operation of this Infinite, this Perfectness.

The following passage from Feuerbach's all-important second chapter, on " The Essence of Religion," is specially instructive.

" Consciousness of God is self-consciousness ; knowledge of God is self-knowledge. . . . But this is not to be understood as affirming that the religious man is directly aware of this identity ; for, on the contrary, ignorance of it is fundamental to the peculiar nature of religion."—" Man first of all sees his nature as if *out of* himself before he finds it in himself. . . . Religion is the childlike condition of humanity ; the child sees his nature—man—out of himself. In childhood a man is an object to himself, under the form of another man. Hence the historical progress of religion consists in this : that what by an earlier religion was regarded as objective, is now recognised as subjective ; that is, what was formerly contemplated and worshipped as God, is now perceived to be something *human*. What was at first religion becomes at a later period idolatry.

. . . Man has given objectivity to himself, but has not recognised the object as his own nature ; a later religion takes this forward step : every advance in religion is therefore a deeper self-knowledge. But every particular religion excepts itself—and necessarily so, otherwise it would no longer be religion—from the fate, the common nature, of all religions. . . . It is our task to show that the antithesis of divine and human is altogether illusory ; that it is nothing else than the antithesis between human nature in general and the human individual " (pp. 68, 69 ; Eng. Tr. pp. 12, 13).

Here we have, I think, a profoundly true reading of history side by side with a colossal paradox,—a paradox which is indeed absolutely necessary to this philosophy, but which does not follow from this reading of history, a paradox which, from its very character, demands the strictest proof. Yet no such proof is forthcoming ; whilst all the presumptions derivable from man's other, non-religious, experiences, and from the special nature and effects of this religious attestation itself, are very decidedly against it.

Thus it is indeed certain that later stages of religion do generally look upon the earlier stages as so many sheer idolatries ; and that the strongly religious man, as such, is generally reluctant to concede an element of truth to those earlier stages. Such a man readily sees, in those earlier stages, a mere deification of the worshipper's worst passions, and as readily fails to perceive any traces of a similar projection in his own religious conviction and practice. Hence, no doubt, an important peculiarity in the phenomenology of religion is here laid bare. Yet it is plain that, unless the Irishman's argument be sound that, because a certain stove will save him half his fuel, therefore two such stoves will save it all, there is no necessary consequence from such admixture of illusion with truth to the negation of every and all truth,— to the denial of the operative presence of some non-human reality within this long series of human apprehensions.

Again, it is true that religion has hitherto moved, upon the whole, from seeing God as it were visibly in the visible, outside world to experiencing Him in the operations of the human conscience and in the necessary laws and ideals of the human mind. Yet much in recent science and philosophy, and in the general movement of men's minds and requirements, points to future developments when men at large will again see in Nature (now encouraged to do so by science and philosophy themselves) not finally a mechanism, nor a blind impulsion and warfare of forces, but once again, yet now much more deeply than ever, a world which (in proportion to its degree and scale of reality) is purposive—a world indicative of, because preparatory for,

mind, love and will. The strict and sharp delimitation of Nature
and of Spirit, of mathematico-physical and of historico-philo-
sophical methods and of their respective special fields, has been
very necessary and has produced most fruitful results in both
directions. Yet it is obvious that they must be somehow conceived as operating within one great inter-connected world, at
however various levels of reality. Indeed this inter-connection
is continually being shown by the manner in which any earnest,
well-conducted enquiry of any one kind promptly benefits all
other enquiries of whatsoever other kind ; and this, as much to
the surprise of, say, the discoverer in biology as of the student
of religion.

And in the study of the history of religion there is certainly
no necessity for the mind which here knows most, and knows
with the greatest critical discrimination and reproductive sympathy, about the endless variations and stages of religion, to
recognise in this apparent chaos just nothing but a pretentious
effusion, a sheer projection, of the variations of the vain heart
of man. Such utter scepticism cannot be a necessary conclusion ;
since, were it so, such daring yet religiously tempered critics as
William Robertson Smith, Paul de Lagarde, C. P. Tiele, Edvin
Lehmann, could never have existed. For in the case of these
scholars, and of many another now living critically trained mind,
the intolerable insufficiency of all mere Immanence, the conviction that that very history testifies to the immanence of the
Transcendent, has certainly not been weakened ; it has somehow
been quickened by or during such strenuous studies.

We undoubtedly find something closely analogous in the
history of man's other experiences and cognitions. What a
dreary waste is the history of philosophy, of politics, of ethics
themselves, except to the man who is imbued with the strongest
philosophical, political, ethical sense,—the man who knows
where to look for truth and fruitfulness, and who is at the same
time trained in historical—that is in patient, grateful, mag-
nanimous—imagination ! It may be retorted that in religion
we are dealing not, as in philosophy, politics, ethics, only with
principles and ideas, but primarily, according to our own insistence, with a great self-revealing Reality ; and that hence we
may expect in religion, from the first, a greater freedom from

absurdities. But we can point, in arrest of judgment, to the notorious history of the natural sciences. Also these sciences are primarily busy with facts and existences which reveal their own selves to the observing mind. Indeed these sciences deal with objects which are, of necessity, more readily discernible and more easily describable than could ever be those of religion. For in science the self-revelation is largely to our senses ; the objects revealed do not claim to be more, and are indeed mostly less, than human ; and the dispositions required for their accurate ascertainment are of necessity not as deep, delicate and costly as are those required in the case of religion. Yet especially the early history of the natural sciences is, at first sight, a continuous reeling from one gross absurdity to another hardly less gross.

The general conditions and circumstances and the specific effects of the religious attestation itself also strongly point the other way. For here we have to do, not with this or that particular attestation, nor even with this or that persistent concomitant of this whole range and succession of human experience, but with this entire kind of human life—one held by mankind at large to be the highest and the deepest life attainable by man. And yet this life is declared to consist in a sheer projection, by the individual human mind, of the general, but purely immanental, human requirements and ideals, although this individual mind is, whilst practising such a sheer projection, admittedly so entirely unaware of what it is doing that it actually considers itself, the projector, to be the creation of its own projection. But in real experience doubts may arise within the religious mind against this or that concomitant or element of its present faith,—it may even entirely lose faith in this or that particular religion, yet it does not *pari passu* lose faith in trans-subjective, transcendent, superhuman Reality as such. And let it be particularly noted that, according to Feuerbach, the whole force of religion proceeds precisely from what is sheer illusion in it ; for it is just only that inversion, that attribution by the soul of the most objective validity and transcendent worth to this its mere projection of a self utterly shut up within this self's own sheer human musings, which gives religion all its specific power. The same, precisely the same, content which, when seen

in its "true" place and character, leaves men cold or only
superficially moved, becomes, when seen by them in its "false"
place and character, the most profoundly, often the most terribly,
powerful force known to history. Yet not all the recitals of the
childishnesses, the moral abuses, and the intellectual trials and
complications, traceable in and alongside of the various religions
of the world, can make any at all just student overlook religion's
magnificent services to mankind,—the most heroic patience and
courage, the noblest purity, the most self-oblivious love and
service, and withal the keen sense of the givenness of man's
very capacities, of the pathetic mystery of his life, and of the
entrancing depth of the Reality that touches and pervades it.
It is impossible to see why Plato, Aristotle, Leibniz and Kant,
and why again Pheidias and Michael Angelo, Raphael and
Rembrandt, Bach and Beethoven, Homer and Shakespeare are
to be held in deepest gratitude, as revealers respectively of
various kinds of reality and truth, if Amos and Isaiah, Paul,
Augustine and Aquinas, Francis of Assisi and Joan of Arc are
to be treated as pure illusionists in precisely what constitutes
their specific greatness.

The following group of passages will now conclude our
examination of Feuerbach.

" If you doubt the objective truth of the predicates (of God),
you must also doubt the objective truth of the subject whose
predicates they are. If the predicates are anthropomorphisms,
the subject of them is an anthropomorphism too. If love, goodness, personality, and the rest, are human attributes, so also is
the subject which you presuppose; the existence of God, the
belief that there is a God, are anthropomorphisms, presuppositions purely human " (p. 74; Eng. Tr. p. 17).—" Originally,
man makes truth dependent upon existence; subsequently,
existence dependent upon truth " (p. 77; Eng. Tr. p. 19).—
" Not the attribute of the divinity, but the divineness or deity
of the attribute, is the first true Divine Being."—Hence " he
alone is the true atheist to whom the predicates of the Divine
Being—for example, love, wisdom, justice—are nothing; not
he to whom merely the subject of these predicates is nothing.
And in nowise is the negation of the subject necessarily also
a negation of the predicates considered in themselves. These

have an intrinsic, independent reality. They force their recognition upon man by their very nature; they prove, they attest themselves. It does not follow that goodness, justice, wisdom are chimeras, because the existence of God is a chimera; nor that they are truths, because this is a truth. The idea of God is dependent on the idea of justice, of goodness, of wisdom, . . . but the converse does not hold " (p. 79; Eng. Tr. p. 21).—" Religion knows nothing of anthropomorphisms; to it they are not anthropomorphisms. . . . They are pronounced to be images only by the understanding which reflects on religion, and which, while defending them, yet, before its own tribunal, denies them " (p. 84; Eng. Tr. pp. 24, 25).

I take these several positions in an order of my own.

It is certainly contrary to the facts that religion, as such, " knows nothing of anthropomorphisms," *i.e.* that religion, as such, is unaware of the inadequacy of all human thought and language to the realities, even simply as these are experienced by the soul. " O the depth of the wisdom and the knowledge of God! How unsearchable are his judgments, his ways past tracing out!" This cry of St. Paul (Rom. xi. 33) expresses the very soul of religion. " One of the greatest favours bestowed transiently on the soul in this life is to enable it to see so distinctly, and to feel so profoundly, that . . . it cannot comprehend Him at all. . . . In heaven those who know Him most perfectly, perceive most clearly that He is infinitely incomprehensible." This experience and reflection of the peasant St. John of the Cross (*A Spiritual Canticle*, stanza viii. 10) only places in the very centre of attention that which persistently accompanies, as a delicate background and presupposition, all deep spiritual experience, and which indeed can be found to some degree even in the less spiritual religions. True, philosophical reflection and natural science bring perplexities to the religious mind, and there is *some* connection between a man's growth in such other insights and his analysis and theory of his religious experience. Yet the influence of philosophy and of science upon religious experience itself appears to be primarily the furnishing of obstacles and stimulants, of tests and purifications; and certainly the sense of *awe*, derived by the religious soul from its vivid apprehension of the greatness of the Reality, a Reality experienced as so much deeper and richer than the soul can ever express, is specifically different from any sense of *uncertainty* as to the existence and the superhuman nature of the Reality underlying and occasioning this apprehension. Healthy mysticism and genuine scepticism are thus intrinsically opposites.

The predicates which the believer finds inherent to the subject " God," indeed whatsoever he says or can say, believe or wish, as to God, are undoubtedly expressed within the limits of, and in accordance with, the human nature in which they are experienced or thought. " Everything that is apprehended by any apprehending being, is apprehended according to the manner of this being's apprehension," is continuously insisted upon by St. Thomas, the prince of the Scholastics, who here, as usual, follows Aristotle. (So, *e.g.*, in the *Summa Theologiae*, First Part, 75th Question, Article 5c.) Man can never jump out of his own skin. Yet this in no way decides how widely that skin may stretch, nor what, nor how much of, Reality really affects man and is presumably apprehended by him with some genuine knowledge. Indeed man is found to possess somehow, in very certain fact, a more or less continuous, often most painful, sense of the inadequacy of any and all merely human mode and degree both of existence and of apprehension. And this sense is too fundamentally human, and too demonstrably impels him towards, yet never to rest in, his noblest achievements in science and philosophy, in art, in ethics, in life generally, for it to be anything but suicidal for man himself ever, in the long run and deliberately, to declare this sense to be sheer illusion, or (what is practically the same, and equally inadequate) to find in this sense nothing but the merely human race-instinct. There then remains no way out of scepticism, where scepticism is least tolerable and where it is most ruinous, than to carry right up into religion what we believe and practise in our practical life and in our science. Just as we simply admit the existence of countless realities, more or less different from, though only lower than or equal to ourselves ; and as we frankly grant the real influence of these realities upon ourselves and our real knowledge of them, since such influence and knowledge are prior to, and are the material of, our discursive reasoning about them : so also let us simply admit the existence of a perfect Reality, sufficiently like us to be able to penetrate and to move us through and through, the which, by so doing, is the original and persistent cause of this our noblest dissatisfaction with anything and all things merely human. Certainly no other explanation has ever been given which does not sooner or later mis-state or explain away the very data, and the immense dynamic forces of the data, to be explained. But this, the only adequate, explanation moves us on at once, from the quicksands of religion as illusion, to the rock of Religion as the witness and vehicle of Reality.

Of course, this dim or vivid general sense of the Perfect, of all-sustaining Spirit, operates in men and is describable by them only in human terms; but this very fact and the believer's ready admission of it make the persistent witness to the Reality all the more striking. Feuerbach's own later history shows most instructively that the question of existence *does* matter; that, sooner or later, it demands a categorical answer. It shows also how precarious, with denials as sweeping and as absolute as are those in his *Wesen des Christenthums*, is the persistence of the sense, here still so delicate and apparently so vigorous, of the possibility, indeed of the frequent reality, of costly, self-oblivious love and devotion amongst men and for men, without any superhuman beliefs at all. Indeed even in this his chief work, and according to the author's own actual procedure, which is often strangely ignored by himself, existence *does* matter. For here the subject of those predicates of love, wisdom, etc., is even passionately declared to exist; it is indeed not God, but it is mankind, conceived as an intensely real reality. But when Feuerbach comes to write his *Wesen der Religion*, " mankind " has become an abstraction, and only two realities remain: utterly determinist, immoral Nature and hopelessly selfish, sensual, cruel individual men. Here also then existence matters; indeed here it matters supremely.

RELIGION AND REALITY

IN " Religion and Illusion " we rapidly surveyed the main peculiarities to be found in religion at large throughout human
history. These peculiarities were four : Universality, as wide for
religion as for man's other deeper peculiarities ; Importance,
traceable also where man seems without the religious sense ;
Self-differentiation from the other modes and ranges of human
life, in proportion as religion grows deep and delicate ; and
Super-humanity—the sense of Givenness, Reality, Otherness,
Super-humanness, as characterising the Ultimate Object and
deepest Cause of religion. We next noted the chief objections to
allowing any specific evidential value to this last peculiarity—the
superhuman intimations ; we noted the difficulties against the
admission that these intimations really take us beyond individual
men's idle fancies or egoistic selfishnesses, or, at best, beyond
projections, by the human individual, of the deepest, yet purely
human, needs and ideals of the human race. The human race
itself and the less than human realities around it are taken, by
such an objector, as the sole realities of which we men are truly
cognizant. And lastly we took the chief articulations of such a
purely human, illusionist, explanation of religion, as furnished
by Ludwig Feuerbach at his immanentist best, and we attempted,
in connection therewith, some preliminary discriminations of the
whole question.

In " Religion and Reality " I now propose to concentrate
more fully upon the deepest of the four religious peculiarities
—upon the Evidential, Revelational quality of religion, its
intimations of Superhuman Reality, and to meet more systematically the chief objections to the trans-human validity of these
intimations. But I want first to make plain how much this final
exposition intends to cover, and in what way it intends to operate.

The following pages, then, will chiefly consider Revelation,
but also, in some measure, Miracle, Creation and Personality,
—since these four experiences or concepts are all closely connected with the points in need of elucidation against the Pure
Immanentists. But this study excludes any equal consideration

of Evil, Suffering, Sin. It excludes these great facts, because
they do not directly obstruct, even if they do not directly aid,
the question as to the evidential worth of the superhuman
intimations. If the answer to the objections against the evidential
value of these intimations, and against the reasonableness of the
four experiences and concepts closely connected with these
intimations, turns out successful, then, and only then, will it
be worth while to study these great realities as objections to
the Theism for which we have then found good grounds. Evil,
Suffering, Sin, can then be taken as difficulties which are possibly
incapable of any complete solution, yet which, even so, would
not of themselves abolish the evidential value we have discovered
in the superhuman intimations of religion.

It might indeed be contended that Evil, Suffering, Sin—
that the awful reality and significance of these things—themselves form a large part of the superhuman intimations of religion.
But such a contention is based, I believe, on several confusions
of thought. The intimations we here study are of a Superhuman
Ultimate Reality; and this ultimate reality, in proportion as
religion grows deeply and delicately religious, is apprehended
as good, happy and holy. All this doubtless is always apprehended
in conjunction, and in contrast, with other, different qualities
of the apprehending man himself; and these qualities, it may
well be urged, are felt to be evil, painful, sinful. Yet the apprehension of the man's qualities by the man himself are, in any
case, only the occasion and concomitant of the same man's
apprehension of the Superhuman. It may even be questioned
whether a man's apprehensions of the human which are in the
most close contact and in the most constant contrast with the
same man's apprehensions of the Superhuman, are indeed Evil,
Suffering, Sin. I believe those closest and most constant concomitants of the superhuman intimations to be, in actual fact,
the feelings of Weakness, Instability, Dependence. And these
feelings and apprehensions are clearly involved, as concomitant
contrasts, in the experiences and concepts of Revelation, Miracle,
Creation and Personality, which we deliberately include in our
study.

As to the form of the following exposition, it may well seem
rather a clearing away of objections than a direct establishment

of positive facts. But this would only be an appearance. For the exposition assumes throughout the actual, indeed the admitted, existence of these intimations, whether illusory or not. The exposition has as little the need, as it would have the power, to construct these intimations ; it simply finds them and describes and analyses them as best it can. The argument gets under way only upon the admission that religion, in fact, is always penetrated by these intimations ; and the argument reaches port the moment these intimations are allowed really to be what they themselves claim to be. This study has thus to be taken in direct connection with actual life ; the two, thus taken together, are free from any indirectness or ingenuity. The claim to transhuman validity continues upon the whole as present, operative, clear, in the religious intimations, as it continues present, operative, clear, in the intimations of the reality of an external world. And as our removal of objections to the reality of an external world necessarily establishes its reality for us—because *there* is the vivid impression, the sense of a trans-human reality all around us, which clamours to be taken as it gives itself, and which was only refused to be thus taken because of those objections ; so now our removal of objections to the reality of the Superhuman Reality necessarily establishes its reality for us —since *there*, again, is the vivid impression, the sense of a still deeper, a different, trans-human Reality which penetrates and sustains ourselves and all things, and clamours to be taken as It gives Itself.

I

We first take, then, the characteristics of the objects apprehended by the religious mind.

1. Here it seems clear that the apparently endless variations which exist simultaneously between one entire religion and another entire religion, and even between single mind and single mind, or which show successively in one and the same religion, and even in one and the same mind, indeed that the crude childishness of much that most individuals and most religions think and represent their experience and its Object to be,

do not, of themselves, condemn the position that a great trans-subjective superhuman Reality is being thus, variously and ever inadequately, yet none the less actually, apprehended by such groups or persons. The Reality, extant and acting upon and within the world distinct from the human mind, and upon and within those human minds and spirits themselves, can indeed be taken as the determining occasion, object, and cause of man's long search for and continuous re-finding of God; of the gradual growth in depth and in delicacy of man's religious apprehensions; of man finding his full rest and abiding base in the religious experience and certainty alone; and of man simultaneously becoming ever more conscious both of the need of the best, and of the inadequacy of all, human categories and definitions to express this really experienced Reality.

There is nothing intrinsically unreasonable in this, unless we are to become simple sceptics also in Ethics and Politics, indeed in Natural Science itself, since, in these cases also, we readily find a closely similar, bewildering variation, both simultaneous and successive,—we find similar childish beginnings, and similar slow and precarious growth. In Natural Science the earth and the sun are assuredly really extant, and rocks, plants and animals have been with man since first man appeared upon the earth. Yet innumerable crude fancies, each variously contradicting the others, have been firmly believed for ages about these very certain realities; nor are these same realities, even now, free from mysteries greater certainly by far than is all we know with certainty about them. Indeed the reality of the external world in general can be called in question, as certainly as can the reality of the spiritual world and of God; the reality of both these worlds can be argued or willed away, as a mere subjective illusion or projection, by this or that person, or group of persons, for a while. But neither of these worlds can, with strict consistency, ever be thus dissolved by any single man; and neither of these worlds will ever, consistently or not, be thus dissolved in permanence by any considerable body of men, for reasons to be given presently. And note that the very closeness and interiority of the chief evidences and experiences of religion render the clear perception and true explication of their content and significance, in certain important respects, indefinitely more difficult

c

than is the analogous attempt with regard to the external world ; and that such greater difficulty is characteristic of every advance in depth, richness and reality in the subject-matters of whatsoever we may study. Thus the science of the soul is indefinitely richer in content, but far more difficult, than is the science of shells.

2. But we have also to face the widespread violation, in the earlier religions (even where these are already above nature-worship), of truthfulness, purity, justice, mercy, as these fundamental moral and spiritual qualities and duties are understood in the later religions ; and the fact that much of such improvement as occurs (in what, if not the very heart of religion, is surely closely connected with it) appears to proceed, not from religion, but from the growth of civilisation, of the humane spirit, and this largely in keen conflict with the representatives of superhuman religion. These are doubtless grave objections. For if Religion be, at bottom, the fullest self-revelation of the Infinite Perfect Spirit in and to man's finite spirit, and if indeed this self-revelation takes place most fully in Religion, how can this self-revealing Spirit, just here, and precisely through the belief in the Superhuman, here most operative, instigate, or at all events allow, and thus often render at the least possible, terrible crimes of deception, lust, injustice, cruelty ? How can It require the aid of man's non-religious activities against man's religious apprehensions ?—Here if we care to remain equitable, we shall have to bear in mind the following.

Man's personality, the instrument of all his fuller and deeper apprehensions, is constituted by the presence and harmonisation of a whole mass of energies and intimations belonging to different levels and values ; and not one of these can (in the long run and for mankind at large) be left aside or left unchecked by the others, without grave drawback to that personality. Religion is indeed the deepest of energisings and intimations within man's entirety, but it is not the only one; and though through Religion alone God becomes definitely revealed to man as Self-conscious Spirit, as an Object, as *the* Object, of direct, explicit adoration, yet those other energies and intimations are also willed by God and come from Him, and (in the long run and for mankind at large) are necessary to man's health and balance even in religion itself.

So also the Æsthetic Sense alone conveys the full and direct intimations of the Beautiful; yet it nevertheless requires, for its healthy, balanced functioning, the adequate operation of numerous other energies and intimations, from the senses up to mental processes, in the man who apprehends the Beautiful.

Such an at all adequate and balanced development of any one group of energies and intimations, let alone of the entire personality, is of necessity, except in rare souls or in rare moments of ordinary souls, a difficult and a slow process. It has been so certainly with ethics and humaneness. It has been so still more with religion.

It is important too, throughout all these somewhat parallel growths, especially those of Ethics and Religion, always to compare the conviction, command, or practice of one time, race or country, not with those of much later times or of quite other races or communities, but with the, closely or distantly, preceding habits of one and the same race and community. Thus in Ethics, polygamy should be compared, not with monogamy, but with polyandry; and polyandry again with promiscuous intercourse. And in Religion the imprecatory Psalms and the divine order to exterminate the Canaanites should be compared, not with the Sermon on the Mount, but with purely private *vendetta*. We thus discover that, in many cases which now shock us, the belief that God had spoken was attached to genuine, if slight, moves or to confirmations of moves in the right direction; and in all such cases the belief was, so far, certainly well-founded.

Doubtless more or less self-delusion in religion must at all times have occurred, and must be still occurring, both in individuals and even in the larger groups; and doubtless, had religion never existed, certain special kinds of self-delusion would not have operated amongst men. Yet man cannot, without grave damage, do without Religion; for he cannot, in the long run, formally deny all Reality to a Subject in which man's highest inevitable ideals can find a persistent home and be harmoniously alive; nor can he attain to the vivid apprehension and steady affirmation of such a Reality except by Religion. Ethics, Philosophy, Science, all the other special strivings of man, have indeed the right and the duty persistently to contribute their share— a share indispensable (in the long run and in various, largely indirect, ways) in awakening, widening, sweetening man's imagination, mind, emotions, will; and thus to aid him also in his preparation for, and in his interpretation of, the visitations of God's Spirit. But (again in the long run and in various, often strangely unexpected, yet terribly efficacious ways) these various activities, though not directly religious, cannot fail themselves to suffer inevitably, if men *will* go further,—if they will deny all reality to the persistent object of all living Religion. Our gratitude most rightly goes out to those men who, from whatsoever quarter, have helped to awaken, widen, sweeten man in general, and in ethical, philosophical, scientific directions in particular, even though those men may have had but little specific Religion, indeed even if (often more sinned against than sinning) they have vehemently combated the only form of specific, hence superhuman, Religion which they knew. But a gratitude no less sincere is due to those men also who indeed failed to understand the worth, and who opposed the growth, of such other activities, yet who preserved the sense of the specific character of Religion,—that it deals primarily, not with ideas, but with realities, and that a certain superhumanness is of the very essence of all full Religion.

3. The points where the affirmations seemingly essential to all superhuman religion appear to be hopelessly contradicted by Philosophy or Science have been taken by us as four: the experiences of Revelation and of Miracle, and the conceptions of Creation and of Personality. The first two will be considered presently in connection with the philosophical problems.

As to Creation, it is plain that no sheer beginnings, however much we may attempt to conceive them in terms and images of the latest Natural Science, are picturable, or clearly thinkable, by us at all. Yet assuredly all the finite life, even all the ordering of matter, such as is directly known to us in our visible universe, are known to us only with marks of having had a beginning. Natural Science cannot indeed start otherwise than with already extant diffused matter, and cannot but tend to speak as though this matter, by its purely immanental forces, groups itself into such and such combinations, and proceeds to ever more complex and interior results. Yet that " already extant," that presupposition demanded for the purposes of Science, and so as to secure to Science a situation in which it begins to have a subject-matter at all—surely exhausts all that such Science requires, and all that it can confidently teach us, concerning the eternity or non-eternity of matter. Again, the successive advents of vegetable, animal, human life upon our planet introduce differences delicately, powerfully different in kind, especially when any one of these lives is compared with inorganic matter, yet also when any one such life is compared with any other of these several lives. And finally, the adaptations, in these several organisms, of their life to its environment (even if simply caused, at the observational level of Natural Science, by survival of the fittest amongst a mass of variations) always pre-supposes the original presence and the persistent repetition of variations deserving to be thus selected. We thus, still, get in Natural Science, if not a clear and complete proof of an Eternal Wisdom creating and ever sustaining all things, yet many a fact and problem which indicate how largely modal, where at all certain, is Evolution. Evolution in reality still gives us, at most and at best, not the ultimate *why* but the intermediate *how*; whilst the points of central religious importance here appear to be, not so much the non-eternity, as the createdness, of all finite realities.

Thus St. Thomas can teach us that the Eternity of the material universe would not be incompatible with its Creation, and that only Creation is intrinsically essential to Theism; although the Jewish-Christian Revelation has now taught us that, as a matter of fact, the universe is not only a creature but a non-eternal one. And indeed it appears certain that what religion here centrally cares for is " the mysterious and permanent relation between the moving changes we know in part, and the Power (after the fashion of that operation, unknown) which is " Itself unmoved all motion's source." [1]

As to the Personal God, it has now become a prevalent fashion angrily to proclaim, or complacently to assume, the utter absurdity of anything Personal about the Infinite; since Personality, of every degree and kind, essentially implies, indeed largely consists of, limitations of various kinds, and is a gross anthropomorphism the moment we apply it to anything but man himself. Yet it is interesting to note the readiness with

[1] Rev. P. N. Waggett, in *Darwinism and Modern Science* (1909), p. 490.

which these same thinkers will hypostatise parts, or special functions, of our human personality, and will indeed do so largely with concepts which we know to be specially characteristic of spatially extended bodies. Thus Thought or Love or Law, or even Substance, nothing of all this is, for such thinkers, anthropomorphic or sub-human; but anything personal is rank anthropomorphism. Yet it is only self-conscious spirit that we know well, since it alone do we know from within. Self-conscious spirit is immensely rich in content; and self-conscious spirit is by far the widest and yet deepest reality known to us at all. True, Natural Science and even Philosophy do not, of themselves, fully find the Personal God, since Natural Science is not, as such, busy with the like ultimate questions, and since Philosophy (as we shall show presently) appears, of itself, to bring us indeed to certain more than human orders or laws, but hardly fully to the Orderer. But there is nothing intrinsically unreasonable in thinking of the ultimate Cause, Ground and End of the world as certainly not less than, as somehow not all unlike, what we know our own self-conscious mind, feeling and will to be, provided we keep the sense that God is certainly not just one Object amongst other objects, or even simply one Subject amongst other subjects; and that, though variously present and operative in all subjects and objects, He is not only more perfect than, but distinct and different from, them all. In so thinking we find in, or we attribute to, the supreme Reality what we ourselves possess that is richest in content, that is best known to us, and that is most perfect within our own little yet real experience—we have done what we could; and life and history abound with warnings how easy it is here to go apparently further and to fare in fact very much worse.

Indeed we can safely hold with Lotze, not only that Personality is compatible with Infinitude, but that the personality of all finite beings can be shown to be imperfect precisely because of their finitude, and hence that " Perfect Personality is compatible only with the conception of an Infinite Being; finite beings can only achieve an approximation to it." [1]

---

[1] *Grundzüge der Religionsphilosophie* (ed. 1884), pp. 45, 46.

II

The general philosophical difficulties appear to be met by the following facts and observations.

1. Man's actual experiences, the *data* with which he starts, are never (as a certain current in modern philosophy might easily lead us to believe) simply impressions which are felt by man at the time of his receiving them as purely subjective, or which are conclusively shown to be merely subjective by philosophical analysis, or which in reason man ought to assume to be merely subjective unless a strict demonstration of their trans-subjectivity be forthcoming. The *data* of man's actual experience, on the contrary, are subject *and* object, each giving to and taking from the other ; the two, and not the one only, are (somehow and to some co-relative extent) included within the single human consciousness. And since only an outlook so purely *solipsistic* as to be destructive of the assumptions necessary to any and all coherent reasoning can, in the long run, deny the reality of something, indeed also of some mind or minds, other than, and distinct from, our own minds ; and since these our minds are doubtless surrounded by and related to such other various realities : the rational presumption is that the spontaneous and universal testimony of these our minds (after deduction of such points or forms as can be clearly shown to be simply subjective) is truly indicative of the several trans-subjective realities which these experiences so obstinately proclaim. Kant's interestingly unconscious self-contradiction here,—that we can know nothing whatever about trans-subjective reality, yet that we know for certain it is in no sense like what even our deepest and most closely criticised experiences indicate it to be—can doubtless not be maintained as reasonable by any mind once vividly aware of the inconsistency. We shall have, on the contrary, to say that, by the very nature of things, we cannot indeed get clean out of our mind, so as to compare things as they are outside it with the same things as we experience them within it ; yet that we have every solid reason for, and no cogent reason against, holding that the objects most persistently apprehended by our deeper experience as trans-subjectively real, and whose acceptance by us as

thus real brings light, order and fruitfulness, in the most unexpected ways and into the most remote places of our life and
work, are indeed trans-subjectively real and are, in themselves,
not all unlike to, not disconnected with, what we thus apprehend
them to be.

We doubtless know nothing completely, nothing adequately,
not even ourselves; we know nothing directly from within
except ourselves. Yet we do not know only ourselves, or other
things only through reasoning them out from this our self-
knowledge. But, in the endless contacts, friendly, hostile, of
give, of take, between ourselves and the objects of all kinds
which act upon us, and upon which we act in some degree or
way, we do not obtain, of ourselves a real knowledge, and of the
other things a merely subjective impression as to their mere
appearance; but such contacts always simultaneously convey
some real experience, some real knowledge, both of ourselves
and of the objects thus experienced, and indeed of each precisely
on occasion, and because, of the other.

But can I thus experience and know God? The question is,
in the first instance, *not whether I can, but whether I do*. It is
true that, outside the specifically religious life and apprehension,
there is no vivid experience of God as a Distinct Reality, as the
Supreme Subject, as Self-Conscious Spirit. Nor, even in the
religious life, is God so apprehended except on occasion of and
in contrast to other, different, lesser realities. Yet even outside
such specifically religious experiences, in all the larger human
apprehensions and endeavours, wheresoever they become entirely
serious and fully conscious of their own essential presuppositions
and necessary ideals, there is found to exist, ineradicably, the
sense of a More-than-merely-subjective, whether individually
or even generally human, without which those larger apprehensions and endeavours would lose all ultimate worth and
justification.

This More-than-merely-subjective was admirably brought out,
as regards Ethics, by Fichte in 1800. " Let us suppose you go
and sow seed in a field : so much as this may be reckoned as
your own act alone. But you no doubt sow, not simply to sow,
but that your seed may germinate and may bear fruit. The
latter, the future harvest—however much your sowing may be

a necessary condition for it—is no more your action, but the
aim of your action. We have here two things, and not one."
" Now in all your actions which show visibly in the world of
sense, you always reckon in this way upon *two* things :—upon a
first thing, which is solely produced by yourself, and upon a
second thing, which exists and which acts entirely independently
of yourself, and is simply *known* to you,—an eternal Order of
Nature." And thus too in Ethics. " If a man here calls the law
by which a special consequence necessarily follows from any
particular determination of his will, an *Order,* and (in contradistinction from the Order of Nature), a Moral or Intelligible
Order, whence a Moral or Intelligible Coherence, or System,
or World, would arise ; such a man would not, by this procedure,
be placing the Moral Order within the finite moral beings themselves, but outside of [in distinction from] them ; he would
thus assume something in addition to these beings." " Now
here is, according to me, the *place* of Religious Faith,—here, in
this necessary thinking and demanding of an Intelligible Order,
Law, Arrangement, or whatever else you may care to call it,
by which all genuine morality, the interior purity of the heart,
has necessary consequences." [1] But the late Professor Windelband, in his *Praeludien* (1903 and since), and Professor Eucken,
in his *Der Wahrheitsgehalt der Religion* (1904 and since), have
traced out in much detail precisely similar necessitations in the
Theory of Knowledge and in Logic, and again in Æsthetics, where
the worlds of the trans-subjectively True and the trans-subjectively Beautiful are as truly necessary presuppositions as is a
world of the trans-subjectively Good a necessary presupposition
in Ethics. And the late Professor Siegwart and Professor Volkelt
have most thoroughly laid bare the ever-present working of this
trans-subjective intimation and faith in Logic and the Theory of
Knowledge.

Now even with these three more-than-simply-subjective
worlds we have not, it is true, yet reached the Self-conscious
Spirit experienced by Religion. But we have thus established
important points. Man's general, human experience (wheresoever it is sufficiently wide, deep and earnest, sufficiently trustful
of whatever may turn out to be its necessary pre-requisites,

[1] *Sämmtliche Werke,* vol. v., pp. 388, 389, 392, 394.

*C

and sufficiently pressed and analysed) reveals intimations and orders of more than merely human origin, truth and range. Man's general, human experience reveals this Trans-Subjective, Superhuman World in at least three specific forms, on three different sides of his experience. And whether or not there be still another legitimate form and side of human experience, a fourth revelation of the Trans-Subjective, Superhuman World which can bring further light and support to those three, it is certain that, having got as far as those three revelations, it is exceedingly difficult for men at large to retain a vivid faith in those three worlds, and yet deliberately to reject the revelation of Self-conscious Spirit offered to them by Religion. True, the same Fichte, continuously so sure of the reality and more than human character of the Moral World, tells us, in 1798 and 1800, that " this faith is faith full and entire. That living and active Moral Order is itself God ; we do not require and we cannot apprehend any other. There is no ground in reason for going beyond such a Moral Cosmic Order, and, by means of a con-clusion from the effect to the cause, to assume, in addition, a Particular Being as this cause." [1] But then we are left thus at the surely strange, highly abstract, more or less mythical, conception of " an active Ordering." [2] We are thus given an Order which is not a mere *Orderedness,* in which case God and world would be one, and there would be no God ; but an Order which is an *active Ordering,* which is, in so far, distinct from the world it orders ; and yet an Ordering which neither is, nor implies, an *Orderer.* But it is surely entirely doubtful (even apart from what the complete, hence also especially the religious, experience of mankind may convey and require) whether such a strange *intermezzo* of a conception is, in the long run, possible for the human mind. For we have here an active Ordering of a gigantic conflict and confusion, according to abiding, more than human, standards of Truth, Beauty and Goodness, standards not made by, yet recognisable by, the human spirit ; and nevertheless this Ordering and these standards are not to be the effects of Self-conscious Spirit, and are not to be apprehended by such a spirit.

Insistence upon this *intermezzo,* as the ultimate analysis of man's entire legitimate experience, becomes indeed something

---

[1] *Sämmtliche Werke,* vol. v., p. 186.   [2] *Ibid.,* p. 382.

doctrinaire and contradicts the general method and temper which
have led the mind to the point attained, if we *will* maintain it
even after we have been brought face to face with the massive,
varied, persistent witness of the religious sense and life. For
only if we show how and why the logical, the æsthetic and the
ethical life can alone be trusted and not the religious life also,
where it supplies what those three lives all severally seek, can
we consistently accept the deep-lying testimony of the logical,
æsthetic and ethical lives, and, nevertheless, refuse or explain
away the central witness of the religious life. Fichte indeed bids
us " cease to listen to the demands of an empty system," and to
beware lest, by our hypothesis of a Personal God, we make the
first of all objective cognitions, the most certain of all certainties,
to depend upon " ingenious pleadings (*Klügelei*)." [1] Yet the
now immensely abundant testimony of Religion lies before us as
a warning that Fichte here confounded philosophical thinking
and the general idea of religiousness with the specifically religious
experiences themselves. Theological deductions and speculations have indeed at times articulated or analysed, in " ingenious "
ways, the deepest and most delicate experiences of living religion.
Yet these experiences themselves always present their object
as overflowingly existent ; and, in proportion as spirituality
becomes more conscious of its own requirements and more
sensitively discriminating, this object is apprehended as perfect
Self-conscious Spirit, as very Source of all existence and reality.
We can indeed argue against Religion, as mistaken in so doing ;
but that Religion actually does so, and this, not in the form of
deductive reasoning, but in that of intuitive experience, cannot
seriously be denied.

And this Religious Experience is, in fact, interwoven, from first
to last, with the sense of Revelation and the sense of Miracle.

2. As to Revelation, it is remarkable that men's latter-day
pre-occupation with the apparent imperfections in the *content*
of the various religions has frequently blinded them to the
excellence of the *form*, the vehicle of all Religion. For the characteristic form of all Religion is Revelation ; and the various
activities and achievements of human life, wheresoever these
are sufficiently deep to awaken and to hold the entire man and

---

[1] *Sämmtliche Werke*, vol. v., p. 180.

to lead him to some certitude, all possess, in various degrees
and ways, something *revelational* about them.[1]

It is true, of course, that the *naïf* Realism or Objectivism of
classical and mediæval times (so little conscious, upon the whole,
of the always present, and often large, contribution furnished
by the apprehending human Subject to this subject's apprehensions of the Object) led, by the excess of every reaction,
to a sometimes equally one-sided Idealism or Subjectivism, in
which the entire outer and inner world becomes the sheer projection, or at least the purely subjective elaboration, by mankind,
into orders of beauty, truth and goodness, of what is intrinsically
(or what at least is found by us analytically to be) a sheer *caput
mortuum*—just so much dead matter or wild flux and chaotic
impulsions. Yet it is equally true that the newer sciences of
Biology, Sociology and History are now fast bringing us to a third
stage where truth and life will more and more evidently be found
to consist in the fullest and most manifold interaction between
Subject and Object—and this in increasing degrees, according to
the increase in the importance of the subject-matter experienced
or studied. And everywhere in these newer sciences there is a
sense of how much there is to *get*, how rich and self-communi-
cative is all reality, to those who are sufficiently detached from
their own petty subjectivisms. A keen yet reverent study of the
Given appears here,—by a Darwin, be it of but the earth-worm,
and by a Wilken, be it of but the scribblings on ancient potsherds.
And then the greater *Givennesses* are found in those vast Intelligible
Orders, which persistently show themselves anew, wheresoever
human experience is sufficiently pressed, and which so entranced
the great minds of a Kant and of a Fichte. In all these cases we
have an absorption of the Subject in the Object, and a response
—an assuredly gradual, ever only partial, yet a very real, self-
revelation—of the Object to the Subject. In the cases of these
Intelligible Orders we have already something more or less
religious. Indeed the sense of *Givenness*, of *Prevenience*, of a
Grace, of something transcendent having in part become Immanent to our human world as a Fact within this factual world,
and of this Fact as alone rendering even possible that sense of

---

[1] See Mr. Clement C. J. Webb's excellent exposition in *Problems in the Relations
between God and Man* (1911), pp. 28 ff.

Givenness—all these experiences are already present in the apprehension and affirmation of those Intelligible Orders as truly extant. And yet it is only the specifically religious experience which gives us Revelation at its fullest, not only as to Revelation's content but also as to Revelation's form. For Religion alone brings the vivid revelation of Spirit other than the human—a Spirit so perfect and so richly real as Itself to be the ultimate, overflowingly self-conscious cause of man's very capacity for apprehending It. Nevertheless, such a Self-manifestation of Perfect Spirit, once found and accepted, gives a base, a setting and a crown to all those other self-manifestations of the lesser realities—a base, a setting and a crown which their graduated series, taken as a whole, so greatly requires and which indeed it dimly and semi-consciously prepares yet cannot itself effectuate. And this same Self-manifestation of Spirit and the human spirit's response to It, render superfluous all attempts, always more or less hopeless, to construct God *à priori*, or even to demonstrate Him, from the facts of nature and of human life, by any single, deductive argument of a strictly constraining force. Because Spirit, God, works in our midst and in our depths, we can and we do know Him; because God has been the first to condescend to us and to love us, can we arise and love Him in return. "Do you wake?" asks St. Bernard. "Well, He too is awake. If you arise in the night time, if you anticipate to your utmost your earliest awaking, you will already find Him waking—you will never anticipate His own awakeness. In such an intercourse you will always be rash if you attribute any priority, any predominant share to yourself; for He loves both more than you love, and before you love at all." [1] The prevenience of God becomes thus the crown and final guarantee of all the other, minor preveniences which variously bring us the materials and occasions for our other kinds of knowledge and conviction—from the crystal and the plant on to the animal and man.

3. The experience of Miracle, when discriminated in the higher religions and by maturely spiritual souls, appears to be composed, in its essence, of three, yet only of three, vivid, interdependent apprehensions. There is the vivid apprehension of something *unique* being experienced or produced, *hic et nunc*,

[1] *Sermons on the Canticle of Canticles*, lxix. 8.

in this particular experiencing soul. There is the vivid apprehension that this unique experience comes from the One Divine *Spirit* to this particular human spirit. And there is the vivid apprehension that this effect of Spirit upon spirit is not restricted to the human spirit alone, but that the Spirit can affect, and in any particular instance is actually affecting, in more or less striking, most real ways, the very *body* and its psychical, indeed even its physical conditions and environment, and the visible exterior conditions and history of mankind. All our previous considerations have prepared us thus to conceive Reality as, in proportion to its depth, an ever nearer and nearer approach to the Concrete Universal, to the unique embodiment of a universally valuable type ; to discover, in this tendency, throughout the successive stages of realities, to ever increasing typical uniqueness, the increasingly large operation of the actually extant Concrete Universal, God ; and to recognise, as we retrace these stages, that neither does God's Spirit live all aloof from man's spirit, nor does man's spirit live all aloof from man's body or from this physical body's physical environment. On the contrary, throughout reality, the greater works in and with and through the lesser, affecting and transforming this lesser in various striking degrees and ways. To at least this degree in these ways does Miracle, and the belief in Miracle, thoroughly belong to the permanent experience of mankind, and to the adequate analysis of this experience. Grave difficulties arise only when these three central experiences are interpreted as meaning that the spiritual or psychical or physical effects of Miracle constitute direct breaches within (as it were) the phenomenal rind and level of natural reality—breaches which can be strictly demonstrated to be such by Natural Science itself. This opinion, if pressed, requires of Natural Science (whose subject-matter is essentially limited to that level and that constituent of reality or appearance where strict continuity or repetitive law can be found or applied) to discover its object in what suspends or contradicts these characteristics, and hence is outside its special range and cognisance. Wherever such suspension or contradiction could be discovered, Science would have nothing to work upon, and could only wait till it again found something more or less continuous or repetitive.

III

It is doubtless the practical difficulties which, more largely
than all the other objections put together, explain the *doctrinaire*
aloofness or the angry set-purpose to be found extant and operative, more or less in all times and places, against Religion, as soon
as Religion appears in its full specific and articulate form—
i.e. as a conviction and claim of the Superhuman. For as men
look back into the past, or even carry the effects of the past within
their very blood, they perceive or feel that, if not Religion in its
roots, yet at least the various theologies and the various sects
and churches have, in all sorts of times and places, ways and
degrees, protected and perpetuated, or occasioned and increased,
impoverishments, divisions, oppressions, obvious or obscure,
yet very real, within men's inner lives, or as between man and
man, or between one group of men and other groups. And in
all such cases the sanction or stimulus to such grave inhibitions
or complications appear to have sprung precisely from the supposed superhuman character of some revelation, command or
institution. Such a work as Andrew White's *History of the
Warfare of Science and Theology* (1903) shows, in full detail,
how largely the Science, Philosophy, Medicine, Politics, Life
generally, which we all practise or profit by, have been established
at the price of conflict, more or less costly, with such Superhuman
Claims. Hence we are bound to show how and why those blights
or deadlocks were not produced by the Superhuman Claims as
such, and indeed how and why a Superhuman Conviction, rightly
understood and wisely practised, remains our sole ultimate
guarantee against Fanaticism on the one hand and Scepticism on
the other.

1. It is plain, for one thing, that this whole practical question
is greatly complicated by the fact that (even more than the other
circles of the higher human endeavours,—Science, Art, Ethics)
Religion always brings with it, Religion indeed always more or
less requires, such things as association, organisation, institutions.
Religious Institutions indeed habitually insist upon two most
precious principles and practices which the other, non-religious,
circles do not and cannot thus vividly apprehend and directly

inculcate ; yet these same Institutions also tend to enforce these principles and practices by means which are accountable for certainly the greater amount of the bitterness felt by so many serious, clean-lived men against those very principles and practices themselves.

Such Institutions, then, most rightly maintain the Superhuman Claim as essential to Religion ; they emphasise Religion as essentially Revelation, as man's deepest experience of the ultimate Reality through the action of that Reality Itself,—a Reality which both underlies and crowns all our other, lesser strivings and *givennesses*. And such Institutions, again, most rightly emphasise the great difference in amount, purity, and worth of the spiritual truth and life to be found even within the sincerest and most entirely positive convictions and practices of the several religions of mankind.[1] Here we have two immense services rendered by the higher Religious Institutions to the abiding truths, to the ultimate basis of man's worth ; services absolutely without serious parallel, as to their depth and range, in any other quarter.

Yet that superhuman, revelational Religion has, in the rough and tumble of life, and by and for the average institutionalist, been too often conceived as though arising *in vacuo*, and hence as though able, even in the long run, to dispense with, or to starve, the other activities and necessities of man ; or, again, as though not only Religion but Theology were a divine communication—as though God Himself communicated intrinsically adequate, mathematically precise formulations of Religion. And thus we get a starving of all that is not directly religious in man or an arrest of theological improvement. We get an insistence upon a direct and decisive jurisdiction, by a deductive theology and institutional administration, over the results of (indeed over the very methods and necessities specific to) man's other activities and apprehensions, in Science and Æsthetics, in Historical Research, Politics and Ethics, and in Philosophy. And in proportion as this is actually effected, Religion becomes bereft of the material, the friction, the witnesses so essential to the health and fruitfulness of man in general and of Religion in particular. The material

---

[1] See, as to this second point, the admirable discriminations of J. N. Farquhar in *The Crown of Hinduism* (1915), pp. 26-33.

is lost ; for man's full other experiences, which, pressed, yield
so firm a foundation for specific Religion, are here prevented
from being thus full and from being thus pressed. The friction
between Religion and Ethics, and between Theology and Science
and Philosophy, so necessary to bring out the fullest powers of
each and the deep underlying mutual need which in the living
man, each has of all the others, is eliminated ; since all these
several activities, except that of the official Theology, have,
previous to all possibility of wholesome clashing, been carefully
deprived of all their specific weapons of attack and of defence.
And the witnesses for religion disappear ; for what is a witness
who has, by forcible suppressions or modifications of his
testimony, been rendered " safe " beforehand ?

And again, as to all the religions of mankind other than their
own, such great Institutions tend, in their average representatives
and disciples, to speak and act as though it were Indifferentism
ever to discover *some* religious truth and life as present in such
other religions, in however various degrees and ways. The
whole conception of varyingly intense and varyingly precious
feelings after God ; of stages of growth and of light ; of more
or less error and corruption mixed with more or less of truth
and of health ; of the test and measure of such truth and health
lying indeed within the deepest practice and the fundamental
convictions of the most richly and most specifically religious of
the great religious bodies—with these as most fully explicating
whilst exceeding the previous illuminations and gropings of
man's soul : such a conception is clearly difficult to every fully
organised Religious Institution.

2. The all-important facts here are, however, that no Orthodoxy
explicitly denies such a general position ; and that no Orthodoxy
achieves its own deepest function except it explicitly admits and
genially practises this its very genuine implication. And is it
really so difficult, precisely for men so rightly concentrated
upon the reality of God and of His operativeness throughout
the world at large, and especially throughout the world of souls,
to find thus His traces, though doubtless in very different degrees
of clearness and of worth, even where their possessors are not
awake to their source, or even where they turn angrily against
the bearers of a fuller message ? Unless the whole Christian

Church is wrong in insisting upon the Old Testament as the Word of God, unless St. Paul was wrong in preaching God to the heathen Athenians as " Him Whom they had ignorantly worshipped," and unless our Lord Himself was wrong in coming, " not to be ministered to, but to minister," some such attitude cannot but be the right one, however difficult to our poor human passions it may persistently remain.

Even amongst the rigorist Primitive Christians and amongst harsh Mediæval Churchmen, such mild and comprehensive convictions and characters have as certainly occurred as the fierce feelings and persecuting proceedings of others amongst their contemporaries. And it would clearly be utterly *a priori* and arbitrary to construe these convictions and characters as springing from, or as leading to, indifference. The Church Father Lactantius and the Popes St. Gregory the Great and Alexander II. were no less certain of, and no less zealous for, Superhuman Religion—for the supreme truth of Christianity and of Catholicism, than were the Church Father St. Augustine or the Popes St. Pius V. and Paul IV. But the former combined, with this their all-pervading and all-crowning faith, a keen sense for the natural virtues, as the inviolable pre-requisites, concomitants and consequences of the Supernatural Life ; for the elements of truth and goodness present in all men and in all religions ; for the essentially free character of the act and habit of faith ; and for the irreplaceable persuasiveness of love ; whereas the latter were all but exclusively engrossed in the specifically religious virtues, in the completest religion, in this religion's scholastic and juridical formulation, and in the influence and utility of pressure, fear, commands, obedience. But both groups, in their several ways, are equally discriminative, equally zealous, equally superhuman.

3. The dispositions and acts of the mild and comprehensive group appear now to be as true and as wise as ever, and to require no more than certain further discriminations. We religious men will have to develop, *as part of our religion,* the ceaseless sense of its requiring the *nidus,* materials, stimulant, discipline, of the other God-given, non-religious activities, duties, ideals of man, from his physical and psychical necessities up to his æsthetic, political and philosophical aspirations. The autonomy,

competition, and criticism of the other centres of life will have thus to become welcome to religion for the sake of religion itself. We religious men again will have to develop, *as part of our religion*, a sense, not simply of the error and evil, but also of the truth and the good, in any and every man's religion. We will have to realise, with Cardinal John de Lugo, S.J. (who died in See p. 284 1660), that the members of the various Christian sects, of the Jewish and Mohammedan communions, and of the non-Christian philosophies, who achieved and achieve their salvation, did and do so in general simply by God's grace aiding their good faith instinctively to concentrate itself upon, and to practise, those elements in the cultus and teaching of their respective sect, communion or philosophy, which are true and good and originally revealed by God.[1] And, finally, we religious men, especially we Catholic Christians, will indeed never drop the noble truth and ideal of a universal unity of cultus and belief, of one single world-wide Church, but we will conceive this our deathless faith in religious unity as being solidly realisable only if we are able and glad to recognise the rudimentary, fragmentary, relative, pædagogic truth and worth in religions other than our own,—a worth which, as regards at least Judaism and Hellenism, the Roman Church has never ceased to practise and to proclaim.

To conclude.

We have found reason to hold that all actually lived Religion is, in proportion to the depth and delicacy of its spirituality, always simultaneously conscious of two closely interconnected things : *the more than human reality of the Object of its experience*, which Object indeed Itself reveals Itself in, and makes real, this experience, AND *the abiding difference between even this its present experience and the great Reality thus experienced and revealed*. And, in this twin consciousness, living Religion is like every other truly live apprehension. No true scientist, artist, philosopher, no moral striver, but finds himself, at his best and deepest moments, with the double sense that some abiding, transsubjective, other-than-human or even more-than-human reality, or force, or law, is manifesting itself in his experiences ; and yet that these very experiences, and still more his reasoned abstracts

[1] *De Fide*, Disputatio xii., No. 50, seqq.

of them, give but a very incomplete, ever imperfect, conception of those trans-subjective realities.

And now let us suppose that all such conviction of a real contact with Superhuman Reality were to be lost by humanity at large ; and that neither general life, in its deepest necessities, nor the historical religions, in their special answers, would any longer be admitted as witnesses to anything but just so much sheer projection of merely human, although racial, fancies. Thus, the spiritual deeps, beckoning us on to their ever further, never exhaustible, exploration, and the spiritual atmosphere, in and through which mankind has ever, with varying degrees of consciousness as to this medium, perceived things finite, would go. And in lieu of Mysterious Reality, to be ever more closely pressed and more deeply penetrated, we should be environed by an importunate mystification which, surely, men would attempt to eliminate at any and every cost. Such men, bereft of all atmosphere, such " men of the moon," would, of necessity, end by being sure that they knew all there is to know, or, at least, that they or their fellow-men could thus know all there is to know : hence they would represent the very acme of intolerance. For, in truth, abstractions of his own mind and projections of his own wishes, if and where taken by man to be in very deed no more than himself, and to correspond to nothing outside of or higher than himself, will, in the long run, be incapable of satisfying man ; and hence they will be unable to check his passions, good or evil. The Fanaticism which in man, as long as he is man, will always lurk within the folds of his emotions, and which in religious men springs, not from their superhuman belief as such, but from their ignorance or misunderstanding of certain pre-requisites and conditions essential to the healthy and fruitful working of Superhuman Religion (that gift and act and habit, so free and yet so firm, within poor yet rich, complex, many-levelled man)—will, in such a supposed attempt at a purely immanental life, no doubt at first (if it have no other man's supernatural belief to tilt against) roam about loose and restless. But Fanaticism, in such a case, would soon attach itself to some sheer Secularism—to what such a pure Immanentist would at first admit to be merely such ; it would next attempt solemnly to proclaim and to believe such a

Secularism to be somehow great or even unique, and to enforce
it as such; and then, unless simple assent to the Trans-
Subjective Intimations returned, even this kind and degree of
conviction and Fanaticism would be succeeded by a Scepticism,
more sincere but more destructive than even this Secularism
itself.

Are cultivated West Europeans really coming, for good and
all, to such a condition of alternate or of simultaneous irreligious
fanaticism and utter scepticism? Surely, no. For if religious
faith and hope and love are free gifts of God and free virtues
of man, and if they are, in some respects, specially difficult for
such Europeans, yet the present keenness of irritation, amongst
so many of these men, against the very terms of Transcendence
and the Superhuman, is demonstrably, in great part, a quite
understandable reaction against still widely prevalent ways of
conceiving and of applying (*i.e.* of enforcing) the Superhuman
and Religion. The presence and pressure of the motives for
General Religion, and the answering evidences and aids of
Specific, Characteristic Religion (as these latter culminate, for
us Europeans, in the Jewish-Christian Revelation and Spiritual
Society) remain, on and on, too strongly rooted in the very
nature and necessities of the spiritual world which environs and
penetrates us all, for them not, more or less continuously, to
keep or to raise us above such irritation and reactions against the
Supernatural as such. And once a man is thus free from a
specially dangerous, because inverted and hence unnoticed,
dependence upon the faults and excesses of others, he will be
able to find, to love and to practise (by means of and within
the great Historical Institutions) deep Superhuman Religion, and
this without repelling other souls, where these are sincere and
serious in their own degree and kind.

Some years ago alarm grew rife concerning the safety of
Winchester Cathedral, discovered to be undermined by water-
courses; and expert divers, in full diving dress, plunged down
through the springs to the swamps and sands—the foundations
so daringly accepted by the original builders of the majestic
edifice. The divers found the great oaken beams, as laid by those
first builders upon those shifting natural foundations, still,
for the most part, serviceably sound. Yet some of these beams

required replacing; and the guardian architects decided to replace them all by great concrete piers. We too, in this study, have been probing foundations—those of Religion. But here we have found the foundations to consist of rock—two inter-dependent, interclamped rock-masses : the general, dim and dumb Religiosity—the more or less slumbering sense and need of the Abiding and Eternal; and the concrete, precise and personal Religion—the clear answer to that confused asking, and, with this answer, the now keen articulation of that dim demand. And both that general dull sense and this special definite presentment were found by us in actual life,—found by us there as Givennesses of an evidential, revelational, an other-than-human, a more-than-human quality. Yet here also, in our own subject-matter, as there in the case of the Cathedral, some renovation or re-arrangement of the structure reared more or less directly upon the ancient and abiding foundations appeared to be demanded. Nevertheless in this, the religious case, the desirable repairs turned out to consist essentially, not in preventing shift-ing, swampy foundations from spreading their sapping influence upwards, but, on the contrary, in eliminating, from the various stages of builders' work reared upon the sound and solid rock-foundations, whatsoever may impede those stages from full reception of this soundness and solidity. And we found the dispositions necessary for the unhampered spreading through-out the whole of life of the soundness resident in the deepest roots—in Superhuman Religion, to be three : the soberly auto-nomous development of the several non-religious faculties and of the non-religious associations of man; the ready recognition, by any one religion, of elements of worth variously present in the other religions, together with the careful avoidance of all attempts at forced conformity; and a careful respect for the methods intrinsic to history and philosophy, even where these analyse or theorise the documents and experiences of religion itself. Thus will all men of good faith be laid open to the appeal, so full of aid to the best that is in them, of Superhuman Religion in its profound life and reality.

3

PROGRESS IN RELIGION[1]

THE difficulties are deep and delicate which confront any man
at all well acquainted with the fuller significance of Religion and
of Progress, who attempts clearly and shortly to describe or
define the ultimate relations between these two sets of fact and
conviction. It is plain that Religion is the deeper and richer
of the two terms; and that we have here, above all, to attempt
to fathom the chief elements and forces of Religion as such,
and then to see whether Progress is really traceable in Religion
at all. And again it is clear that strongly religious souls will,
as such, hold that Religion answers to, and is occasioned by, the
action, within our human life and needs, of great, abiding, living
non-human Realities; and yet, if such souls are at all experienced
and sincere, they will also admit—as possibly the most baffling
of facts—that the human individuals, families, races, are relatively
rare in whom this sense and need of Religion is strongly, sensitively active. Thus the religion of most men will either all
but completely wither or vanish before the invasion of other
great facts and interests of human life—Economics or Politics
or Ethics, or again, Science, Art, Philosophy; or it will, more
frequently, become largely assimilated, in its conception, valua-
tion, and practice, to the quite distinct, and often subtly different,
conceptions, valuations, and practices pertaining to such of
these other ranges and levels of human life as happen here to
be vigorously active. And such assimilations are, of course,
effected with a particular Philosophy or Ethic, mostly some
passing fashion of the day, which does not reach the deepest laws
and standards even of its own domain, and which, if taken as
Religion, will gravely numb and mar the power and character

[1] An Address to the Summer School Meeting at Woodbroke (Birmingham),
1916. Reprinted from *Progress and History*, edited by F. S. Marvin, Oxford
University Press, 1916.

of such religious perception as may still remain in this particular soul.

I will, then, first attempt some discriminations in certain fundamental questions concerning the functioning of our minds, feelings, wills. I will next attempt short, vivid descriptions of the chief stages in the Jewish and Christian Religions, with a view to tracing here what may concern their progress ; and will very shortly illustrate the main results attained by the corresponding peculiarities of Confucianism, Buddhism, and Mohammedanism. And I will finally strive to elucidate and to estimate, as clearly as possible, the main facts in past and present Religion which concern the question of religious " Progressiveness."

I

I begin with insisting upon seven discriminations which, even only forty years ago, would have appeared largely preposterous to the then fashionable philosophy.

First, then, our Knowledge is always wider and deeper than is our Science. I know my mother, I know my dog, I know my favourite rose-tree ; and this, although I am quite ignorant of the anatomical differences between woman and man ; of the psychological limits between dog and human being ; or of the natural or artificial botanical order to which my rose-plant belongs. Any kind or degree of consciousness on my part as to these three realities is a knowledge of their content. "Knowledge is not simply the reduction of phenomena to law and their resolution into abstract elements ; since thus the unknowable would be found well within the facts of experience itself, in so far as these possess a concrete character which refuses translation into abstract relations." So Professor Aliotta urges with unanswerable truth.[1]

And next, this spontaneous awareness of other realities by myself, the reality Man, contains always, from the first, both matter and form, and sense, reason, feeling, volition, all more or less in action. Sir Henry Jones insists finely : " The difference between the primary and elementary data of thought on the one

[1] *The Idealistic Reaction against Science*, Engl. tr. 1914, pp. 6, 7.

hand, and the highest forms of systematised knowledge on the other, is no difference in kind, analogous to a mere particular and a mere universal ; but it is a difference of articulation." [1]

Thirdly, direct, unchallengeable Experience is always only experience of a particular moment ; only by means of Thought, and trust in Thought, can such Experience be extended, communicated, utilised. The sceptic, to be at all effective, practises this trust as really as does his opponent. Thought, taken apart from Experience, is indeed artificial and arid ; but Experience without Thought, is largely an orderless flux. Philosophers as different as the Neo-Positivist Mach and the Intuitionist Bergson, do indeed attempt to construct systems composed solely of direct Experience and pure Intuition ; and, at the same time, almost ceaselessly insist upon the sheer novelty, the utter unexpectedness of all direct Experience, and the entire artificiality of the constructions of Thought—constructions which alone adulterate our perceptions of reality with the non-realities repetition, uniformity, foreseeableness. Yet the amazing success of the application of such constructions to actual Nature stares us all in the face. " It is indeed strange," if that contention be right, " that facts behave as if they too had a turn for mathematics." Assuredly " if thought, with its durable and coherent structure, were not the reflection of some order of stable relations in the nature of things, it would be worthless as an organ of life." [2]

Fourthly, both Space and Time are indeed essential constituents of all our perceptions, thoughts, actions, at least in this life. Yet Time is perhaps the more real, and assuredly the richer, constituent of the two. But this rich reality applies only to Concrete or Filled Time, Duration, in which our experiences, although always more or less successive, interpenetrate each other in various degrees and ways, and are thus more or less simultaneous. An absolutely even flow of equal, mutually exclusive moments, on the contrary, exists only for our theoretical thinking, in Abstract, Empty, or Clock time. Already, in 1886, Professor James Ward wrote : " In time, conceived as physical, there is no trace of intensity ; in time, as psychically experienced,

---

[1] *A Critical Account of the Philosophy of Lotze*, 1895, p. 104.
[2] Aliotta, *op. cit.*, pp. 89, 187.

duration is primarily an intensive magnitude."[1] And in 1889 Professor Bergson, in his *Essai sur les Données Immédiates de la Conscience*, gave us exquisite descriptions of time as we really experience it, of " duration strictly speaking," which " does not possess moments that are identical or exterior to each other."[2] Thus all our real soul life, in proportion to its depth, moves in Partial Simultaneity; indeed it apprehends, requires and rests, at its deepest, in an overflowingly rich Pure Simultaneity.

Fifthly, Man is Body as well as Soul, and the two are closely interrelated. The sensible perception of objects, however humble, is always necessary for the beginning, and (in the long run) for the persistence and growth, of the more spiritual apprehensions of man. Hence Historical Persons and Happenings, Institutions, affording Sensible Acts and Contacts, and Social Corporations, each different according to the different ranges and levels of life, can hardly fail to be of importance for man's full awakening—even ethical and spiritual. Professor Ernst Troeltsch, so free from natural prejudice in favour of such a Sense-and-Spirit position, has become perhaps the most adequate exponent of this great fact of life, which is ever in such danger of evaporation amidst the intellectual and leading minority of men.

Sixthly, the cultivated modern man is still largely arrested and stunted by the spell of Descartes, with his insistence upon immediate unity of outlook and perfect clearness of idea, as the sole, universal tests, indeed constituents, of truth. " I judged that I could take for my general rule that the things which we conceive very clearly and very distinctly are all true "—these and these alone.[3] Thus thenceforth Mathematics and Mechanics have generally been held to be the only full and typical sciences, and human knowledge to be co-extensive with such sciences alone. Yet Biology and Psychology now rightly claim to be sciences, each with its own special methods and tests distinct from those of Mathematics and Mechanics. Indeed, the wisest and most fruitful philosophy is now coming to see that " Reality generally eludes our thought, when thought is reduced to mathematical formulas."[4] Concrete thought, contrariwise, finds full

[1] *Encycl. Brit.*, " Psychology," 11th ed., p. 577.
[2] Ed. 1898, p. 90.
[3] *Discours sur la Méthode*, 1637, IVe Partie.
[4] Aliotta, *op. cit.*, p. 408.

room also for History, Philosophy, Religion, for each as furnishing rich subject-matters for Knowledge or Science, of a special but true kind.

Seventhly. Already Mathematics and Mechanics absolutely depend, for the success of their applications to actual Nature, upon a spontaneous correspondence between the human reason and the Rationality of Nature. The immensity of this success is an unanswerable proof that this rationality is not imposed, but found there, by man. But Thought without a Thinker is an absurd proposition. Thus faith in Science is faith in God. Perhaps the most impressive declaration of this necessary connexion between Knowledge and Theism stands at the end of that great work, Christoph Sigwart's *Logik*. " As soon as we raise the question as to the real *right*," the adequate reason, " of our demands for a correspondence, within our several sciences, between the principles and the objects of the researches special to each, there emerges the need for the Last and Unconditional Reason. And the actual situation is not that this Reason appears only on the horizon of our finite knowledge," as Kant would have it. " Not in thus merely extending our knowledge lies the significance of the situation, but in the fact that this Unconditional Reason constitutes the presupposition without which no desire for Knowledge (in the proper and strict sense of the word) is truly thinkable." [1]

And lastly, all this and more points to philosophical Agnosticism as an artificial system, and one hopelessly inadequate to the depths of human experience. Assuredly Bossuet is right : " man knows not the whole of everything " ; and mystery, in this sense, is also of the essence of all higher religion. But what man knows of anything is that thing manifested, not essentially travestied, in that same thing's appearances. We men are most assuredly realities forming part of a real world-whole of various realities ; those other realities continuously affect our own reality ; we cannot help thinking certain things about these other realities ; and these things, when accepted and pressed home by us in action or in science, turn out, by our success in this their utilisation, to be rightly apprehended by us, as parts of interconnected, objective Nature. Thus our knowledge of Reality is real as far as it goes, and philosophical Agnosticism is a *doctrinaire* position. We can say with Herbert Spencer, in spite of his predominant Agnosticism, that " the error " committed by philosophers intent upon demonstrating the limits and conditions of consciousness " consists in assuming that consciousness contains *nothing but* limits and conditions, to the entire neglect of that which is limited and conditioned." In reality " there is some thing which alike forms the raw material of definite thought and remains after the definiteness, which thinking gave to it, has been destroyed." [1]

II

Let us next consider five of the most ancient and extensively developed amongst the still living Religions : the Israelitish-Jewish and the Christian religions shall, as by far the best known to us and as the most fully articulated, form the great bulk of this short account ; the Confucian, Buddhist, and Mohammedan religions will be taken quite briefly, only as contrasts to, or elucidations of, the characteristics found in the Jewish and Christian faiths.   All this in view of the question concerning the relations between Religion and Progress.

1. We can roughly divide the Israelitish-Jewish religion into three long periods ; in each the points that specially concern us will greatly vary in clearness, importance, and richness of content.

The first period, from the time of the founder Moses and the Jewish exodus out of Egypt to the appearance of the first great prophet Elijah (say 1300 B.C. to about 860 B.C.) is indeed but little known to us ; yet it gives us the great historical figure of the initial lawgiver, the recipient and transmitter of deep ethical and religious experiences and convictions.   True, the Code of King Hammurabi of Babylon (between 1958 and 1916 B.C.; or, according to others, about 1650) anticipates many of the laws of the *Book of the Covenant* (Exod. xx. 22–xxiii. 33), the oldest amongst the at all lengthy bodies of laws in the Pentateuch ; and, again, this Covenant appears to presuppose the Jewish settlement in Canaan (say in 1250 B.C.) as an accomplished fact. And, indeed, the Law and the books of Moses generally have undoubtedly

[1] *First Principles*, 6th ed., 1900, vol. i., p. 67.

passed through a long, deep, wide, and elaborate development, of which three chief stages, all considerably subsequent to the Covenant-Book, have, by now, been established with substantial certainty and precision. The record of directly Mosaic sayings and writings is thus certainly very small. Yet it is assuredly a gross excess to deny the historical reality of Moses, as even distinguished scholars such as Edward Meyer and Bernhard Stade have done. Far wiser here is Wellhausen, who finds, in the very greatness and fixity of orientation of the development in the Law and in the figure of the Lawgiver, a conclusive proof of the rich reality and greatness of the Man of God, Moses. Yet it is Hermann Gunkel, I think, who has reached the best balanced judgement in this matter. With Gunkel we can securely hold that Moses called God Yahweh, and proclaimed Him as the national God of Israel ; that Moses invoked Him as " Yahweh is my banner "—the divine leader of the Israelites in battle (Exod. xvii. 15) ; and that Yahweh is for Moses a God of righteousness—of the right and the law which he, Moses, brought down from Mount Sinai and published at its foot. Fierce as may now appear to us the figure of Yahweh, thus proclaimed, yet the soul's attitude towards Him is already here, from the first, a religion of the will : an absolute trust in God (" Yahweh shall fight for you, and ye shall hold your peace," Exod. xiv. 14), and a terrible relentlessness in the execution of His commands—as when Moses orders the sons of Levi to go to and fro in the camp, slaying all who, as worshippers of the Golden Calf, had not been " on Yahweh's side " (Exod. xxxii. 25–29) ; and when the chiefs, who had joined in the worship of Baal-Peor, are " hung up unto Yahweh before the sun " (Num. xxv. 1–5). Long after Moses the Jews still believed in the real existence of the gods of the heathen ; and the religion of Moses was presumably, in the first instance, " Monolatry " (the adoration of One God among many) ; but already accompanied by the conviction that Yahweh was mightier than any other god—certainly Micah, " Who is like Yahweh ? " is a very ancient Israelitish name. And if Yahweh is worshipped by Moses on a mountain (Sinai) and His law is proclaimed at a spring, if Moses perhaps himself really fashioned the brazen serpent as a sensible symbol of Yahweh, Yahweh nevertheless remains without visible representation in or on the Ark; He is never conceived as the sheer equivalent of natural forces; and all mythology is absent here—the vehement rejection of the calf-worship shows this strikingly. Michael Angelo, himself a soul of fire, understood Moses well, Gunkel thinks.[1]

The second period, from Elijah's first public appearance (about 860 B.C.) to the Dedication of the Second Temple (516 B.C.), and on to the public subscription to the Law of Moses, under Ezra (in 444 B.C.), is surpassed, in spiritual richness and import-ance, only by the classical times of Christianity itself. Its begin-ning, its middle, and its end each possess distinctive characters.

The whole opens with Elijah, " the grandest heroic figure in all the Bible," as it still breathes and burns in the First Book of Kings. " For Elijah there existed not, in different regions, forces possessed of equal rights and equal claims to adoration, but everywhere only one Holy Power that revealed Itself, not like Baal, in the life of Nature, but like Yahweh, in the moral demands of the Spirit " (Wellhausen).

And then (in about 750 B.C.) appears Amos, the first of the noble " storm-birds " who herald the coming national destruc-tions and divine survivals. " Yahweh was for these prophets above all the god of justice, and God of Israel only in so far as Israel satisfied His demands of justice. And yet the special relation of Yahweh to Israel is still recognised as real; the ethical truth, which now stood high above Israel, had, after all, arisen within Israel and could only be found within it." The two oldest lengthy narrative documents of the Pentateuch— the Yahwist (J) and the Ephraemite (E)—appear to have been composed, the first in Judah in the time of Elijah, the second in Israel at the time of Amos. J gives us the immortal stories of Paradise and the Fall, Cain and Abel, Noah and the Flood ; E, Abraham's sacrifice of Isaac ; and the documents conjointly furnish the more naive and picturesque parts of the grand accounts of the Patriarchs generally—the first great narrative stage of the Pentateuch. God here gives us some of His most exquisite self-revelations through the Israelitish peasant-soul. And Isaiah of Jerusalem, successful statesman as well as deep seer, still vividly lives for us in some thirty-six chapters of that great

[1] Article, " Moses," in *Die Religion in Geschichte und Gegenwart*, 1913.

collection the "Book of Isaiah" (i.–xii., xv.–xx., xxii.–xxxix.).
There is his majestic vocation in about 740 B.C., described by
himself, without ambiguity, as a precise, objective revelation
(chap. vi.) ; and there is the divinely impressive close of his long
and great activity, when he nerves King Hezekiah to refuse the
surrender of the Holy City to the all-powerful Sennacherib,
King of Assyria : his assurance that Yahweh would not allow
a single arrow to be shot against it, and would turn back the
Assyrian by the way by which he came—all which actually
happens as thus predicted (chap. xxxvii.).

The middle of this rich second period is filled by a great
prophet-priest's figure, and a great prophetical priestly reform.
Jeremiah is called in 628 B.C., and dies obscurely in Egypt in
about 585 B.C. ; and the Deuteronomic Law and Book is found
in the Temple, and is solemnly proclaimed to, and accepted by,
the people, under the leadership of the High Priest Hilkiah
and King Josiah, "the Constantine of the Jewish Church,"
in 628 B.C. Jeremiah and Deuteronomy (D) are strikingly cog-
nate in style, temper, and injunctions ; and especially D contrasts
remarkably in all this with the documents J and E. We thus
have here the second great development of the Mosaic Law.
Both Jeremiah and Deuteronomy possess a deeply interior,
tenderly spiritual, kernel and a fiercely polemical husk—they
both are full of the contrast between the one All-Holy God to
be worshipped in the one Holy Place, Jerusalem, and the many
impure heathen gods worshipped in so many places by the
Jewish crowd. Thus in Jeremiah Yahweh declares : " This
shall be my covenant that I will make with the house of Israel :
I will write my law in their hearts : and they shall all know me,
from the least to the greatest : for I will remember their sin
no more " (xxxi. 33, 34). And Yahweh exclaims : " My people
have committed two evils : they have forsaken me, the fountain
of living waters, and have hewn out cisterns that can hold no
water." " Lift up thine eyes unto the high places . . . thou hast
polluted the land with thy wickedness." " Wilt thou not from
this time cry unto me : My Father, thou art the guide of my
youth ? " (ii. 13, iii. 2, 4). And Deuteronomy teaches magnificently : " This commandment which I command you this day,
is not too hard for thee, neither is it far off. It is not in heaven,

neither is it beyond the sea, that thou shouldest say: Who shall go up for us to heaven or over the sea, and bring it unto us? But the word is very nigh unto thee, in thy mouth and in thy heart, that thou mayest do it " (xxx. 11–14). And there are here exquisite injunctions—to bring back stray cattle to their owners; to spare the sitting bird, where eggs or fledglings are found; to leave over, at the harvest, some of the grain, olives, grapes, for the stranger, the orphan, the widow; and not to muzzle the ox when treading out the corn (xxii. 1, 6, 7; xxiv. 19; xxv. 4). Yet the same Deuteronomy ordains: " If thine own brother, son, daughter, wife, or bosom friend entice thee secretly, saying, let us go and serve other gods, thine hand shall be first upon him to put him to death."   Also " There shall not be found with thee any consulter with a familiar spirit . . . or a necromancer.   Yahweh thy God doth drive them out before thee." And, finally, amongst the laws of war, " of the cities of these people (Hittite, Amorite, Canaanite, Perizzite, Hivite, Jebusite) thou shalt save alive nothing that breatheth, as Yahweh thy God hath commanded thee " (xii. 2–5 ; xiii. 6, 9 ; xviii. 10–13 ; xx. 16, 17).   Here we must remember that the immorality of these Canaanitish tribes and cults was of the grossest, indeed largely unnatural, kind ; that it had copiously proved its terrible fascination for their kinsmen, the Jews ; that these ancient Easterns, e.g. the Assyrians, were ruthlessly cruel at the storming of enemy cities ; and especially that the morality and spirituality, thus saved for humanity from out of a putrid flood, was (in very deed) immensely precious.   One point here is particularly far-sighted—the severe watchfulness against all animism, spiritism, worship of the dead, things in which the environing world of the Jews' fellow Semites was steeped.   The Israelitish-Jewish prophetic movement did not first attain belief in a Future Life, and then, through this, belief in God ; but the belief in God, strongly hostile to all those spiritisms, only very slowly, and not until the danger of any infusion of those naturalisms had become remote, led on the Jews to a realisation of the soul's survival with a consciousness at least equal to its earthly aliveness.   The Second Book of Kings (chaps. xxii., xxiii.) gives a graphic account of King Josiah's rigorous execution of the Deuteronomic law.

The end of this most full second period is marked by the now
rapid predominance of a largely technical priestly legislation
and a corresponding conception of past history ; by the inception
of the Synagogue and the religion of the Book ; but also by
writings the most profound of any in the Old Testament, all
presumably occasioned by the probing experiences of the Exile.
In 597 and 586 B.C. Jerusalem is destroyed and the majority of
the Jews are taken captives to Babylon ; and in between (in 593)
occurs the vocation of the prophet-priest Ezekiel, and his book
is practically complete by 573 B.C. Here the prophecies as to
the restoration are strangely detailed and schematic—already
somewhat like the apocalyptic writers. Yet Ezekiel reveals to
us deathless truths—the responsibility of the individual soul for
its good and its evil, and God Himself as the Good Shepherd
of the lost and the sick (xviii. 20–32 ; xxxiv. 1–6) ; he gives us
the grand pictures of the resurrection unto life of the dead bones
of Israel (chap. xxxvii.), and of the waters of healing and of life
which flow forth, ever deeper and wider, from beneath the
Temple, and by their sweetness transform all sour waters and
arid lands that they touch (xlvii. 1–12). A spirit and doctrine
closely akin to those of Ezekiel produced the third, last, and most
extensive development of the Pentateuchal legislation and
doctrinal history—in about 560 B.C., the Law of Holiness (Lev.,
chaps. xvii.–xxvi.) ; and in about 500 B.C., the Priestly Code. As
with Ezekiel's look forward, so here with these Priests' look
backward, we have to recognise much schematic precision of
dates, genealogies, and explanations instinct with technical
interests. The unity of sanctuary and the removal from the feasts
and the worship of all traces of naturalism, which in Jeremiah,
Deuteronomy, and the Second Book of Kings appear still as
the subject-matters of intensest effort and conflict, are here
assumed as operative even back to patriarchal times. Yet it can
reasonably be pleaded that the life-work of Moses truly involved
all this development ; and even that Monotheism (at least,
for the times and peoples here concerned) required some such
rules as are assumed by the Priestly Code.

And P gives us the great six days' Creation Story with its
splendid sense of rational order pervasive of the Universe, the
work of the all-reasonable God—its single parts good, its totality

D

very good ; and man and woman springing together from the
Creator's will. But the writer nowhere indicates that he means
long periods by the " days " ; each creation appears as effected
in an instant, and these instants as separated from each other by
but twenty-four hours.

In between Deuteronomy and the Priestly Code, or a little
later still, lies probably the composition of three religious works
full, respectively, of exultant thanksgiving, of the noblest insight
into the fruitfulness of suffering, and of the deepest questionings
issuing in child-like trust in God. For an anonymous writer
composes (say, in 550 B.C.) the great bulk of the magnificent
chapters forty to fifty-five of our Book of Isaiah — a pæan of
spiritual exultation over the Jews' proximate deliverance from
exile by the Persian King Cyrus. In 538 B.C. Cyrus issues the
edict for the restoration of the Jews to Judæa, and in 516 the
Second Temple is dedicated. Within this great Consolation
stands (xlii. 1–4 ; xlix. 1–6 ; l. 4–9 ; lii. 13–liii. 12) the poem
on the Suffering Servant of Yahweh—the tenderest revelation
of the Old Testament—apparently written previously in the
Exile, say in 570–560 B.C. The Old Law here reaches to the very
feet of the New Law—to the Lamb of God who taketh away the
sins of the world. And the Book of Job, in its chief constituents
(chaps. i.–xxxi., xxxviii.–xlii.), was probably composed when
Greek influences began—say in about 480 B.C., the year of
the battle of Thermopylæ. The canonisation of this daringly
speculative book indicates finely how sensitive even the deepest faith and holiness can remain to the apparently unjust
distribution of man's earthly lot.

Our second period ends in 444 B.C., when the priest and scribe
Ezra solemnly proclaims, and receives the public subscription
to, the Book of the Law of Moses—the Priestly Code, brought
by him from Babylon.

The Jewish last period, from Ezra's Proclamation 444 B.C.
to the completion of the Fourth Book of Ezra, about A.D. 95,
is (upon the whole) derivative. Amos, Isaiah, Jeremiah were
absorbed in the realities of their own epoch-making times,
and of God's universal governance of the world past and future ;
Daniel now, with practically all the other Apocalyptic writers
in his train, is absorbed in those earlier prophecies, and in

ingenious speculations and precise computations as to the how
and the when of the world's ending. The Exile had given rise
to the Synagogue, and had favoured the final development and
codifying of the Mosaic law ; the seventy years' intermission
of the Temple sacrifices and symbolic acts had turned the worship,
which had been so largely visible, dramatic, social, into the
praying, singing, reading, preaching of extant texts, taken as
direct and final rules for all thought and action, and as incapable
of additions or interpretations equal in value to themselves.
Yet thus priceless treasures of spiritual truth and light were
handed down to times again aglow with great—the greatest
religious gifts and growths ; and indeed this literature itself
introduced various conceptions or images destined to form a
largely fitting, and in the circumstances attractive, garment for
the profound further realities brought by Christianity.

In the Book of Daniel (written somewhere between 165 and
163 B.C.) all earthly events appear as already inscribed in the
heavenly books (vii. 10), and the events which have still really
to come consist in the complete and speedy triumph of the
Church-State Israel against King Antiochus Epiphanes. But
here we get the earliest clear proclamation of a heightened life
beyond death—though not yet for all (xii. 2). The noble vision
of the four great beasts that came up from the sea, and of one
like unto a Son of Man that came with the clouds of heaven
(chap. vii.), doubtless here figures the earthly kingdoms, Babel,
Media, Persia, Greece (Alexander), and God's kingdom Israel.

The Psalter was probably closed as late as 140 B.C. ; some
Psalms doubtless date back to 701—a few perhaps to David
himself, about 1000 B.C. The comminatory Psalms, even if
spoken as by representatives of God's Church and people, we
cannot now echo within our own spiritual life ; any heightened
consciousness after death is frequently denied (e.g. vi. 5 : " in
the grave who shall give thee thanks ? " and cxv. 17 : " the dead
praise not the Lord ")—we have seen the impressive reason of
this ; and perhaps a quarter of the Psalms are doubles, or pale
imitations of others. But, for the rest, the Psalter remains as
magnificently fresh and powerful as ever : culminating in the
glorious self-commitment (Ps. lxxiii.), " I was as a beast before
Thee. Nevertheless I am continually with Thee. Whom have I

in heaven but Thee? and there is none upon earth that I desire
beside Thee." The keen sense, present throughout this amazingly
rich collection, of the reality, prevenience, presence, protection
—of the central importance for man, of God, the All-Abiding,
finds thus its full, deathless articulation.

Religiously slighter, yet interesting as a preparation for
Christian theology, are the writings of Philo, a devout, Greek-
trained Jew of Alexandria, who in A.D 40 appeared before the
Emperor Caligula in Rome. Philo does not feel his daringly
allegorical sublimations as any departures from the devoutest
Biblical faith. Thus " God never ceases from action ; as to burn
is special to fire, so is action to God "—this in spite of God's
rest on the seventh day (Gen. ii. 2). " There exist two kinds of
men : the heavenly man and the earthly man." [1] The long Life
of Moses [2] represents him as the King, Lawgiver, High Priest,
Prophet, Mediator. The Word, the Logos (which here everywhere hovers near, but never reaches, personality) is " the first-
born son of God," " the image of God " ; [3] its types are " the
Rock," the Manna, the High Priest's Coat ; it is " the Wine
Pourer and Master of the Drinking Feast of God." [4] The majority
of the Jews, who did not accept Jesus as the Christ, soon felt
they had no need for so much allegory, and dropped it, with
advantage, upon the whole, to the Jewish faith. But already
St. Paul and the Fourth Gospel find here noble mental raiment
for the great new facts revealed by Jesus Christ.

2. The Christian Religion we will take, as to our points, at
four stages of its development—Synoptic, Johannine, Augustinian, Thomistic.

The Synoptic material here specially concerned we shall find
especially in Mark i. 1 to xv. 47 ; but also in Matt. iii. 1 to
xxvii. 56, and in Luke iii. 1 to xxiii. 56. Within the material thus
marked off, there is no greater or lesser authenticity conferred
by treble, or double, or only single attestation ; for this material
springs from two original sources—a collection primarily of
doings and sufferings, which our Mark incorporates with some
expansions ; and a collection primarily of discourses, utilised
especially by Matthew and Luke in addition to the original

[1] Ed. Mangey, vol. i., pp. 44, 49.   [3] Ibid., pp. 80-179.
[2] Ibid., pp. 308, 427.   [4] Ibid., pp. 213, 121, 562, 691.

Mark. Both these sources contain the records of eye-witnesses, probably Saints Peter and Matthew.

The chronological order and the special occasions of the growths in our Lord's self-manifestation, or in the self-consciousness of His human soul, are most carefully given by Mark and next by Luke. Matthew largely ignores the stages and occasions of both these growths, and assumes, as fully explicit from the beginning of the Ministry, what was manifested only later on or at the last ; and he already introduces ecclesiastical and Christological terms and discriminations which, however really implicit as to their substance in Jesus's teaching, or inevitable (as to their particular form) for the maintenance and propagation of Christianity in the near future, are nevertheless still absent from the accounts of Mark and Luke.

The chief rules for the understanding of the specific character of our Lord's revelation appear to be the following. The life and teaching must be taken entire ; and, within this entirety, each stage must be apprehended in its own special peculiarities. The thirty years in the home, the school, the synagogue, the workshop at Nazareth, form a profoundly important constituent of His life and teaching—impressively contrasted, as they are, with the probably not full year of the Public Ministry, even though we are almost completely bereft of all details for those years of silent preparation.

The Public Ministry, again, consists of two strongly contrasted parts, divided by the great scene of Jesus with the Apostles alone at Cæsarea Philippi (Mark viii. 27–33 ; Luke ix. 18–22 ; Matt. xvi. 13–23). The part before is predominantly expansive, hopeful, peacefully growing; the part after, is concentrated, sad, in conflict, and in storm. To the first part belong the plant parables, full of exquisite sympathy with the unfolding of natural beauty and of slow fruitfulness ; to the second part belong the parables of keen watchfulness and of the proximate, sudden Second Coming. Both movements are essential to the physiognomy of our Lord. And they are not simply differences in self-manifestation ; they represent a growth, a relatively new element, in His human soul's experience and outlook.

The central doctrine in the teaching is throughout the Kingdom of God. But in the first part this central doctrine appears

as especially upheld by Jesus's fundamental experience—the
Fatherhood of God.   In the second part the central doctrine
appears as especially coloured by Jesus's other great experience
—of Himself as the Son of Man.   In the earlier part the Kingdom is presented more in the spirit of the ancient prophets,
as predominantly ethical, as already come in its beginnings,
and as subject to laws analogous to those obtaining in the natural
world.   In the second part the coming of the Kingdom is presented more with the form of the apocalyptic writers, in a purely
religious, intensely transcendent, and dualistic outlook—especially this also in the Parables of Immediate Expectation—as not
present but future (Matt. xix. 28) ; not distant but imminent
(Matt. xvi. 28 ; xxiv. 33 ; xxvi. 64) ; not gradual but sudden
(Matt. xxiv. 27, 39, 43) ; not at all achieved by man but purely
given by God (so still in Rev. xxi. 10).

To the earlier part belongs the great Rejoicing of Jesus
(Matt. xi. 25-30 ; Luke x. 21, 22).   The splendid opening,
" I thank Thee, Father—for so it hath seemed good in Thy
sight," and the exquisite close, special to Matthew, " Come unto
Me—and my burthen is light," raise no grave difficulty.   But
the intermediate majestic declaration, " All things are delivered
unto Me by the Father—neither knoweth any man the Father
save the Son and he to whomsoever the Son will reveal him,"
causes critical perplexities.

I take this declaration to be modelled upon actual words of
Jesus, which genuinely implied rather than clearly proclaimed
a unique relation between the Father and Himself.   Numerous
other words and acts involve such a relation and Jesus's full
consciousness of it.   Thus His first public act, His baptism,
is clearly described by Mark as a personal experience, " He saw
the heavens opened " and heard a heavenly voice " Thou art
my beloved Son, in whom I am well pleased " (i. 10, 11). Already
in the first stage Jesus declares the Baptist to be " more than a
prophet " (Matt. xi. 9), yet claims superiority over him and over
Solomon (xi. 11 ; xii. 42).   His doctrine is new wine requiring
new bottles (Mark ii. 22) ; indeed His whole attitude towards
the law is that of a Superior, who most really exhorts all, " Learn
of Me."   And soon after Cæsarea Philippi He insists to the people :
" Whosoever shall be ashamed of Me in this generation, of him

also shall the Son of Man be ashamed, when He cometh in the glory of the Father " (Mark viii. 38). The most numerous cures, physical, psychical, moral, certainly performed by Him, appear as the spontaneous effect of a unique degree and kind of spiritual authority; and the sinlessness attributed to Him throughout by the apostolic community (2 Cor. v. 21; Heb. iv. 15; John viii. 46; 1 John ii. 29) entirely corresponds to the absence, in the records of Him, of all traits indicating troubles of conscience and the corresponding fear of God. And this His unique Sonship is conjoined, in the earliest picture of Him, with an endless variety and combination of all the joys, admirations, affections, disappointments, desolations, temptations possible to such a stainless human soul and will. We thus find here a comprehensiveness unlike the attitude of the Baptist or St. Paul, and like, although far exceeding, the joy in nature and the peace in suffering of St. Francis of Assisi.

The Second Part opens with the great scene at Cæsarea Philippi and its sequel (given with specially marked successiveness in Mark viii. 27-x. 45), when, for the first time in a manner beyond all dispute, Mark represents Jesus as adopting the designation " the Son of Man " in a Messianic and eschatological sense. For our Lord here promptly corrects Peter's conception of " Messiah " by repeated insistence upon " the Son of Man " —His glory yet also His sufferings. Thus Jesus adopts the term of Daniel vii. 13 (which already the Apocalypse of Enoch had understood of a personal Messiah) as a succinct description of His specific vocation—its heavenly origin and difference from all earthly Messianism; its combination of the depths of human weakness, dereliction, sufferings with the highest elevation in joy, power and glory; and its connexion of that pain with this triumph as strictly interrelated—only with and through the Cross, was there here the offer and the acceptance of the Crown.

As to the Passion and Death, and the Risen Life, four points appear to be central and secured. Neither the Old Testament nor Jewish Theology really knew of a Suffering Messiah. Jesus Himself clearly perceived, accepted, and carried out this profound new revelation. This suffering and death were conceived by Him as the final act and crown of His services—so in Mark x. 44, 45 and Luke xxii. 24-7. (All this remains previous to, and

independent of, St. Paul's elaborated doctrine as to the strictly
vicarious and juridical character of the whole.) And the Risen
Life is an objectively real, profoundly operative life—the visions
of the Risen One were effects of the truly living Jesus, the Christ.

The Second Christian Stage, the Johannine writings, are fully
understandable only as posterior to St. Paul—the most enthusiastic and influential, indeed, of all our Lord's early disciples,
but a convert, from the activity of a strict persecuting Pharisee,
not to the earthly Jesus, of soul and body, Whom he never knew,
but to the heavenly Spirit-Christ, Whom he had so suddenly
experienced. Saul, the man of violent passions and acute interior
conflicts, thus abruptly changed in a substantially *pneumatic*
manner, is henceforth absorbed, not in the past Jewish Messiah,
but in the present universal Christ ; not in the Kingdom of God,
but in *Pneuma*, the Spirit. Christ, the second Adam, is here a
life-giving spirit, as it were an element that surrounds and penetrates the human spirit ; we are baptised, dipped, into Christ,
Spirit ; we can drink Christ, the Spirit. And this Christ-Spirit
effects the universal brotherhood of mankind, and articulates
in particular posts and functions the several human spirits, as
variously necessary members of the one Christian society and
Church.

Now the Johannine Gospel indeed utilises considerable
Synoptic materials, and does not, as St. Paul, restrict itself to
the Passion and Resurrection. Yet it gives us, substantially, the
Spirit-Christ, the Heavenly Man ; and the growth, prayer,
temptation, appeal for sympathy, dereliction, agony, which,
in the Synoptists, are still so real for the human soul of Jesus
Himself, appear here as sheer condescensions, in time and space,
of Him who, as all things good, descends from the Eternal Above,
so that we men here below may ascend thither with Him. On
the other hand, the Church and the Sacraments, still predominantly implicit in the Synoptists, and the subjects of costly
conflict and organisation in the Pauline writings, here underlie,
as already fully operative facts, practically the entire profound
work. The great dialogue with Nicodemus concerns Baptism ;
the great discourse in the synagogue at Capernaum, the Holy
Eucharist—in both cases, the strict need of these Sacraments.
And from the side of the dead Jesus flow blood and water, as

those two great sacraments flow from the everliving Christ; whilst at the Cross's foot He leaves His seamless coat, symbol of the Church's indivisible unity. The Universalism of this Gospel is not merely apparent: " God so loved the world " (iii. 16), " the Saviour of the world " (iv. 42)—this glorious teaching is traceable in many a passage. Yet Christ here condemns the Jews—in the Synoptists only the Pharisees ; He is from above, they are from below; all those that came before Him were thieves and robbers ; He will not pray for the world—" ye shall die in your sins " (xvii. 9 ; viii. 24) ; and the commandment, designated here by Jesus as His own and as new, to " love one another,' is for and within the community to which He gives His " example " (xv. 12 ; xiii. 34)—in contrast with the great double commandment of love proclaimed by Him, in the Synoptists, as already formulated in the Mosaic Law (Mark xii. 28–34), and as directly applicable to every fellow-man—indeed, a schismatic Samaritan is given as the pattern of such perfect love (Luke x. 25–37).

Deuteronomy gained its full articulation in conflict with Canaanite impurity ; the Johannine writings take shape during the earlier battles of the long war with Gnosticism—the most terrible foe ever, so far, encountered by the Catholic Church, and conquered by her in open and fair fight. Also these writings lay much stress upon Knowing and the Truth : " this is life eternal, to know Thee, the only true God and Jesus Christ whom Thou hast sent " (xvii. 3) ; symbolism and mysticism prevail very largely ; and, in so far as they are not absorbed in an Eternal Present, the reception of truth and experience is not limited to Christ's earthly sojourn—" the Father will give you another Helper, the spirit of truth who will abide with you for ever " (xiv. 16). Yet here the knowing and the truth are also deeply ethical and social : " he who doeth the truth cometh to the light " (iii. 21) ; and Christ has a fold, and other sheep not of this fold—them also He must bring, there will be one fold, one Shepherd; indeed, ministerial gradations exist in this one Church (so in xiii. 5–10 ; xx. 3–8 ; xxi. 7–19). And the Mysticism here is but an emotional intuitive apprehension of the great historical figure of Jesus, and of the most specifically religious of all facts—of the already overflowing operative existence, previous

*D

to all our action, of God, the Prevenient Love. " Not we loved God (first), but He (first) loved us," " let us love Him, because He first loved us," " no man can come to me, unless the Father draw him "—a drawing which awakens a hunger and thirst for Christ and God (1 John iv. 10, 19 ; John vi. 44 ; iv. 14 ; vi. 35).

The Third Stage we can find in St. Augustine, who, born a North African Roman (A.D. 354) and a convert (A.D. 386) from an impure life and Manichæism, with its spatially extended God, wrote his *Confessions* in 397, lived to experience the capture and sack of Rome by Alaric the Goth, 410, composed his great work, *The City of God*, amidst the clear dissolution of a mighty past and the dim presage of a problematical future, and died at Hippo, his episcopal city, in 430, whilst the Vandals were besieging it. St. Augustine is more largely a convert and a rigorist even than St. Paul when St. Paul is most incisive. But here he shall testify only to the natures of Eternity and of real time, a matter in which he remains unequalled in the delicate vividness and balance of his psychological analysis and religious perception. " Thou, O God, precedest all past times by the height of Thine ever-present Eternity ; and Thou exceedest all future times, since they *are* future, and, once they have come, will be past times. All thy years abide together, because they abide ; but these our years will all be, only when they all will have ceased to be. Thy years are but One Day—not every day, but To-Day. This Thy To-Day is Eternity." [1] The human soul, even in this life, has moments of a vivid apprehension of Eternity, as in the great scene of Augustine and Monica at the window in Ostia (Autumn, 387). And this our sense of Eternity, Beatitude, God, proceeds at bottom from Himself, immediately present in our lives ; the succession, duration of man is sustained by the Simultaneity, the Eternity of God : " this day of ours *does* pass within Thee, since all these things " of our deeper experience " have no means of passing unless, somehow, Thou dost contain them all." " Behold, Thou wast within, and I was without . . . Thou wast with me, but I was not with Thee." " Is not the blessed life precisely *that* life which all men desire ? Even those who only hope to be blessed would not, unless they in some manner already possessed the blessed life, desire to be blessed, as, in reality,

[1] *Conf.* x., 13, 2.

it is most certain that they desire to be." [1] Especially satisfactory is the insistence upon the futility of the question as to what God was doing in Time before He created. Time is only a quality inherent in all creatures ; it never existed of itself.[2]

And our fourth, last Christian Stage shall be represented by St. Thomas Aquinas (A.D. 1225–74), in the one great question where this Norman-Italian Friar Noble, a soul apparently so largely derivative and abstractive, is more complete and balanced, and penetrates to the specific genius of Christianity more deeply, than Saints Paul and Augustine with all their greater directness and intensity. We saw how the deepest originality of our Lord's teaching and temper consisted in His non-rigoristic earnestness, in His non-Gnostic detachment from things temporal and spatial. The absorbing expectation of the Second Coming, indeed the old, largely effete Græco-Roman world, had first to go, the great Germanic migrations had to be fully completed, the first Crusades had to pass, before—some twelve centuries after Nazareth and Calvary—Christianity attained in Aquinas a systematic and promptly authoritative expression of this its root-peculiarity and power. No one has put the point better than Professor E. Troeltsch : " The decisive point here is the conception, peculiar to the Middle Ages, of what is Christian as Supernatural, or rather the full elaboration of the consequences involved in the conception of the Supernatural. The Supernatural is now recognised not only in the great complex miracle of man's redemption from out of the world corrupted by original sin. But the Supernatural now unfolds itself as an autonomous principle of a logical, religious and ethical kind. The creature, even the perfect creature, is only Natural—is possessed of only natural laws and ends ; God alone is Supernatural. Hence the essence of Christian Supernaturalism consists in the elevation of the creature, above this creature's co-natural limitations, to God's own Supernature." The distinction is no longer, as in the Ancient Church, between two kinds (respectively perfect and relative) of the one sole Natural Law ; the distinction here is between Natural Law in general and Supernature generally. " The Decalogue, in strictness, is not yet the Christian Ethic. ' Biblical ' now means revealed, but not necessarily

Christian ; for the Bible represents, according to Aquinas, a process of development which moves through universal history and possesses various stages. The Decalogue is indeed present in the legislation of Christ, but as a stage preliminary to the specifically Christian Ethic. The formula, on the contrary, for the specifically Christian Moral Law is here the Augustinian definition of the love of God as the highest and absolute, the entirely simple, Moral end—an end which contains the demand of the love of God in the stricter sense (self-sanctification, self-denial, contemplation) and the demand of the love of our neighbour (the active relating of all to God, the active interrelating of all in God, and the most penetrating mutual self-sacrifice for God). This Ethic, a mystical interpretation of the Evangelical Preaching, forms indeed a strong contrast to the This-World Ethic of the Natural Law, Aristotle, the Decalogue and Natural Prosperity ; but then this cannot fail to be the case, given the entire fundamental character of the Christian Ethic." [1]

Thus the widest and most primitive contrasts here are, not Sin and Redemption (though these, of course, remain), but Nature (however good in its kind) and Supernature. The State becomes the complex of that essentially good thing, Nature ; the Church the complex of that different, higher good, Supernature ; roughly speaking, where the State leaves off, the Church begins.

It lasted not long, before the Canonists and certain ruling Churchmen helped to break up, in the consciousness of men at large, this noble perception of the two-step ladder from God to man and from man to God. And the Protestant Reformers, as a whole, went even beyond Saints Paul and Augustine in exclusive preoccupation with Sin and Redemption. Henceforth the single-step character of man's call more than ever predominates. The Protestant Reformation, like the French Revolution, marks the existence of grave abuses, the need of large reforms, and, especially on this point, the all but inevitable excessiveness of man once he is aroused to such " reforming " action. Certainly, to this hour, Protestantism as such has produced, within and for religion specifically, nothing that can seriously compare, in massive, balanced completeness, with the

[1] *Die Soziallehren der christlichen Kirchen und Gruppen*, 1912, pp. 263–65.

work of the short-lived golden Middle Age of Aquinas and Dante. Hence, for our precise purpose, we can conclude our Jewish and Christian survey here.

3. Only a few words about Confucianism, Buddhism, Mohammedanism, as these, in some of their main outlines, illustrate the points especially brought out by the Jewish Christian development.

Confucianism admittedly consists, at least as we have it, in a greatly complicated system of the direct worship of Nature (Sun, Moon, Stars especially) and of Ancestors, and of a finely simple system of ethical rules for man's ordinary social intercourse. That Nature-worship closely resembles what the Deuteronomic reform fought so fiercely in Israel; and the immemorial antiquity and still vigorous life of such a worship in China indicates impressively how little such Nature-worship tends, of itself, to its own supersession by a definite Theism. And the Ethical rules, and their very large observance, illustrate well how real can be the existence, and the goodness in its own kind, of Natural, This-World morality, even where it stands all but entirely unpenetrated or supplemented by any clear and strong supernatural attraction or conviction.

Buddhism, in its original form, consisted neither in the Wheel of Reincarnation alone, nor in *Nirvana* alone, but precisely in the combination of the two; for that ceaseless flux of reincarnation was there felt with such horror, that the *Nirvana*— the condition in which that flux is abolished—was hailed as a blessed release. The judgment as to the facts—that all human experience is of sheer, boundless change—was doubtless excessive; but the value-judgment—that if life be such pure shiftingness, then the cessation of life is the one end for man to work and pray for—was assuredly the authentic cry of the human soul when fully normal and awake. This position thus strikingly confirms the whole Jewish and Christian persistent search for permanence in change—for a Simultaneity, the support of our succession.

And Mohammedanism, both in its striking achievements and in its marked limitations, indeed also in the presentations of it by its own spokesmen, appears as a religion primarily not of a special pervasive spirit and of large, variously applicable maxims, but as one of precise, entirely immutable rules. Thus we find here something not all unlike, but mostly still more rigid than, the post-Exilic Jewish religion—something doubtless useful for certain times and races, but which could not expand and adapt itself to indefinite varieties of growths and peoples without losing that interior unity and self-identity so essential to all living and powerful religion.

III

Let us now attempt, in a somewhat loose and elastic order, a short allocation and estimate of the facts in past and present religion which mainly concern the question of Religion and Progress.

We West Europeans have apparently again reached the fruitful stage when man is not simply alive to this or that physical or psychic need, nor even to the practical interest and advantage of this or that Art, Science, Sociology, Politics, Ethics ; but when he awakens further to the question as to why and how these several activities, all so costly where at all effectual, can deserve all this sacrifice—can be based on anything sufficiently abiding and objective. The history of all the past efforts, and indeed all really adequate richness of immediate outlook, combine, I think, to answer that only the experience and the conviction of an Objective Reality distinct from, and more than, man, or indeed than the whole of the world apprehended by man as less than, or as equal to, man himself, can furnish sufficiently deep and tenacious roots for our sense and need of an objective supreme Beauty, Truth, and Goodness—of a living Reality which is already overflowingly that which, in lesser degrees and ways, we small realities cannot altogether cease from desiring to become. It is Religion which, from first to last, but with increasing purity and power, brings with it this evidence and conviction. The sense of the Objective, Full Reality of God, and the need of Adoration are quite essential to Religion, although considerable philosophers, who are largely satisfactory on the more immediate questions raised by Æsthetics and even by Ethics, and who are sincerely anxious to do justice also to the

religious sense, are fully at work to explain away these essential
characteristics of all wideawake Religion.   Paul Natorp, the
distinguished Plato-scholar in Germany, the short-lived pathetic-
ally eloquent M. Guyau in France, and, above all, Benedetto
Croce, the large encyclopædic mind in Italy, have influenced or
led much of this movement, which, in questions of Religion,
has assuredly not reached the deepest and most tenacious
teachings of life.

The intimations as to this deepest Reality certainly arise
within my own mind, emotion, will ; and these my faculties
cannot, upon the whole, be constrained by my fellow-mortals ;
indeed, as men grow more manysidedly awake, all attempts at
any such constraint only arrest or deflect the growth of these
intimations.   Yet the dispositions necessary for the sufficient
apprehension of these religious intimations—sincerity, conscientiousness, docility—are not, even collectively, already Religion,
any more than they are Science or Philosophy.   With these dispositions on our part, objective facts and living Reality can reach
us—and, even so, these facts reach us practically always, at
first, through human teachers already experienced in these
things.   The need of such facts and such persons to teach them
are, in the first years of every man, and for long ages in the
history of mankind, far more pressing than any question of
toleration.   Even vigorous persecution or keen exclusiveness of
feeling have—pace Lord Acton—saved for mankind, at certain
crises of its difficult development, convictions of priceless worth
—as in the Deuteronomic Reform and the Johannine Writings.
In proportion as men become more manysidedly awake, they
acquire at least the capacity for greater sensitiveness concerning
the laws and forces intrinsic to the various ranges and levels of
life ; and, where such sensitiveness is really at work, it can
advantageously replace, by means of the spontaneous acceptance of such objective realities, the constraints of past ages—
constraints which now, in any case, have become directly mis-
chievous for such minds.   None the less will men, after this
change as before, require the corporate experience and manifestation of religion as, in varying degrees and ways, a permanent
necessity for the vigorous life of religion.   Indeed, such corporate
tradition operates strongly even where men's spiritual sense seems

most individual, or where, with the retention of some ethical
nobility of outlook, they most keenly combat all and every
religious institution.   So with George Fox's doctrine of the
Divine Enlightenment of every soul separately and without
mediation of any kind, a doctrine derived by him from that highly
ecclesiastical document, the Gospel of St. John ; and with many
a Jacobin's fierce proclamation of the rights of Man, never far
away from sayings of St. Paul.

   This permanent necessity of Religious Institutions is primarily
a need for men who will teach and exemplify, not simply Natural,
This-World Morality, but a Supernatural, Other-World Ethic ;
and not simply that abstraction, Religion in General or a Religious
Hypothesis, but that rich concretion, this or that Historical
Religion.   In proportion as such an Historical Religion is deep
and delicate, it will doubtless contain affinities with all that is
wholesome and real within the other extant historical religions.
Nevertheless, all religions are effectual through their own special
developments, where these developments remain true at all.
As well deprive a flower of its " mere details " of pistil, stamen,
pollen, or an insect of its " superfluous " antennæ, as simplify
any Historical Religion down to the sorry stump labelled " the
religion of every honest man."   We shall escape all bigotry,
without lapsing into such most unjust indifferentism, if we
vigorously hold and unceasingly apply the doctrine of such a
Church theologian as Juan de Lugo.   De Lugo (A.D. 1583–1660),
Spaniard, post-Reformation Roman Catholic, Jesuit, Theological
Professor, and a Cardinal writing in Rome under the eyes of
Pope Urban VIII., teaches that the members of the various
Christian sects, of the Jewish and Mohammedan communions,
and of the heathen religions and philosophical schools, who
achieve their salvation, do so, ordinarily, simply through the aid
afforded by God's grace to their good faith in its instinctive concentration upon, and in its practice of, those elements in their
respective community's worship and teaching, which are true
and good and originally revealed by God.[1]   Thus we escape all
undue individualism and all unjust equalisation of the (very
variously valuable) religious and philosophical bodies ; and yet
we clearly hold the profound importance, next to God's sanctify-

---

[1] *De Fide*, Disp. xix., 7, 10 ; xx., 107, 194.

ing grace, of the single soul's good faith and religious instinct, and of the worship or school, be they ever so elementary and imperfect, which environ such a soul.

A man's religion, in proportion to its depth, will move in a Concrete Time which becomes more and more a Partial Simultaneity. And these his depths then more and more testify to, and contrast with, the Fully Simultaneous God. Because man thus lives, not in an ever-equal chain of mutually exclusive moments, in Clock Time, but in Duration, with its variously close interpenetrations of the successive parts; and because these interpretations are close in proportion to the richness and fruitfulness of the durations he lives through: he can, indeed he must, conceive absolutely perfect life as absolutely simultaneous. God is thus not Unending, but Eternal; the very fullness of His life leaves no room or reason for succession and our poor need of it. Dr. F. C. S. Schiller has admirably drawn out this grand doctrine, with the aid of Aristotle's Unmoving Action, in *Humanism*, 1903, pp. 204–27. We need only persistently apprehend this Simultaneity as essential to God, and Succession as varyingly essential to all creatures, and there remains no difficulty—at least as regards the Time-element—in the doctrine of Creation. For only with the existence of creatures does Time thus arise at all—it exists only in and through them. And assuredly all finite things, that we know at all, bear traces of a history involving a beginning and an end. Professor Bernardino Varisco, in his great *Know Thyself*, has noble pages on this large theme.[1] In any case we must beware of all more or less Pantheistic conceptions of the simultaneous life of God and the successive life of creatures as but essential and necessary elements of one single Divine-Creaturely existence, in the manner, *e.g.*, of Professor Josiah Royce, in his powerful work *The World and the Individual*, second series, 1901. All such schemes break down under an adequate realisation of those dread facts Error and Evil. A certain real independence must have been left by God to reasonable creatures. And let it be noted carefully: the greatest theoretic difficulty against all Theism lies in the terrible reality of Evil; and yet the deepest adequacy, in the actual toil and trouble of life, of this same Theism, especially

[1] *Cognosci Te Stesso*, 1912, pp. 144–47.

of Christianity, consists in its practical attitude towards, and
success against, this most real Evil. Pantheism, on the contrary,
increases, whilst seeming to surmount, the theoretical difficulty,
since the world as it stands, and not an Ultimate Reality behind
it, is here held to be perfect ; and it entirely fails really to trans-
mute Evil in practice. Theism, no more than any other outlook,
really explains Evil ; but it alone, in its fullest, Jewish-Christian
forms, has done more, and better, than explain Evil : it has fully
faced, it has indeed greatly intensified, the problem, by its noble
insistence upon the reality and heinousness of Sin ; and it has
then overcome all this Evil, not indeed in theory, but in practice,
by actually producing, in the midst of deep suffering and through
a still deeper faith and love, souls which are the living expression
of the deepest beatitude and peace.

The fully Simultaneous Reality awakens and satisfies man's
deepest, most nearly simultaneous life, by a certain adaptation of
its own intrinsic life to these human spirits. In such varyingly
"incarnational" acts or action the Non-Successive God Himself
condescends to a certain Successiveness; but this, in order to help
His creatures to achieve as much Simultaneity as is compatible
with their several ranks and calls. We must not wonder if,
in the religious literature, these condescensions of God the non-
successive largely appear as though they themselves were more
or less non-successive ; nor, again, if the deepest religious consciousness tends usually to conceive God's outward action, if
future, then as proximate, and, if present, then as strictly instantaneous. For God in Himself is indeed Simultaneous; and
if we try to picture Simultaneity by means of temporal images
at all, then the instant, and not any period long or short, is
certainly nearest to the truth—as regards the form and vehicle
of the experience.

The greater acts of Divine Condescension and Self-Revelation,
our Religious Accessions, have mostly occurred at considerable
intervals, each from the other, in our human history. After
they have actually occurred, these several acts can be compared
and arranged, according to their chief characteristics, and even
in a series of (upon the whole) growing content and worth—
hence the Science of Religion. Yet such Science gives us no
power to produce, or even to foresee, any further acts. These

great Accessions of Spiritual Knowledge and Experience are
not the simple result of the conditions obtaining previously
in the other levels of life, or even in that of religion itself; they
often much anticipate, they sometimes greatly lag behind, the
rise or decline of the other kinds of life. And where (as with the
great Jewish Prophets, and, in some degree, with John the
Baptist and Our Lord) these Accessions do occur at times of
national stress, these several crises are, at most, the occasion for
the demand, not the cause of the supply.

The mostly long gaps between these Accessions have been
more or less filled up, amongst the peoples concerned, by
varyingly vigorous and valuable attempts to articulate and
systematise, to apply in practice, and rightly to place (within the
other ranges of man's total life) these great, closely-packed
masses of spiritual fact, or to elude, to deflect, or directly to
combat them, or some of their interpretations or applications.
Now a fairly steady improvement is possible, desirable, and
largely actual, in the critical sifting and appraisement, as to the
dates of the historical documents, and as to the actual reality
and details of these Accessions; in the philosophical articulation of their doctrinal and evidential content; in the finer understanding and wider application of their ethical demands; and
in the greater adequacy (both as to firmness and comprehensiveness) of the institutional organs and incorporations special to
these same Accessions. All this can and does progress, but mostly
slowly, intermittently, with short violent paroxysms of excess
and long sleepy reactions of defect, with one-sidedness, travesties,
and—worst of all—with worldly indifference and self-seeking.
The grace and aid of the Simultaneous Richness are here also
always necessary; nor can these things ever really progress
except through a deep religious sense—all mere scepticism
and all levelling down are simply so much waste. Still, we can
speak of progress in the Science of Religion more appropriately
than we can of progress in the Knowledge of Religion.

The Crusades, the Renaissance, the Revolution, no doubt
exercised, in the long run, so potent a secularising influence,
because men's minds had become too largely other-worldly—
had lost a sufficient interest in this wonderful world; and hence
all those new, apparently boundless outlooks and problems were

taken up largely as a revolt and escape from what looked like a prison-house—religion. Yet through all these violent oscillations there persisted, in human life, the supernatural need and the supernatural call. In this need and in this call God is the greatest central interest, love and care of the soul. We must look to it that both these interests and Ethics are kept awake, strong and distinct within a costingly rich totality of life : the Ethic of the honourable citizen, merchant, lawyer—of Confucius and Bentham; and the Ethic of the Jewish Prophets at their deepest, of the Suffering Servant, of our Lord's Beatitudes, of St. Paul's great eulogy of love, of Augustine and Monica at the window in Ostia, of Father Damian's voluntary death as a leper amidst the lepers in the far-away, antipodean seas. The Church is the born incorporation of this Supernatural Pole, as the State is of the other, the Natural Pole. The Church indeed should, at its lower limit, also encourage the This-world Stage ; the State, at its higher limit, can, more or less consciously, prepare us for the Other-World Stage. Both spring from the same God, at two levels of His action ; both concern the same men, at two stages of their need and of their call. Yet the primary duty of the State is turned to this life ; the primary care of the Church, to that life—to life in its deepest depths.

Will men, after this great war, more largely again apprehend, love, and practise this double polarity of their lives ? Only thus will the truest progress be possible in the understanding, the application, and the fruitfulness of Religion, with its great central origin and object, God, the beginning and end of all our true progress, precisely because He Himself already possesses immeasurably more than all He helps us to become,—He Who, even now already, is our Peace in Action, and even in the Cross is our abiding Joy.

BOOKS FOR REFERENCE

I. 1. Oswold Külpe, *The Philosophy of the Present in Germany*. English translation. London : George Allen, 1913.

2. J. McKeller Stewart, *A Critical Exposition of Bergson's Philosophy*. London : Macmillan, 1913.

Il. 1. R. H. Charles, *A Critical History of the Doctrine of a Future Life.* London : A. & C. Black, 1899.

2. Ernest T. Scott, *The Fourth Gospel.* Edinburgh : T. & T. Clark.

III. 1. Aliotta, *The Idealistic Reaction against Science.* English translation. Macmillan.

2. F. C. Schiller, *Humanism,* Macmillan, 1903.

3. C. C. J. Webb, *Group Theories of Religion and the Individual,* Allen and Unwin, 1916.

4

ON THE PRELIMINARIES TO RELIGIOUS BELIEF AND ON THE FACTS OF SUFFERING, FAITH AND LOVE [1]

MY DEAR MRS. N.,

Please allow me, before I attempt to explain some matters of fact and of reality, to suggest to you, with a little detail and vividness, certain habits of mind and certain spiritual practices, which (I am very sure) are simply necessary for any true apprehension of those facts and realities. I do so all the more because, even if I fail altogether in my striving to help you as regards those facts, I shall have been of some use to you if I succeed in winning you, however little, to these general dispositions of soul.

I

These dispositions I have had to gain and to practise for myself, now during forty years ; and I am very sure that, if I see at all steadily and profitably, it is owing to these habits of soul. I find them to be three.

1. I write, then, to you at all, only because I believe you to be, or (at least) to wish to be, in the great fundamental disposition in which alone my suggestions, which anyone could make to you as to the facts, can do some little good, and not much harm. That is, I assume you to be non-contentious and non-controversial ; to be athirst for wisdom, not for cleverness ; to be humble and simple, or (at least) to feel a wholesome shame at not being so ; to be just *straight*, and anxious for some light, and ready to pay for it and to practise it. I take you to be determined not to stop

[1] Written to V. N. on the death, after a long illness, of her little daughter of eighteen months, in answer to the question, " how such suffering could be permitted by a God said to be all-good and all-powerful ? " January, 1914.

and worry over such facts or expressions of my communication
as you may not understand or may not like ; but quietly to
move on to, and then to rest and browse amongst, such facts and
feelings as here may gently attract and feed your spirit. Drop
brain, open wide the soul, nourish the heart, purify, strengthen
the will : with this, you are sure to grow ; without this, you are
certain to shrink.

How much you can learn, as I myself have learnt, from watching cattle dreamily grazing and ruminating in their pastures !
See how the sagacious creatures, without any theory or inflation
of mind, instinctively select the herbs and grasses that suit
and sustain them ; and how they peacefully pass by what does
not thus help them ! They do not waste their time and energy
in tossing away, or in trampling upon, or even simply in sniffing
at, what is antipathetic to them. Why should they ? Thistles
may not suit *them* ; well, there are other creatures in the world
whom thistles *do* suit. And, in any case, are they the police of
this rich and varied universe ?

You see, no human being can possibly divine, in all respects and
degrees, the every want of a fellow-soul, even at any one of this
soul's stages. And yet no soul can really advance just simply
by itself ; either books, or letters, or pictures, or the words or
actions of others are, sooner or later, and more or less, always
necessary, always indeed operative within us, for good or for
evil, or for both. Hence the profound importance for the soul,
for every soul, to be, to become, always to re-become, outward-
moving, humbly welcoming, generously interpretative. For only
thus could even an angel from Heaven help it at all, since thus,
and thus only, will it not be *fine* and *blasé* ; will it readily see how
much is being offered to it by which it can grow and overcome
its old self, and even its present self ; and will it gratefully
accept and utilise that which is now submitted to it, even where
it has somewhat to modify, so as to make fit, this valuable help.

Thus I assume that you will nowhere, in what follows, either
attempt to force yourself to accept it against your best—your
quiet—light and instinct ; nor allow yourself to tilt against,
and to judge as wrong or false, what does not, at least not at
once, bring to your own soul some real light and strength. You
will judge it all only as suiting yourself, or as not suiting yourself ;

and even this much of judging, if you want to grow, will have to be done looking up to God, with a gentle imploring, and not down upon man, with self-sufficingness.

You will never get, you will never deserve to get, light, unless you become, unless you realise that (at your best) you are :

> An infant crying in the night ;
> An infant crying for the light,
> And with no language but a cry.

In this way the very faults and limitations (sure to be plentifully present) in what follows, will actually become further aids, because occasions of growth, for your soul, since thus you will be stimulated to practise that peace and patience, humility and love without which we cannot really advance in these fundamental quests.

2. My further preliminary is as follows. Gently learn to see the reasonableness, the need, the duty, and quietly strive to gain the habit, of dropping all insistence upon great and continuous clearness—upon *your* degree, *your* kind of evidence in these deepest things. For these things *are* the deepest things, are they not ?

Here I mean that, if these things that we are after are not merely figments, or at least mere abstractions, of our brains, but are real in themselves, and distinct from our minds, then they *must be* dim and difficult for our minds—for our analysis and reasoning. Pray get this point quite definite and firm,—that to require clearness in proportion to the concreteness, to the depth of reality, of the subject-matter is an impossible position,—I mean a thoroughly unreasonable, a self-contradictory habit of mind.

This is so, because only abstract ideas, and only numerical and spatial relations are quite clear, utterly undeniable, and instantly transferable from soul to soul ; and these ideas and relations are thus entirely transparent, because they do not involve any affirmation of particular existences (of realities)—at least they do not directly involve any such affirmation. Thus, for instance, "largeness," "smallness," "fullness," "emptiness," and, again, "one," "two," "seven"; "five and five are ten," "six times six are thirty-six," "the part is smaller than the whole," "a straight line is the shortest route between any two points ";

" one extended thing cannot occupy the same space as another similarly extended thing " : all this is absolutely clear. It is all absolutely clear, yes ; but just because here we have nowhere affirmed the *existence* or *reality* of anything whatsoever. We have only asserted that our mind possesses the ideas of " largeness," " smallness," " fullness," " emptiness " ; but whether anything distinct from our mind, and of these ideas of our mind, exists in correspondence to these ideas—*that* remains quite unsettled. We have, again, affirmed that *if* there exist realities, say apples, we can number them as one, two, seven apples ; and if there exist five eggs and other five eggs, then the total of all these eggs will be ten ; and if there exist six sets of six nuts each, we shall have a collection of thirty-six nuts. But whether there really exists one single apple, one single egg or nut, not all this clearness and neat reasoning has established in the very least.

All stands differently, indeed contrariwise, with affirmations of real existence, and of real qualities attaching to such existences.

As you doubtless know, even the reality of any outside world— especially the existence of material objects—of sun and moon, of rocks and rivers—their existence, or (at least) that we can at all know that they exist—has been denied by philosophers of distinction. And we have to admit that it is a complicated and tedious business to prove these philosophers to be wrong ; that no one argument quotable against them is, taken alone, entirely clear and utterly irresistible.

Again, most philosophers deny that we, human individuals, possess any direct knowledge of the nature, the character of other human individuals, however near and dear to us ; they maintain that our knowledge, in all such cases, is always of ourselves alone, and that we then get, beyond this our sole real knowledge, only our ever faulty and fallible interpretation of essentially ambiguous signs—of peculiarities of gesture, tone, look, which reach us, or seem to reach us, from those other beings. I believe myself that, where we love, we possess, or can develop, direct instinct and intuition in such matters. Nevertheless, however the case may really stand, the process, indeed the result itself, of our knowledge of our fellows, is not simple and clear. On the contrary, the process is most subtle and complex; and the result, at its best, is indeed most rich and vivid, but distinctly not simple and "clear"—it can be resisted even by ourselves, and it can only very rarely be transferred, with any ease, to others, however closely these others may be connected with us.

Certainly with regard to animals—even with respect to our dogs that we know and love best, we are often in the dark as to what is their momentary disposition and requirement. But how instructive it is to watch precisely such animals thus dear to us —I mean their knowledge and love of us, and their need of us and of our love! Our dogs know us and love us, human individuals, from amongst millions of fairly similar other individuals. Our dogs know us and love us thus most really, yet they doubtless know us only vividly, not clearly; we evidently strain their minds after a while—they then like to get away amongst servants and children; and, indeed, they love altogether to escape from human company, the rich and dim, or (at best) the vivid experiences—the company that is above them, to the company of their fellow-creatures, the company that affords so much poorer but so much clearer impressions—the level company of their brother-dogs. And yet, how wonderful! dogs thus require their fellow-dogs, the shallow and clear, but they also require us, the deep and dim; they require indeed what they can grasp; but they as really require what they can but reach out to, more or less— what exceeds, protects, envelopes, directs them. And, after a short relaxation in the dog-world, they return to the bracing of the man-world.

Now pray note how if religion is right—if what it proclaims as its source and object, if God be real, then this Reality, as superhuman, *cannot possibly* be clearer to us than are the realities, and the real qualities of these realities, which we have been considering. The source and object of religion, if religion be true and its object be real, *cannot*, indeed, *by any possibility, be as clear to me even as I am to my dog*. For the cases we have considered deal with realities inferior to our own reality (material objects, or animals), or with realities level to our own reality (fellow human beings), or with realities no higher above ourselves than are we, finite human beings, to our very finite dogs. Whereas, in the case of religion—if religion be right—

we apprehend and affirm realities indefinitely superior in quality and amount of reality to ourselves, and which, nevertheless (or rather, just because of this), anticipate, penetrate and sustain us with a quite unpicturable intimacy. The obscurity of my life to my dog, must thus be greatly exceeded by the obscurity of the life of God to me. Indeed the obscurity of plant life—so obscure for my mind, because so indefinitely inferior and poorer than is my human life—must be greatly exceeded by the dimness, for my human life, of God—of His reality and life, so different and superior, so unspeakably more rich and alive, than is, or ever can be, my own life and reality.

You may well ask here : " But what protection, then, do you leave me against mere fancy and superstition ? Will we not, thus, come to believe, to pretend to believe, in reality *because* the affirmations of it are obscure ? And are not all sorts of nonsense, of bogies, of chimeras, obscure ? What evidence, then, remains for these, the most sweeping and important of all affirmations ? Ought we not to be careful, indeed exacting, as to proof, exactly in proportion to the importance of the matters that solicit our adhesion ? And how otherwise can we be careful than in demanding clearness for the proof, in precise proportion to the importance of the subject-matter ? "

The answer here is not really difficult, I think.

Note, pray, how Darwin acquired certainty, and remark the nature of the certainty he acquired, concerning the character, the habits, indeed (in part) the very existence of fly-trap plants and of orchids, of earthworms and of humming-birds. He was always loving, learning, watching ; he was always " out of himself," doubling himself up, as it were, so as to penetrate these realities so much lowlier than himself, so different from himself. He had never done and finished ; what he learnt to-day had to be re-learnt, to be supplemented and corrected to-morrow, yet always with the sense that what he had learnt was, not his own mind and its fancies and theories, but realities and their real qualities and habits. His life thus moved out into other lives. And what he thus discovered was, not clear, but vivid ; not simple, but rich ; not readily, irresistibly transferable to other minds, but only acquirable by them through a slow self-purification and a humble, loving observation and docility like unto his own. His own conclusions deserved, and indeed demanded credit, because so many different facts, facts often widely apart from each other, converged to these conclusions; and because, on the other hand, these same conclusions, once accepted, illumined so large a body of other facts—facts which, otherwise, remained quite dark or strange anomalies. Indeed these conclusions, once accepted, led on to the discovery of numerous facts which had been unknown, unsuspected until then. Yet these very conclusions, since this is the process and the nature of their proof, were not and are not irresistible at any one moment and because of any one single fact or argument. Indeed, to this hour, even the most reasonably assured of the conclusions of Darwin have certain clear objections against them, objections which we cannot solve. So also even Copernicanism—that mathematically clear doctrine concerning the rotation of the earth around the sun—has certain objections standing over against it, which we cannot solve.

So it always is, in various degrees, with all our knowledge and certainty concerning existences, realities, and concerning the real qualities and nature of these realities. We get to know such realities slowly, laboriously, intermittently, partially; we get to know them, not inevitably nor altogether apart from our dispositions, but only if we are sufficiently awake to care to know them, sufficiently humble to welcome them, and sufficiently generous to pay the price continuously which is strictly necessary if this knowledge and love are not to shrink but to grow. We indeed get to know realities, in proportion as we become worthy to know them,—in proportion as we become less self-occupied, less self-centred, more outward-moving, less obstinate and insistent, more gladly lost in the crowd, more rich in giving all we have, and especially all we are, our very selves. And we get to know that we really know these realities, by finding our knowledge (dim, difficult, non-transferable though it be) approving itself to us as fruitful; because it leads us to further knowledge of the realities thus known, or of other realities even when these lie apparently quite far away; and all this, in a thoroughly living and practical, in a concrete, not abstract, not foretellable, in a quite inexhaustible way.

Thus we find, through actual experience and through the

similar experiences of our fellow-men, that the right and proper
test for the adequacy of abstractions and of spatial, numerical,
mechanical relations is, indeed, clearness and ready transferableness; but that the appropriate test for the truth concerning
existences and realities is vividness (richness) and fruitfulness.
The affirmations which concern abstractions and relations may
be ever so empty and merely conditional; if they are clear
and readily transferable, they are appropriate and adequate.
The affirmations which concern existences and realities may be
ever so dim and difficult to transmit; if they are rich and fruitful,
they are appropriate and true. Thus in neither set of affirmations
do we assent without evidence and proof; but in each set we
only require *the kind* of evidence and proof natural to this particular set. And our exactingness can increase, ought indeed to
increase, with the increase in the importance of the affirmations
put forward within either set. But in the mathematical abstract
set, I will require more and more clearness and ready transferableness, the wider and the more universal is the claim of a
particular proposition; whereas in the existential concrete set
I will require, in proportion to the importance of the existence
affirmed, more and more richness and fruitfulness (I mean
fruitfulness also in fields and levels other than those of the
particular reality affirmed).

Of course, whether or no the affirmations of religion are thus,
not indeed clear, but vivid (rich), and, not indeed readily
transferable, but deeply and widely fruitful, is here in no way
or degree prejudged. We are only busy, so far, with our method
and our standard,—not with the answer we shall get, but with
the question we have a right to ask. And though even with this
method and standard—with these by themselves—we may be
unable to acquire religion, we most certainly will never gain
religion without them, and still less in opposition to them.
Without the acceptance of such a temper of mind, or at least
without striving after, or some wish for, such a disposition, it
is worse than waste of time to enter upon the questions of fact;
worse than simple waste,—because we are then certain to come
away from such a study more rebellious and empty, or more
despairing and bitter, or considerably more sceptical, than we
came or could come to it.

3. In writing out for you these experiences that are continually before me, I think I have been leading up, quite naturally, to the last predisposition which I myself strive hard to practise, and which I will now invite you to appreciate and attempt. Those two habits of mind are indeed the necessary preparations for this last and third habit, or rather they readily issue in a third habit—the one I would now propose. Ever since I have had, ever since I *could* have children, I have felt myself a creature enriched with the noble duty of giving on the largest scale— with the obligation to possess a reserve of light and life and love— a reserve for dearest little beings who would not have existed but for myself. I have not, it is true, created these beings ; yet it was because I chose to marry, to be and to act as a husband and a possible father, that these particular beings became possible, and that, when they actually came, they possessed many a physical and temperamental peculiarity of my own, good, bad and mixed. And if I, and still more my wife, possess thus a unique share and responsibility, under God, in the physical existence, and even in the psychical peculiarities of our children, have I not, has she not, a deep, indeed unique, share and responsibility, under God, in their spiritual life, spiritual health and spiritual growth ?

Of course, I know well how often facts confront us which seem to show that the care of parents, precisely in these deepest matters, avails nothing, indeed that it tends to irritate the children and to drive them the other way. I know well, too, how widespread just now is the theory, and still more the tacit assumption, that all such spiritual matters are unfitted to children, that human beings can understand them at all, and can judge them in any way fairly, only when they are grown men, and hence that our children have the right, when they *are* grown men, to find themselves facing these questions quite unfettered by early bias in any direction.

And yet our own deepest instincts and experiences, once they are at all awake to the teeming possibilities, for good and for evil, of our children, and especially as we become alive and sensitive to the deeper and deepest realities, to the religious Realities, cannot sincerely and abidingly acquiesce in these or similar cold, and even cynical calculations. For nothing is more

certain than that, if children can easily be taught too many
practices and too many doctrines, or can be taught even but few
practices and doctrines in a thoroughly inappropriate way ; if,
as they grow older, we can easily drive them away by much
reasoning or by want of alert understanding of their wants, which
are always largely quite individual: nevertheless, these same
children are immensely impressionable to *personality*, not indeed
to what those around them say or even do, but to what they *are*
and to whether or not these seniors are simple and sincere, and
full of love or no. Thus what every child requires is life and love,
—life and love offered to it long before any explanation or analysis ;
the child requires such overflowing love as freely as it requires
the mother's breast.   And for the purposes of the child's hungry
soul, the mother's soul must possess, must it not ?, the spiritual
food, just as, for the infant's hungry body, the mother's breast
must possess the appropriate physical food.   And the history
of great souls shows, upon the whole very plainly I think, how
profound has been, in most cases, the influence of, not what
the mother taught or said or did, but what she *was*.

Now if it is important that we poor parents should thus *be*,
we must lead lives of faith, of trust, of risk. All spiritual life and
love have ever to begin afresh, and thus, only thus, they discover,
indeed create conditions, if old yet ever new, and if countless
yet unique. And see, how delightful ! The very predispositions,
the habits of mind, which we have found to be simply necessary
for our own awaking and growth as individual souls, turn out
here to be precisely the dispositions which fit us to understand
and to awaken our children. For we have, from the first, been
seeking, not even truth, but reality ; not a system or a theory,
nothing abstruse or straining. Indeed we have not found, even
as to method, more than that we must learn peacefully to browse
amongst, and instinctively to select from, the foods, or seeming
foods, proposed to our souls ; and that we must seek reality and its
knowledge in action and through self-purification, and must find
the tests of what is reality and what is its knowledge in the vividness (richness) and in the fruitfulness of what claims to be
spiritually true and spiritually known. Yet these means and tests,
if we but practise them humbly, silently, generously, more and
more instinctively, will certainly make us deeper, homelier,

more genial, better : they will bring us into ever closer and wider
contact with our children ; they cannot, of themselves, annoy or
strain even the most sensitive of these our little ones.

Oh, may we become ever richer in self-giving, in the joy and
perpetual youth of its ever extending, its unspeakable delights !
The children's Father indeed, he too can be, and ought to become,
such a self-giver ; but what cannot and ought not the Mother
to be and to become in these magnificent respects ? Yet neither
Father nor Mother will ever become thus truly rich except they
become poor and little in their own eyes ; and, again, they will
never become thus sufficiently, profoundly little, except with
and because of the consciousness of God, the great Reality which
then so solidly sustains and so delightfully dwarfs them. Only
prostrate at the foot of " the world's great altar-stairs " will the
parent become and remain sufficiently humble, homely and holy
for his or her unique sufferings, joys and duties, to bud and
blossom as they are silently required to flourish by the souls of
their little ones.

II

As to the facts, I will attempt to be very short, since if you
have accepted, and are practising, or even trying to practise,
the three dispositions described at some length, you will discover, I think, that the answers—the " explanations "—as to
these facts—the kind and degree of answers and " explanations "
we thus require for (and in) a humble and homely, warm and
working action and self-donation, will largely suggest themselves,
more or less untaught, to your own heart.

1. There is, then, your impression that Happiness indeed helps
us to believe in a Higher Power, and that your own years of
happiness were gradually building up some kind and degree
of Faith within you; but that Suffering acts contrariwise—that
this your keen, deep trouble has swept all that budding faith
away.

How natural, inevitable is this impression—at least until we
awaken, very widely and sensitively, to the wonderful witness
of history and to the no less mysterious testimony of our own

deepest spirit, and, through these evidences, to another, a fuller
set of truths !

For if I look back upon the long and varied history of mankind, and if I call to mind the numerous souls, of the most
different races, temperament, social grade, education, whom
I have known intimately well, what do I see ?   I see, as a
mysterious but most real, most undeniable fact—that it is precisely the deepest, the keenest sufferings, not only of body but
of mind, not only of mind but of heart, which have occasioned
the firmest, the most living, the most tender faith.   It was during
the desolation and unspeakable cruelties of the Assyrian and
Babylonian Exiles, that Jeremiah learnt the love of God as
written, not on tables of stone, but on the living heart of man ;
that Ezechiel realised God to be the Good Shepherd going after
His wandering, weary and lost sheep ;   and that—doubtless
then—Psalms were composed of an unspeakable magnificence
of unconquerable certainty as to God, the soul's unfailing refuge,
its one sure lover and support.   It was under the awful persecution by King Antiochus Epiphanes that the Maccabees
developed their grand faith.   It was more even than by the
peaceful lake and on the quiet mountain side—it was in Gethsemane and on Calvary that the trust and love of Jesus awoke
to their fullest.   And so, in their lesser, various degrees with
Stephen and St. Paul ;   and, under the Emperor Hadrian, with
the touching Jewish martyr, Rabbi Akiba.   Christianity at large
grew spiritually deep and tender under the terrible early persecutions lasting, with few breaks, during some two hundred
years and more.   The faith and fervour of the Jews, since their
dispersion, has, very certainly, suffered but little because of
the persecutions they endured, deeply unjust though these
persecutions substantially were ;   their faith and fervour, as in
the case of Christians, have suffered far more from wordly
prosperity where and when this has come.   Thus also the German
people, largely sceptical when the first Napoleon woke them up
to pain and humiliation, learnt again to pray, and, in the strength
as much of faith in God as of love of country, effected their
national liberation.

And case upon case has passed, in real life, before my eyes,
of awful physical suffering (I am thinking of my own dear sister),

E

of deep anguish of soul (I am thinking of a sweet saint of God, a washerwoman whose feet I wish I could become worthy to kiss), of various other, all delicately individual cases, in which (sometimes only slowly and after imperfect beginnings, sometimes heartwholly from the first) the soul's faith, service, love, devotedness, tenderest abandonment, and acceptance of God, of His will, of His beauty, so largely hidden behind these black bars and dread purifications, were splendidly, magnificently awakened and sustained.

And pray note particularly that *of course* suffering merely as such, suffering alone does not, cannot soften or widen any soul ; it can thus, of itself and alone, only harden, narrow and embitter it. Hence what I here witness to,—and these facts are as certain as that the earth spins round the sun,—is explicable only by the presence, the operation of a power, a reality, so immensely powerful and real as to counteract and greatly to exceed the suffering and this suffering's natural effects. This power comes from God,—comes, and can come, only from the fact that He exists—that He exists most really, and that His reality and aid are more real and more sustaining by far than is all this suffering and all the soul's natural sensitiveness and weakness in face of such dread pain.

I take, then, your impression to be most natural, but not yet to reach the great facts and depths of history at large, of individual souls still now around us, nor, at bottom, of your own spirit even as it is already,—for is not, already now, this your distress at the apparent loss of all your budding faith, a very sure sign that you still possess some very real faith, pressing to be more ?

2. There is also your *most* natural, indeed your absolutely true thought that " one cannot reconcile these things with any theory of a ' loving ' Father." And you feel that " Faith must somehow come to terms with the enigma of suffering."

Here again I look first at the large facts across history, and then to my experience of many souls, including my own. And everywhere thus without me and within me I see that Christianity has, from the first, been very precisely fronting and overcoming the enigma of suffering. True, Christianity has not " explained " suffering and evil ; no one has done so, no one can do so,—Christianity has no more done so than any of the philosophies or sciences, although, unfortunately, apologists for religion too often speak and write as though Christianity had really done so, or, at least, as though it could do so. Here once more all the exigencies of " clearness " are thoroughly out of place. Yet Christianity, in further articulation of many a deep intuition in the Exilic writings of the Old Testament, has done two things with regard to suffering—two things quite other indeed than " explanation," yet two things greater, more profound and profitable for us than ever could be such a satisfaction of our thirst for clear intellectual comprehension.

Christianity, then, has, from the first, immensely deepened and widened, it has further revealed, not the " explanation "—which never existed for us men,—but the fact, the reality, the awful potency and baffling mystery of sorrow, pain, sin, things which abide with man across the ages. And Christianity has, from the first, immensely increased the capacity, the wondrous secret and force which issues in a practical, living, loving transcendence, utilisation, transformation of sorrow and pain, and even of sin. It is the literal fact, as demonstrable as anything that has happened or will happen to our human race can ever be, that Christianity, after some two centuries of the most terrific opposition, conquered—that it conquered in an utterly fair fight—a fight fair as regards the Christian success,—the philosophy of Greece and the power of Rome ; indeed that it even conquered Gnosticism, that subtle New Paganism of the thousand elusive hues and forms, that Protean error so very dear to all over-ripe, *blasé* civilisations. It is the simple fact that Christianity conquered ; and it is equally the simple fact that it did so, above all because of what it actually achieved with regard to suffering.

For Christianity, without ever a hesitation, from the first and everywhere, refused to hold, or even to tolerate, either the one or the other of the two only attempts at self-persuasion which, then as now, possess souls that suffer whilst they have not yet found the deepest. Christianity refused all Epicureanism,—since man cannot find his deepest by fleeing from pain and suffering, and by seeking pleasure and pleasures, however dainty and refined. And it refused all Stoicism,—since pain, suffering, evil are not fancies and prejudices, but real, very real ;

and since man's greatest action and disposition is not self-sufficingness or aloofness, but self-donation and love. Christianity refused these theories, not by means of another theory of its own, but simply by exhibiting a Life and lives—the Life of the Crucified, and lives which continually re-live, in their endless various lesser degrees and ways, such a combination of gain in giving and of joy in suffering. Christianity thus gave to souls the faith and strength to grasp life's nettle. It raised them, in their deepest dispositions and innermost will, above the pitiful oscillations and artificialities of even the greatest of the Pagans in this central matter,—between eluding, ignoring pain and suffering, and, animal-like, seeking life in its fleeting, momentary pleasures ; or trying the nobler yet impossible course,—the making out that physical, mental, moral pain and evil are nothing real, and the suppressing of emotion, sympathy and pity as things unworthy of the adult soul. Christianity did neither. It pointed to Jesus with the terror of death upon Him in Gethsemane ; with a cry of desolation upon the Cross on Calvary ; it allowed the soul, it encouraged the soul to sob itself out. It not only taught men frankly to face and to recognise physical and mental pain, death, and all other, especially all moral evils and sufferings as very real ; it actually showed men the presence and gravity of a host of pains, evils and miseries which they had, up to then, quite ignored or at least greatly minimised. And yet, with all this—in spite of all such material for despair, the final note of Christianity was and is still, one of trust, of love, of transcendent joy. It is no accident, but of the very essence of the mystery and of the power of faith, it springs from the reality of God and of His action within men's souls, that, as the nobly joyous last chapters of Isaiah (Chap. xl. to the end) contain also those wondrous utterances of the man of sorrows, so also the serenity of the Mount of the Beatitudes leads, in the Gospels, to the darkness of Calvary.

Pray believe me here : it is to Christianity that we owe our deepest insight into the wondrously wide and varied range throughout the world, as we know it, of pain, suffering, evil ; just as to Christianity we owe the richest enforcement of the fact that, in spite of all this, God *is*, and that He is good and loving.

And this enforcement Christianity achieves, at its best, by actually
inspiring soul after soul, to believe, to love, to live this wondrous
faith.

Hence all attempts to teach Christianity anything on this
central matter of pain and suffering would be, very literally,
to " teach one's grandmother to suck eggs." For the very
existence of the problem—I mean man's courage to face it,
together with sensitiveness as to its appalling range and its
baffling mystery—we owe, not to philosophy nor to science,
still less to their own untutored hearts, but to religion—above
all to the Jewish and Christian religion.

And note, please, that the alternative is not between " this
or that non-religious view, denial, or scepticism which *does*
explain suffering and evil," and " religious faith, especially
Christianity, which *does not* explain them." No : this is a purely
imaginary alternative : for there is no unbelief as there is no
faith, there is no science as there is no popular tradition, which
does or can explain these things.   The real alternative is :
" irreligion, which still oscillates between Epicureanism and
Stoicism, systems which remain variously unreal and unhuman
with regard to suffering, and which know only how to evade
or to travesty pain and to deny sin," and " religion, which fully
fronts, indeed extends and deepens indefinitely our sense of,
suffering and sin, and which, nevertheless, alone surmounts
and utilises them." Thus once again, not clearness, not any
ready transferableness, but efficacious power and integrating
comprehensiveness appear as the true, decisive tests.

3. You feel—this is your keenest, yet also your most fruitful
suffering—that what has happened is cruel, cruel ; is what
yourself, you, imperfect as you are, would have given your life
to prevent. How, then, you wistfully ask, can you possibly love
and trust such a power, if it exist at all,—a power, which, in
this case, shows itself so deaf to the most elementary and legitimate, to the most sacred of your longings and your prayers ?
You possessed the darling, and you loved and served it with all
you were ; who possesses and tends it now ?

How I understand ! how keen, how cutting is this pang !

And I look around me, and again I see a similar bewildering
contrast repeated upon an immense scale.   I remember, in our

own day, the earthquake at Messina, with its thousands of cases of seemingly quite undeserved, quite unmitigated anguish, when our own admittedly most imperfect, badly bungling humanity and governments appeared, as so many small dwarfs of pity, alone pitiful, against this awful background of grim havoc and blind fury and cruelty. And, of course, we could all of us add case upon case from history and from our own experience of souls.

But please note well. Where does the keenness of this our scandal come from? Why do we, in all such cases, suffer such feelings of shock and outrage? What makes us, in the midst of it all, persist in believing, indeed persist in acting (with great cost) on the belief, that love and devotedness are utterly the greatest things we know, and deserve the sacrifice of all our earthly gifts, of our very life? Whence comes all this?—The case is, I think, quite parallel with that as to trust in reality generally. Why is it, as to such trust and such reality, that even the most hardened of the sceptics continue to trouble themselves and to trouble us all, if not as to truth, at least as to truthfulness? Why is untruthfulness so very odious? Untruthfulness is certainly most convenient. Why indeed does every at all sane mind find it so intolerable to hold itself to be completely shut up within its own impressions, to admit that these impressions are nothing but illusions, or, at least, are utterly worthless as indications of realities other than its own? Whence springs the suffering—the most keen suffering—of the thought of being thus shut up, if we *are*, in fact, thus shut up within our own purely subjective impressions and fancies? The answer, surely, is that we thus suffer because, in fact, we are *not* thus shut up, because we *do* communicate with realities other than ourselves, and hence that these realities so impress and affect us that only by a painful effort can we, violently and artificially, treat those realities as mere fanciful projections of our own.

Similarly, if there is no source and standard of love, of pity, of giving, of self-donation,—a source and standard abiding, ultimate, distinct from, deeper than ourselves, a source Itself loving, Itself a Lover, and which, somehow profoundly penetrative of ourselves, keeps us poor things, rich with at least this sense of our poverty and with this our inability to abandon love (that very costly thing) as a chimera or a mere fleeting vibration of our nerves : if there is not such a more than human (deeper and higher than human) source and standard, then the real, actual situation becomes wholly rootless and unreasonable, precisely in what it has of admittedly greatest, of most precious and most significant.

Thus, both in the matter of Truth and Reality and in the matter of Love and a Lover, we suffer, when scepticism assails us, because we are *not* simply shut up within our own fancies, because (mysteriously yet most actually) we are penetrated and moved by God, the Ultimate Reality and Truth, the Ultimate Lover and Goodness. We are moved by Him Who *is*, Who is before ever we were, Who is with us from the beginning of our existence, Who is always the first in operation whenever there is interaction between Him and us. Because He *is*, we have our unconquerable sense of Reality ; because He is Love and Lover, we cannot let love go. And it is He Who made the mother's heart ; it is, not simply her love, but, in the first instance, His love, with just some drops of it fallen into the mother's heart, which produce the standard within her which cries out against all that is, or even looks like, blindness and cruel fate.

For remember, please, it is not Judaism, not Christianity, not any kind of Theism that bids us, or even allows us, to hold and to accept as good in themselves the several painful or cruel or wrong things that happen in this our complicated, difficult life. None of these convictions worship Nature, or the World-as-a-whole ; they all, on the contrary, find much that is wrong in Nature as we know it, and in the World-as-a-whole as we actually find it. All such believers worship and adore not Nature but God—the love and the action of God within and from behind the world, but not as though this love and action were every-where equally evident, not as though they directly willed, directly chose, all things that happen and as they happen. On the contrary : these great religions leave such a pure optimism to absolute Idealist philosophers, and to rhapsodising pantheists and poets ; and these religions believe such views, wheresoever they are taken as ultimate, to be either shallow and unreal, or sorry travesties of the facts.

If, then, I be asked to whom I confide those I love when,

after much utterly ineffectual-seeming devotion of my heart, I have seen them suffer fearfully and disappear from my own care and longing, I answer that I confide them to that Reality and Love, to that Real Lover, whose reality and lovingness and penetration of my heart alone make possible and actual my own poor persistent love. Thus my very bitterness and despair over the apparent insult flung at my love by the world as I know it, turns out to be but one more effect of the reality and operativeness of God, and one more reason (again not clear, not readily transferable, but rich and fruitful) for believing and trusting in Him, in Love, the Lover.

Please, in conclusion, to forgive the great length of these leisurely browsings which I love to feel have had to be snatched from hard-worked, laboriously crowded days. And pray be very sure of how keenly I have suffered and I still suffer with your suffering. I beg God to bless these poor little pages, and anything else that may offer itself to you with possibilities of help within it. And I will patiently but unconquerably continue to believe that, in ways and degrees known to God alone, you will attain to Christian humility and trust, to Christian faith, hope and love,—to the joy of utter self-dedication.

Yours very sincerely,

FRIEDRICH von HÜGEL.

II

PAPERS ON THE TEACHING OF JESUS
AND CHRISTIANITY IN GENERAL

5

THE APOCALYPTIC ELEMENT IN THE TEACHING OF JESUS:

ITS ULTIMATE SIGNIFICANCE AND ITS ABIDING FUNCTION [1]

THERE exists a touching medal struck by devotees of Sir Thomas More, after that great life had been done to death by his sensual, savage master. You see there the punning symbol of a syca-more, a " foolish fig-tree "; and the legend beneath runs : " *decisa adhuc dulcescit* "—even when cut down, this (syca-)more smells sweet ! I have often thought this entire medal to be applicable also to Biblical criticism, especially also to the analysis of the Gospels, even of their eschatological elements. We can cut down and break up that noble Biblical tree : somehow, the very fragments still smell sweet ! The fact is that religion thrives, not by the absence of difficulties, but by the presence of helps and powers ; indeed, every step achieved onwards and inwards in such fruitfulness involves new frictions, obscurities, paradoxes, antinomies. Religion achieves its fullest power and balance only in the completest interaction of God, Christ, Church ; and yet each of these great sides and stages of religion contains severally a difficulty so profound and obstinate as to be, in strictness, capable only of delimitation and discrimination— of being rendered bearable for the sake of the light and the power which surround the burden and the darkness ; but incapable, I believe, of any quite direct and entirely clear, easy and readily transferable solution. There is, at the one end, the profound reality of God, and the all-influencing belief in this His reality ; yet there is also the reality of Evil, with its brutal facts and

[1] An Address delivered before the Birmingham Clerical Society (Anglican), October, 1919.

Church

baffling obscurities. And, there is, at the other end, the reality of the Church, so pressingly necessary, so manifoldly fruitful throughout the ages and lands of Christendom; yet there appears also a hampering, a seemingly inevitable hampering, of the other sides, indeed even in part of some of the religious sides and needs, of man's manifold nature. And, in between those two ends, there stands the reality of Jesus and of His immense attraction and beneficence; but there stands at this place also the reality of the *Parousia*—of all the fantastic-seeming teaching concerning a very near universal cataclysm and cosmic regeneration, with Jesus Himself as the visible centre of overwhelming power. It looks indeed as though simply one of these levels, with its own formidable difficulty, were abundantly sufficient for man—a creature, after all, so limited in his capacity for bearing burdens and overleaping obstacles. Nevertheless, the experience of life and the analysis of thought, on the largest scale and in the longest run, show plainly enough, I believe, that the lights and helps of each level are increased and supplemented by those of the other two; whilst the obscurities and obstacles of each level are, somehow, reduced, and in part resolved, by the very darkness and difficulty of the others.

I propose here to examine the helps and difficulties of the middle of these three levels—the problems raised by the Apocalyptic Element in the Teachings of Jesus. To save time I will not discuss, I will merely state as clearly as possible, the main critical conclusions which appear now to be assured or highly probable. I will next draw out certain peculiarities furnished by these conclusions, and I will end by an attempt to fathom the driving forces of all this Eschatology at their deepest, and to appraise their abiding truth and place in the spiritual life.

I

Amongst the (at least apparent) antinomies in the outlook and teaching of Jesus, none is perhaps more immediately striking than is that which obtains between the scenes and sayings which seem to declare or to imply a sunny, continuous, balanced temper— an expansion from within outwards and from below upwards;

and the scenes and sayings which declare or imply a stormy, abrupt, one-sided temper—an irruption from without inwards and from above downwards. The expansive, continuous temper perpetuates and perfects the spirit of the great Prophets during the Hebrew monarchy before the Exile ; the irruptive, sudden movement derives at least its imagery and some of its tone from the Apocalyptic Writers who began to arise already towards the end of the Exile, but especially from the Book of Daniel, composed doubtless as late as 165 or 164 B.C., during the oppression of the Jews in Palestine by the Syrian King Antiochus Epiphanes. It is certainly easy to exaggerate the difference between these two strains ; it is even not absolutely impossible to interpret the entire life and teaching of Jesus as apocalyptic and eschatological from first to last. Nevertheless there *is* a difference of general temper between, on the one hand, the great plant parables, the appeal of the lilies and the birds in the Sermon on the Mount, the blessing of the children, and the sleeping on the storm-tossed ship ; and, on the other hand, the parables of expectation, the urgent appeals to be ready for the Lord who comes as a thief in the night, and the vehement acts in the Temple and the terrifying predictions on the Mount of Olives, during Jesus's last earthly days. I still feel Loisy and Schweitzer to be, on this point, largely over-ingenious and somewhat violent in their handling of the texts and of their delicately cumulative evidences.

But if there indeed exists such a difference, we cannot but place the point of change at Cæsarea Philippi (Mark viii. 27 and parallels, onwards). It is here that, in return for Peter's recognition of His Messianic dignity, Jesus first announces to His disciples His coming Passion, and adds a more insistent note to His call for self-surrender in His followers. And He now promptly introduces the Son of Man as coming to judge all the world upon the clouds of Heaven.

True, even in Jesus's earliest proclamation " the Kingdom of God is at hand," and men are to " repent " (Mark i. 14, 15). Even those earliest addresses seem to imply a public, a world renovation, to occur within that living generation ; and certainly also here the Kingdom, even where it appears as already in course of formation, is conceived as primarily a divine gift.

And here, as simply everywhere in Jesus's own teaching, temper and implications, there already appears the Alternative, the Two Ways, and the Abiding Consequences, Good or Evil, of Good or Evil Choice. Hell, in this general sense, is not simply a part of only the later stage of Jesus's own teaching ; still less is it imported into Jesus's teaching by misunderstanding hearers or reporters. Such Hell indeed is only the natural necessary corollary of Heaven in Jesus's own unchanging scheme. But in the earlier stage there is no violence, no painful suddenness about the world renovation ; nor is there any indication of a Second Coming of Jesus Himself. Whereas at and after Cæsarea Philippi, Jesus, with ever increasing clearness, implies or insists upon *three distinct and several cataclysms* ; historical criticism is doubtless right in refusing to identify any two of them. Thus, already from Cæsarea Philippi onwards Jesus announces, more or less plainly, His own resurrection after His own passion and death ; but this is to be a directly personal rehabilitation, to be witnessed only by His chosen disciples : He will arise in solitude from the grave and will show Himself to them alone. In the last days at Jerusalem, Jesus quite plainly prophesies the early destruction of the Temple. And later than his own death and arising, but earlier than this national destruction, Jesus proclaims a proximate, sudden, God-worked end of the then extant world generally, with Himself descending from heaven as judge of all mankind at this great assize. The death of His own body and the destruction of the Temple were, we see in the Gospel narratives themselves, somehow held mistakenly, by some of his hearers, to have been identified by Himself in His discourses to them ; yet He had really spoken of these two future happenings as two quite distinct things. Similarly the end of the Temple and the end of the world are really distinct events in Jesus's prophecy ; their identification has been rendered at all plausible only by a literary accident—the present position of the " Small Apocalypse " (Mark xiii. 5–37 and parallels) which thus appears as though communicated by Jesus simply in answer to the question of the disciples as to when would occur the destruction of the Temple, seemingly just prophesied by Himself (Mark xiii. 1–4 and parallels). This " Small Apocalypse " is (I believe, rightly) now taken by most critics as largely a Jewish document ; but Professor Percy Gardner assuredly goes too far when he attempts to extend this inauthenticity to all the eschato-logical teaching of Jesus, as found here and elsewhere in the Synoptists. Such, undoubtedly authentic, eschatological teaching appears even in certain verses which form the frame-work of this very Apocalypse ; and is, besides, warranted elsewhere by texts of immense weight and luminous clearness, which stand above all suspicion of a secondary origin. So at Cæsarea Philippi : " verily, I say unto you, there be some of them that stand here, which shall in no wise taste death, till they see the Son of Man coming in His Kingdom " (Matt. xvi. 28). So in Peræa : " verily I say unto you, that ye which have followed me, in the regeneration when the Son of Man shall sit on the throne of His glory, ye shall also sit on thrones, judging the twelve tribes of Israel " (Matt. xix. 28). So on to the Mount of Olives : " immediately after tribulation of those days . . . the stars shall fall from heaven ; and then shall appear the sign of the Son of Man in heaven . . . and they shall see the Son of Man coming in the clouds of heaven with power and great glory " (Matt. xxiv. 29, 30). So at the Last Supper : " but I say unto you, I will not drink henceforth of this fruit of the vine, until that day when I drink it new with you in my Father's Kingdom " (Matt. xxvi. 29). And so when adjured by the High Priest, during His trial, to tell them plainly whether He is the Christ, Jesus not only admits that He is, but adds : " I say unto you, henceforth ye shall see the Son of Man sitting at the right hand of the power and coming on the clouds of heaven " (Matt. xxvi. 64). Thus, as before Cæsarea Philippi the Kingdom was con-ceived prophetically,—as a relatively slow and peaceful growth, and from Cæsarea Philippi onwards it was conceived apocalyptic-ally,—as a sudden and violent irruption ; so also before Cæsarea Philippi the Messiah appears mostly lowly, radiant, and with all-embracing hope, and from Cæsarea Philippi onwards as coming again in the clouds of heaven " with power."

Now this Second Coming is an entirely original conception of Jesus Himself ; no trace of such a conviction can be found in any document previous to His enunciation of it. No Jew had ever before Jesus applied Daniel vii. 13 to a personal Messiah ; they all had taken the verse in its doubtless original meaning, as describing the true Israel as a people humane and from above, in contradistinction to the heathen empires as beastlike—as so many monsters rising up from the ocean below. The personal application is the original work of Jesus, and of the Jesus of the second period. So far all the critics agree with emphasis. There is, however, another doctrine which Jesus launches simultaneously with the Coming on the clouds of heaven, which, I know not really why, is less confidently held, by these same critics, to be Jesus's own discovery—the doctrine of the Suffering Messiah. Nevertheless it is certain that the first Jewish attribution known to us of Isaiah liii. (the Suffering Servant) to a Personal Messiah is that of Trypho in St. Justin's dialogue, written not before A.D. 155 ; whilst as late as A.D. 246 Origen tells of having heard a Jew apply that chapter to the entire Jewish people, dispersed and broken, in order that many proselytes might be gained (*Contra Celsum*, i. 55). It is thus a safe proposition that neither the Old Testament nor the Jews of Jesus's time knew of a Suffering Personal Messiah. The " woes," " birthpangs " of the Messiah meant, of course, only certain public and cosmic disturbances which were to precede and to announce Messiah's first and only coming. As to the origin of the actual description of the Suffering Servant, there is, I think, much to commend the notion of Bernard Duhm that, though the picture was meant by the prophet poet for the Jewish people, as God's missionary amongst the Gentiles, yet that the immensely concrete and moving details of the picture were suggested by a particular Jew, afflicted with leprosy, whose serene resignation and self-immolation for the good of souls had first startled and determined the writer. If so, then Jesus, by applying that prophecy personally, to Himself as Messiah, only reverted, if not to the original meaning, yet to the original occasion of these great Ebed Jahve Lyrics.

II

We have now accumulated a mass of pressing difficulties, of poignant questions. At bottom, they raise the problem, not merely of Jesus's Divinity, or at least of His Inerrancy even with regard to matters of directly religious import, but primarily of the soundness and sanity of His human mind. And even if we succeed in finding room for such teaching within His mind, as the convictions of a supremely sane Jew of well-nigh two thousand years ago, what possible use, what present-day appeal, can we unforcedly still discover in these strange-sounding propositions? And if we do not make some such discovery, is not even the simply human attraction of Jesus ruined, for ourselves, in these our days, beyond all hope of repair? Let us first draw out the following considerations, as preparatory to certain last and deepest probings. I believe that not all the two series combined are too much for the acquisition of some resilience from under the weight of all that Eschatology, once it has thoroughly seized a sensitively awake mind.

1. No doctrine of the Divinity of Christ, no affirmation, even of just simply the normality of the mind of Jesus, are other than out of touch with all the real possibilities of the question, if they do not first recognise that a real Incarnation of God in man can only mean Incarnation in some particular human nature. Man in general is only an idea, it is not a fact, a reality; and God, the supremely factual, utterly real, the creator of the essential facts in man, did not, in the Incarnation, reverse either His own, God's nature, or the reflex of it, the nature of Man. The Incarnation could not, even by Himself, be made other than the entering into, and possession of, a human mind and will endowed with special racial dispositions and particular racial categories of thought. Assuredly this mind and will would be filled and moved by the deepest religious and moral truth and insight; and would be preserved from all essential error concerning the direct objects of the divine indwelling and condescension. Yet this truth and insight would of necessity show, to minds and hearts of other races and times, imaginative and emotional peculiarities —certain omissions, combinations, stresses, outlines, colourings, characteristic of the race and time of the Revealer. Otherwise, the Revealer would begin His career by being simply unintelligible to His first hearers, and even, in the long run, to the large majority of mankind; and He would, in Himself, not be normally, characteristically, man. Now it was most appropriate that the Incarnation, for purposes of religion, should take place in Jewish human nature, since the Jewish people had, already for some

thirteen centuries, furnished forth amongst mankind the purest light and strongest leading in religion. <u>Thus, however, the Revealer could not but imagine, think, feel and will the deepest truths and facts of His mission with Jewish categories, images, emotions.</u> Such a characteristically Jewish category—although, in a lesser degree, it is common to antiquity generally—permeates the Bible from cover to cover, in so far as its writers were Semites in blood and breeding. Everywhere the Divine action is, as such, conceived to be instantaneous. Thus the twenty-four hours of each of the six Days of Creation (in Genesis i.) were very probably conceived by the narrator as almost entirely composed of pauses between the creative acts, these acts themselves being instantaneous. Even St. Teresa could still, in A.D. 1562, consider the suddenness of a vision to be one of the two decisive tests of its divine origin. If then Jesus held that the world's present order would be terminated by an act of God, He could not image and propound this act other than as sudden and rapid. We shall find later on far more ultimate reasons for this category of suddenness ; yet the reason now given appears true and operative so far as it goes.

2. Nowhere, however, does Jesus presuppose or teach a corresponding suddenness of change in man's dispositions or actions, either as everywhere actually operative or even as normally desirable. Hence, as Canon Scott Holland, in his profound *Real Problem of Eschatology*, very acutely observes, the nearness and suddenness of Christ's Second Coming does not weaken but heightens the call to persistent self-purification and uninterrupted service of others. A proximate sharp testing awaits His hearers ; but it will be a testing of, at best, an entire long life of persistent faithfulness. And nowhere does Jesus condemn the essential things, conditions and duties of this life, as intrinsically evil ; His own thought and practice imply and show respect for the human body, reverence for the ties of family and of country, even when these are transcended in a complete, heroic self-abnegation. Even the military career He nowhere condemns—centurions are left by Him as centurions, He even praises them as such with emphasis. And He possesses the leisureliness of mind necessary for the full perception of the beauties or peculiarities of flower and tree ; bird, sheep and

fox; sky, field and lake; of sower, vintner, fisherman and shepherd, mason and housewife; and He disports Himself with children. Immensely earnest and inclusive of the most heroic asceticism as is His life, He can yet be accused of being a wine-bibber, a friend of publicans and sinners. All this tender leisure, observation, forthcoming friendliness—all this genial occupation with the present little things and little friends of God—all this only required the predominant intensity of expectation and detachment, characteristic of the second period of the earthly life of Jesus, to become less central in men's minds and to show itself as constituting, in the permanent scheme, but one of the two great movements of the uniquely wide, deep, various outlook and will of Jesus. The special characteristics of the first stage of the earthly life of Jesus thus come to their full development, in His closest followers, alongside of, alternately with, penetrated by, the special characteristics of the second stage. Thus could Dante find—surely, most rightly—in the Poverello of Assisi—so supremely detached, so expansively attached, so heroic without rigorism, so loving without softness—perhaps the nearest reproduction of the divine paradox of the life of Jesus Himself. On this point also we shall find a still deeper root in the teaching of Jesus, as expressive of the very soul of religion.

3. More and more, after the death of Jesus, did the preaching of the Kingdom, indeed all direct thought of the Kingdom, wane, and did the Church take the place of the Kingdom. This change was, in its essence, simply inevitable, right and beneficent; indeed the conception and the functioning of a Church most justly claim deep implications, nay, definite institutions, in the teaching and acts of Jesus Himself. Mr. Clutton Brock, in his *What is the Kingdom of Heaven?* 1918, very emphatically condemns those who hold that Jesus ever taught or implied a proximate cosmic cataclysm—He really taught and implied only the transfiguring power, given to the pure of heart, to see God here and now, and to see all this Here and Now as, in its essence, already the Kingdom of God. But then Mr. Brock finds himself most instructively baffled—he admits himself deeply surprised—by the fact that (although this purely interior and mystical act and attitude is really all that Jesus meant by the Kingdom)

the Kingdom of God, thus incapable of coming into collision with any of the great public and world facts and forces, should have so rapidly lost its central position in the Christian teaching. In reality, the Kingdom, with its categories of intense proximity, suddenness and cataclysm, soon ceased to be central, even in the minds of Christians, for the simple reason that the given visible world persisted in lasting ; that the vehemence of this group of teachings could not be maintained for long, if the gentler characteristics of the other group of teaching—equally the utterance of Jesus Himself—were to have their full realisation : and that Jesus Himself had given unequivocal indications as to how he would envisage, how He would organise, permanent Christian institutions, did the permanence of the world require —as, in fact, it was now requiring—a corresponding permanence of the Christian organisation.   The acute polemic of Jesus against at least the school of Shammai amongst the Pharisees ; His attitude as critic and new legislator even as regards the Law itself ; and, perhaps above all, His death at the instigation of the Sanhedrin, the great official Churchmen's council of His time and country, readily obscure the nevertheless very certain facts of Jesus's organic conception of all society, civil and religious, and of His actual organising of His apostles and followers. All souls are, indeed, to Jesus, equal in a true sense—they all spring from the one God ; compared with God all their differences are as nothing ; and merely earthly differences do not count as ultimate differences at all. Yet this equality is not interchangeableness, nor a simply individualist, nor again a socialist, equalisation. It is an equality derived from God and operating within humanity at large as this is organised in the family and the religious community. It is an equality rich, elastic, manifold, thorough differentiation into various kinds and degrees of interdependence and mutual service. The very images dearest to Jesus—the Father and his children, the Master and his servants, the Shepherd and his sheep, the King and his subjects—show this plainly, as a quite unchanging characteristic of all His outlook. And Jesus spontaneously acts upon this fundamental conviction when He comes to require a little band of preachers and teachers. As He Himself alone had received the Messianic power and call from the one God, His Father, so He, in turn, selects twelve representatives, endowing them with intrinsic authority and power ; and He places one of them at their head with quite unique gifts and duties. The institution remains small in Jesus's lifetime, not because Jesus objects to a large institution, a Church, or because this small institution is, in any essential point, different from the Church. The institution remains small simply and solely because of the Proximate Expectation : and, with the fading away of the proximity, the Preaching Band automatically becomes the Church. For already in the Preaching Band there is mission, subordination, unitary headship—the genuine religious movement from the One to the Few and thus to the Many ; and from above downwards. The noblest title ever taken by the Popes—the title by which the great ones amongst them stand confirmed, and by which the bad ones amongst them stand condemned—Servant of the Servants of God—is thus in very truth the, varyingly extensive but everywhere real, call and duty of us all. And surely, in spite of the many difficulties, dangers and abuses brought into the world by neglectful or insufficiently Christian Churchmen : the Church, at its best and greatest, has, as a sheer matter of fact, grandly, indeed uniquely, proved this her capacity for preserving and perpetuating the spirit and power of Jesus Christ.

4. We noted above two quite original points in the Eschatology of Jesus : the Suffering of the Messiah, and the Return of this same Messiah in Power and Majesty. They first appear at Cæsarea Philippi in a close interconnection ; let us always keep them thus, as but two constituents of one great fact and law. For only thus, on the one hand, does the picture in Daniel lose every vestige of gratuitousness or inflation ; and only thus, on the other hand, does the picture in Isaiah not express any ultimate scepticism or pessimism. We thus get here, in its acutest richness of interdependent light and shadow, the most original and the most divinely true of all the discoveries and powers of Christianity. Suffering, that very suffering, to escape which, as most real and harmful, or to explain which away, as but the false imagination of men, all the world before Christianity is seen hopelessly fleeing or as hopelessly ignoring : this same suffering, is here both foreknown and suffered through, by the Revealer Himself. And in this concrete case the Suffering

is a very world of the most diverse malignity, humiliation, dereliction, anguish bodily and mental ; and the Sufferer here never ceases to maintain, about all this and about every other sacrifice and suffering throughout the world, both that the pain and the trial and the wicked dispositions which may inflict it or which may be roused by it are most real, most evil, *and* yet that it all, if taken in simple self-abandonment to God, is profoundly operative towards the soul's establishment in an otherwise uncapturable regal beatitude and peace. Without the Cross, Jesus could not ask as much of us, His followers, as He actually does ; without the Crown, He would but teach an heroic Stoicism. Only with the two together, with Joy succeeding, and actually occasioned by, the previous anguish, does His life both fully purify and yet maintain, whilst steadily proposing undared depths of renunciation, man's divinely implanted ineradicable thirst, not indeed for pleasure but for a beatitude abiding in deepest self-oblivion. And here both the Passion and the Power are all, in the first instance, borne for God, borne through God, crowned by God. A virile and wholesome humanitarianism flows indeed necessarily from the heart of Jesus and from men's love of His Spirit ; but they do so, thus wholesomely, because grounded continuously in the primary motive, not of man, but of God.

III

Let us now attempt some five quite final, deepest conclusions.

First, then, as to the conception of all Divine action as proximate and short. There certainly lurks here far more than a merely racial category of thought. Paul de Lagarde, that largely embittered, often unfair, but profoundly instructive scholar, so little known in England, has protested, with volcanic energy and the most angry polemic, against all Jewish thought and feeling on the subject, since the central fact, effect and need of religion, is just exactly its sense of, its thirst for, Eternity, Simultaneity, an experience entirely in the Here and Now. The Present, the Presence, are here intensely felt alone to constitute

religion ; the Past is dust and archæology, the Future is wind
and fanaticism. God, who Himself is ever Here and Now,
is thus loved in a Here and Now act and ecstasy—all Past, all
Future fall away.—There assuredly works here a state of soul, an
apprehension, essential to all genuine spirituality. The same
apprehension gives its special dignity and truth to Quakerism ;
indeed all Mysticism is Mysticism, in proportion as it thus
apprehends and cultivates Presence as the centre of Religion.
Doubtless the noblest intellectual formulation of this great conviction is that of Aristotle in his doctrine of the Unmoving
Energeia—assuredly one more proof of the light given by the
Unincarnate God to non-Jewish, non-Christian souls.   This
very doctrine has been admirably elaborated by Dr. Schiller,
and is re-stated very cogently by Fr. Herbert Walker, S.J. in the
Hibbert Journal for July, 1919. But let us be careful lest the great
experience and doctrine here considered lead us straight into
delusions and morbidities. Doubtless God, in His intrinsic
nature, is non-successive, is outside Time ; doubtless men themselves, in rare moments, can and do experience something like
an arrest, an overleaping of succession ; and indeed unless
man possessed some such faculty, he could not so vividly apprehend God and religion as do all the Mystics. But it does not
follow at all that, because God is simply simultaneous, and
because I am sufficiently simultaneous vividly to apprehend,
and now and then partially to share, that simultaneity of His,
I am simply simultaneous in myself.   It is, of course, this
assumption that man is, or can become, thus simply simultaneous, that man's spirit requires nought else but its own direct
union with the spirit of God alone, which underlies the angry
contempt of all history, institutions, the visible and audible—
of all succession—in all Mystics as such. Nevertheless nothing
is more certain than that man never does nor can get away, for
long, from all succession ; that he is built up into a man of any
sort—inclusively of religious man—in and through his body as
well as his imagination, his reason, his feeling and his will—
bodily things and incitements taking their part also here ; and
that there could be no Quakers, no Mystics, amongst men, were
all men Quakers and Mystics. At bottom, the difference, between
the Mystic as such and the religionist of a more historical or

sacramental type, lies as much in the interesting non-recognition of the mediations always actually at work also in the Mystic, yet always thus ignored or minimised by him, as in the actual preponderance, in this same Mystic, of any directly intuitive element.

2. Again it is very certain that Pure Mysticism and Pantheism are one ; and that they both, by their similar excesses, end by levelling all things down, not up. If any moment, any state, any thing is as good as another, is all engulfed in, is the complete vehicle of, Eternity—then good and evil, true and false, God and World, God and Man, spirit and sense, coalesce.

Now it is profoundly impressive to note how intractable the Synoptic Jesus remains to all purely mystical interpretation : Evelyn Underhill's recent attempt is as able as it is unconvincing. The fact of course is that nothing could be more anti-mystical than is the Proximate Futurism of the authentic Jesus. This Proximate Futurism stands out massively against all Pure Immanentism, all Evolution taken as final cause and not merely as instrument and method. For we must not forget that the favourite method of all Hylozoists, all Monists, has always been the insistence upon immense ranges of time and space, and upon the appearance, little by little, within substances vulgarly dubbed " material," of what are as vulgarly dubbed " spiritual " characteristics. If only you thus manœuvre with little by little, you can delude yourself and others into holding that this exquisite quantification solves the problem of utterly different qualities. It is at this point that Jesus calls a most impressive halt. He points, in the expectation of the Proximate Second Coming, to something not slow of growth, but sudden ; not small and imperceptible, but huge and public ; not produced by the sheer evolution from below of the already extant, but by the descent from without and above, of a newly given, a sheer illapse of quite another quality. Perhaps all the points of this stupendous picture require permanent softening by us His followers, if we would be equally faithful to His earlier, sunnier outlook, and to the ultimate implications of His Spirit as a whole. Yet the magnificent massiveness of the anti-Pantheism here, is a permanent service to religion of the very first magnitude.

3. Let us, however, always remember that, as we have already seen, the suddenness of the crisis to be produced by God in no

wise involves other than persistent dispositions to be cultivated
by man. But indeed there is also another point of persistency
assumed by Jesus throughout; and this point is central in all
Jesus's thought and care. God, the very God Who, in Jesus's
Eschatological picture, appears to act with such utterly dis-
concerting suddenness and discontinuity, is most assuredly
conceived, by this same Jesus, as at bottom profoundly self-
identical, uncapricious, persistent, indeed essentially simultaneous, eternal. It is really because of Jesus's utter certainty of
the unchanging justice and providence of God that, under the
pressure of a proximate earthly defeat of the cause of truth and
right, He vividly foresees a corresponding exaltation of this
same cause. The self-identical God who allowed the defeat will
not fail to execute the triumph. The beautifully naïve parables
which picture God as Father, as Master, as Vineyard Owner or
the like, and which thus of necessity introduce successive acts
and changes of disposition, as though such vicissitudes obtained
in the Divine Nature itself, must very certainly not be pressed
as involving real changes in God. If it can be maintained that
Jesus did not think even of human history in terms of our modern
(largely very problematical) development notions, it can be
contended much more certainly, indeed quite finally, that Jesus
would have rejected with horror any and every doctrine of an
intrinsically changing, or developing, or even simply successive,
God. We can be sure of this, even already simply because Jesus
was a Jew—because, short of overwhelming proof to the contrary,
a religious Jew of the times of Jesus must be assumed to have
been penetrated by such instinctive presuppositions, even if,
as doubtless was the case with Jesus, the particular Jew in question
had not passed through the schools of Hellenistic Judaism, in
which the Nonsuccessiveness of God's nature was very explicitly,
very emphatically taught. We thus secure two great points of
rest and persistence as, so to speak, flanking and framing a line
of movement and change. There is God, at bottom unchanging,
an overflowing richness of ever simultaneous life. And there is
man capable of, called to, about to be tested concerning, stability
—a persistent successiveness of devoted life. The suddenness
is only in the testing and in conversions to a persistent devotedness; and the very Suddenness, in these cases, springs from the

need to express a junction between the Simultaneity of God and
the Successiveness, however steady, of man.   Thus the two
points essential to every real Mysticism are secured, but this in
such a combination with other conditions as to render impossible
all direct derivation of pure Mysticism or Pantheism from the
historical Jesus.

4. Once more. God is indeed the beginning, the middle and
the end, the ceaseless presupposition, of all Jesus's teaching.
His was assuredly the human mind and soul most closely united
with God that ever lived on earth.   The Christian doctrine of
the Divinity of Jesus, which we can trace in all its development
through the Pauline and Johannine writings, through St. Ignatius
of Antioch, St. Justin Martyr, St. Irenæus and Tertullian, on
to the Councils of Nicæa and Chalcedon, till it finds its full
crown at last in the Third Council of the Lateran—is undoubtedly
true and deeply enriching. Yet it can be wisely maintained by
us only if we simultaneously remember that, however truly God
revealed Himself with supreme fullness and in a unique manner
in Jesus Christ, yet that this same God had not left Himself,
still does not leave Himself, without *some* witness to Himself
throughout the ages before Christ, and throughout the countries,
groups, and even individual souls, whom the message, the fact,
of the historic Jesus has never yet reached, or who, in sheer
good faith, cannot understand, cannot see Him as He really
is. The Unincarnate God has thus a wider range, though
a less deep message, than the Incarnate God ; and these two
Gods are but one and the same God, Who, mysteriously, mostly
slowly and almost imperceptibly, prepares or supplements,
expresses and otherwise aids Himself, in each way by the other
way. Thus though of course far from all that passed and passes
for Religion in Paganism can be held by us to be, in its degree
and manner, true and right—to be capable of Christianisation,
indeed itself to serve the fuller apprehension and service of God
and of man ; yet *some* of the great Greek thinkers' thinking, of
the great Roman lawyers' legislation, of the Græco-Roman later
religious philosophies and cults, in very deed sprang from the
Unincarnate God to serve and supplement the God Incarnate.
Only thus can we be freed from anxiety, and can we sincerely
rejoice and be confirmed in our faith in God the Omnipresent,

when we discover how largely the Old Testament Book of Wisdom borrows from Plato, how appreciable is St. Paul's indebtedness to the Greek Mysteries, how much in the form of the Fourth Gospel comes from Philo, how greatly Tertullian learnt from Roman Law, how important was St. Augustine's indebtedness to Plotinus, how almost wholesale was the Dionysian writer's incorporation of Proclus, and how systematic and gratefully avowed was St. Thomas of Aquino's utilisation of Aristotle. Doubtless these appropriations varied in their carefulness, necessity and permanent value ; yet even this most incomplete list surely indicates that the process in general was as legitimate as it has proved fruitful. Christianity could not otherwise have lived and thriven in this world ; and only those who can manage to figure to themselves the world as forsaken by the very God Who made it, and Who sent to it His Son, can, in strictness, be disquieted by such preparations by God Himself for His own fully incarnate coming.

5. Particularly important also is this discrimination in affording a ready Christian means and a full Christian justification for the successive enlargements of man's conception of the world of time and space, and of man's own and of God's own relation to this same world. Even in the teaching of Jesus Himself we have as yet no persistent occupation with souls other than those of the house of Israel—it is to them, to the Palestinian Jews, that His own apostles are sent out by Him. Stephen and his Hellenistic Jewish collaborators already carry the Gospel to the Hellenistic Jews. St. Paul enlarges St. Peter's first evangelising of the Gentiles, and becomes himself emphatically the apostle of the Heathen World. The whole world, the Church's parish— this outlook has never ceased, since then, to actuate the Catholic Church, as this very name implies. Yet though this our earthly world doubtless constitutes the limit of our direct duties and clear knowledge, we have, I believe, passed through experiences and have reached a time which demand a still further deliberate expansion, admittedly of another but, I submit, of a perfectly practicable kind. Such an expansion appears imperative if the deep and tender universalism of the Gospel is not itself to come to appear a parochial sentimentalism. And the point has its urgency, if so symptomatic book as *Foundations* is to count.

For there you find, pretty well throughout, an almost angry vehemence of restriction : that we literally know nothing of God except in and through Jesus, that the whole of sound religion is exclusively concerned with God in His dealings with man—that all over and above this, is the idle guessing of philosophers —and much else substantially to this effect. I know no better cure for this headiness than a careful, frank facing of the trend in the later philosophy of Hegel. For in this later Hegel also you get such a perception as to the actual limits, only that here you see clearly where such limitation very readily leads. In face of the overwhelming probability that there exist worlds upon worlds of intelligent creatures other than man, superior in intelligence to man, Hegel gives us a God Who comes to His own self-consciousness in and through the development of man, a development which culminates in the Prussian State of the Thirties of last century. What appalling Chauvinism ! Yet even without such Pantheistic and humanitarian fanaticisms, the restrictions indicated would slowly but surely spell ruin for religion. For, surely, a religion is doomed which can furnish no emotion appropriate to what I see and surmise every time I look up at the stars at night. And indeed, in other respects also, the outlook considered is narrow to unbearableness; for what is the worth of the homage I pay to Jesus by the refusal to admire and to thank God for, say, Aristotle's doctrine of the Unmoving *Energeia,* or for Plotinus's grand demonstrations of the spaceless character of God ? The position, if taken seriously, ends by caricaturing the true temper of Jesus, Who did indeed ignore much that we have to foster for the sake of careful attention to His spirit, but Who did not thus really exclude, or systematically reject, whatever does not directly come from Himself or is not directly occupied with man's welfare and redemption.

6. A very nest of complications faces us, as soon as we candidly admit, and then attempt selection, combination, or further development amongst, the competing pictures, implications and teachings of Jesus and of His New Testament followers concerning the End. How far are *Kingdom of God, Abraham's Bosom, Paradise, Heaven* identical or at least compatible, or the reverse ? And how far are they, more or less, passing hints and how far permanent revelations ? Even St. Augustine still

inclines to hold that the human soul sleeps from the body's death till the day of the Coming and the Judgment; and he nowhere, I think, clearly decides, for after the Judgment, between a sojourn, limited or not, upon a renovated Earth, and a life strictly in a condition, or place, or both, quite distinct from any renovated humanity alive on a renovated earth. Such an earthly sojourn, for at least a while, we get in the Revelation of St. John; and such Millennarianism has reappeared on and on in the Christian Church, in the Middle Ages; in the movement of Savonarola during the Renaissance; and, in modern England, in Cromwell's Kingdom of the Saints. Indeed recent Socialism, so largely Jewish in its origin, is full of a mostly quite non-religious Millennarianism; whilst even such fervent Christians as the missionary Dr. Hogge and the Rev. Dr. David Cairns have resumed some such an outlook from deep religious motives, yet with an important modification of the stress characteristic especially of the Eschatology of Jesus.

I can but suggest the following discriminations. Even in the Synoptic Gospels alone we get adumbrations and pictures of differing historical provenance and which are more or less incapable of complete harmonisation. For certainly Abraham's Bosom and Paradise hardly appear identical ; and, even if the same, they are clearly distinct from the Sitting upon the Thrones or at the Banquet, which certainly belong to the *Parousia* circle of ideas. St. Paul's Third Heaven can hardly belong to any of these groups ; whereas the Revelation of St. John moves indeed in the *Parousia* circle, yet more of its Eschatology appears to be directly derived from Jewish sources than can similarly be attributed in the Eschatology of the Synoptists. We see from these facts how wide was the freedom and how rich the choice for the Christian Church in its development of a Christian Eschatology.

We can, next, note that all the Christian Eschatological views fall, roughly, into two classes—*the Renovated Earth, the Millennarian Expectation*; and *Heaven, Purgatory, Hell*, which, more and more, in the great orthodox Christian bodies, have, in practice, supplanted the former. The Millennarian class is more clearly rooted in Jesus's actual eschatological utterances, and is more directly in keeping with any strongly stressed doctrine of the resurrection of the body. It goes back, historically, to the Jewish Apocalyptic writers. The Heaven class has more and more come to be felt by Christians of delicate spirituality and wide general cultivation to be the simpler, the more spiritual view, indeed to be the one which most adequately draws out the deepest implications and needs of Theism in general and of Jesus's own great central teachings in particular. This view is indeed compatible with belief in a resurrection of the body (a doctrine which, in some form or other, it is important to retain), but it lends itself less readily to this belief than does the Millennarian view. Historically this Heaven-Purgatory-Hell cycle goes back to Hellenistic Judaism and to Plato.

In the outlook of the average orthodox Christian, for now some ten centuries, it is the Heaven-Purgatory-Hell cycle that forms part of his every-day religion ; with, however, a notable addition and distinction. *The General Judgment and the End of the World*, though these are now placed at an indefinite distance of time, still remain constituents of orthodox belief. Yet *the Particular Judgment*, at the death of each soul, a doctrine belonging to the Heaven class, is doubtless now the more operative conviction ; whereas the doctrine of the End of the World seems to exercise but little influence.

As with the change from Kingdom to Church, so with that from a Renovated Earth to Heaven, we may rest very sure that the deepest reasons and needs slowly determined the Church in this direction. In both, closely interrelated, cases we can, by living the spirit of Jesus, discover how preservative of precisely this spirit are these modifications of the letter. And especially does the great alternative of Heaven-Hell remain true to the whole gist and drift of Jesus's teaching and to the growth of this teaching from first to last, since this teaching was never simply a revelation of a divine cosmic process of universal redemption, but always a warning, an awakening to, a costly, profound alternative of, right or wrong self-determination in view of God's gift and God's call and testing. Millennarianism, on the contrary, mediæval and modern, shows badly as regards sobriety, and is always followed by disillusionment and relaxation, as the inevitable cost of the nervous exaltation and rigorism which inevitably accompany it. Indeed the Millennarianisms of the last sixty years or so, have practically all been without precisely what gave greatness and depth to Jesus's entire Eschatology. For with Jesus the very proximity and suddenness all meant Gift of God, meant God, and meant man's awed moral and spiritual preparation for this Gift which would either cure or kill him; with these Millennarianists, on the other hand, God, Gift, Test, Preparation—all have gone; man and man's work—even pure, unaided human work—have succeeded: and yet this purely human work is proximately, suddenly, to achieve a new heaven and a new earth, an earthly condition which will, of itself, satisfy all the cravings of the human heart and soul. We thus get something essentially hare-brained, inflating, sterilising. We cannot, even if we would, reawaken the first Christian Expectation in the features of its intense belief in a proximate, sudden World Renovation, even though this belief was so grand and true in its ardent faith in God, in His Gift, in our need of Preparation, and in human Life as essentially a Choice and an Alternative. But we will not wish, even if we could, to encourage an Immanentist Millennarianism, an outlook from which have disappeared Alternative, Choice, Preparation, Gift and God.

Indeed even the religiously intended, religiously coloured Millennarianism, will not really work. In this Millennarianism God is fully acknowledged, and the Kingdom, even its proximity and Suddenness, are reconstituted as the Christian central doctrines, yet are interpreted as the coalescence of devoted, heroic human wills to which God has promised millennarian results. For such an outlook is based, historically, upon a grave mis-interpretation of Jesus's meaning, and assumes philosophically a view of human nature and human progress which would make these, and not God and His Perfect Simultaneity, the centre of man's care and striving. Such a view, if it became fixed and full, would bring to already feverish human society only a further contribution of feverishness, indeed the full sanction of such ceaseless tension and intrinsic unrest. Dr. F. Bradley has acutely pointed out that Human Perfection, taken thus absolutely, as a condition attainable suddenly, completely: that such an idea of progress is not a cause or an effect of Theism properly

understood, but always its substitute. You can have as your centre
God ; or you can have as your centre such sudden and complete
human Progress and Perfection : you cannot have both. But
Theism remains fully compatible with man's indefinite improve-
ableness, indeed improvement. Religious men, provided they
care still more for direct spiritual conditions, cannot care too
much for the social, earthly betterment of their fellows ; and
this, most of all, because Grace, Supernature, is fully awakened,
and is given its substrate and material, only by some such setting
in motion of the natural interests and activities of ourselves and
of our fellow-men. In this way our religion will be also thoroughly
social ; but it will bring to this its social outlook a special balance
and sanity, a freedom from exaltations and cynicisms, an indestructible, sober, and laborious hopefulness, which, surely,
constitute exactly the combination so much required and so rare
to find.

7. And what about the entire critical method which, now for
five generations, has been applied by great scholars to delimit, to
fathom, to analyse the figure, the doctrine, the spirit of the
historic Jesus, and this, often with the assumption, or even the
proclamation, that thus only, but that thus really, can we gain
the unadulterated Jesus, as He actually breathed well-nigh two
thousand years ago ? If we take the method thus, as by itself
productive of such a result, we are, very certainly, the victims
of perhaps the most plausible instance of a very natural and
widespread illusion. Professor James Ward and Dr. Pringle
Pattison have, each from a somewhat different starting-point,
admirably brought out the fact I am thinking of. Dr. Ward
compares the two chief methods of Psychology—the Genetic
and the Analytic, and shows how doubtless the perfect knowledge
of anything would be a knowledge of that thing at each of its
stages of growth and becoming, rather than an analysis of the
same thing at its fullest expansion, yet that, as a matter of fact,
the analytic method alone is really completely at our service.
And Dr. Pattison demonstrates the special danger inherent in
the Genetic Method, even where we can most fully apply it.
Let us take the embryology of man. Here the future human
being—in strictness the human being, as he really exists from
conception onwards—is (for all appearances) first a shapeless

material substance, next a plant-like organism, then a mollusc-like, fish-like, bird-like being ; only later on a mammal-like, monkey-like creature, and last of all a clearly human baby. Only God Himself can directly see a human being in those earlier forms ; so that if we *will* treat each of these stages as self-explanatory, as what it appears to us apart from what we know will follow, man *is* a monkey, a fish, a plant, a shapeless material substance—the lowest designation is indeed the most scientific. This method alone is quite clear ; but then, it is also quite inadequate. Human Marriage, under this treatment, becomes a mere pairing of two animals or plants ; the State, a mere herding of wild animals, or the cruel invention of cannibal cave-dwellers. The God of the Jews becomes the mutterings and tremblings of a volcano in the peninsula of Sinai ; indeed one specially " thorough " sage of this school discovers that religion began with, hence that it *is*, the scratching by a cow of an itch upon her back.

It cannot, on the other hand, be denied that the study of Origins properly conducted—that is, conducted with a continuous sense of the reality investigated as it gradually reveals itself in its ever fuller development—does very genuinely deepen, purify and vivify our appreciation of the full reality. For only such study can make us enter (never quite fully, yet with an otherwise unattainable poignancy) into the homely environment, the difficulty and loneliness, the sweat, tears and blood, the obscurities, inhibitions, defeats and difficult conquests, above all into the varying appearances and applications, of the self-identical reality thus studied. The very inevitableness, for an at all human life and teaching, to lose, in course of time, some of the pristine instant attractiveness of its precise pictures and emotions, is thus brought out at its fullest. Yet even this result is attained only by a combination of the Analytic method, which moves back from the life of Jesus as still actually lived in Christ's mystical body, the Church, and of the Genetic method, which starts from the earliest evidence of the earliest stages of Jesus Christ's life on earth and then on across the centuries. If we were restricted to one method only, the Analytic method ought to be preferred, as giving us far more life and reality, indeed as, taken singly, alone capable of furnishing us with genuine life at all.

F

Yet we can, fortunately, work by both ways simultaneously—
we can move from the Christ of the Church, of our prayers, communions and inner life, back to the Jesus of the earliest documents ; and, from this Jesus forwards to the Christ. This double
movement will, if worked devotedly and wisely, really deepen
our sense of the worlds of beauty, truth and goodness, of ideal
help, of ideal reality, of divine facts, offered to us in the Church, in
Jesus Christ, in God.

Two illustrations of the substance of what I have been attempting are often with me. They may help to conclude all with some
vividness. In the Italian Alps I used to love a certain deep, ever
sunless gorge, through which a resounding mountain torrent
was continuously fighting its way, without rest, without fruit.
Why did I love it so ? Doubtless because I realised, amidst
that sterile-seeming uproar, that, down far away, this
torrent would spread itself out as a sunlit, peaceful, fertilising
river, slowly flowing through the rich plains of Piedmont.
So is it with the Apocalyptic Jesus and with the Prophetic
Jesus, indeed with both these Jesuses and the Ever-Present
Christ.

Some years ago the Jesuit Astronomer, Father Perry, was sent
out to a South Pacific station to observe the transit of the Planet
Venus. He sickened of a mortal fever shortly before the transit.
Told of his impending death, he ascertained from the doctor how
long he was likely to retain consciousness, and then planned out
all his duties for within this little span of time. He promptly
received the Last Sacraments and disposed himself religiously
to die. And then he gave himself heartwholly to his present duty
and service of God—to the transit. He made and registered
all the delicate observations with a perfect lucidity and completeness ; and then, the moment the planet had ceased its
apparent contact with the sun, this true, deep Christian fell
back into unconsciousness and death. It seems far from the
Eschatology of Jesus, with its eye upon the little Palestine and
upon a Proximate End of the visible earth and heavens—heavens
all circling, as it seemed, around man upon his little planet ;
far from that to this modern observer, intent upon stellar
vicissitudes of no direct importance to mankind. It seems far,

yet it *is* near, near at least to the complete and fundamental Jesus ; for it is assuredly part of, it is penetrated by, the spirit of Christ living in the Church to bless and to purify all the gifts and calls of the God of Nature by the calls and gifts of the God of Grace.

6

ON THE SPECIFIC GENIUS AND CAPACITIES OF CHRISTIANITY

STUDIED IN CONNECTION WITH THE WORKS OF PROFESSOR ERNST TROELTSCH [1]

I

PERHAPS the subtlest, yet really the greatest, of the difficulties that beset all eirenic endeavours, such as the *Constructive Review* so valiantly represents for our own times and peoples, lie, not without but within,—consist, not in any possible obstruction from a non-perceptive world, but from a certain flatness and unpersuasiveness which, sooner or later, always tend to pervade whatsoever is readily optimistic, studiously pacific, free from all acute stress and strain. Thus even Leibniz, that rich, all-harmonising mind, is he as moving as Tertullian, that vehement, onesided genius, or even as some of Leibniz's own contemporaries, smaller and less balanced, but more concentrated and instinctive than that serene negotiator, of the large wig, amidst the pontiffs and princesses of his day? Probably the best antidote to any such danger is the close study, not directly of the contrasts and conflicts between the already made theologies and cults of the several Churches and Sects, but of the religious life, or at least of its philosophy, still now in the making—of the struggles and successes operative, at this very moment, within some exceptionally capacious mind and deeply spiritual soul. At least, for myself, I can be fully happy in Eirenics only in some such entirely unofficial and unfinal, slow, round-about, far-back and far-onward looking way. And thus I come here to attempt the presentation of the fundamental strivings, and thinkings, in matters of the

[1] Two Papers reprinted from the *Constructive Quarterly* of New York, March, December, 1914.

specific genius, claims and capacities of Christianity, of Professor
Ernst Troeltsch of Heidelberg.

Such a presentation, to be effective, should be clear, yet clearness here is very difficult. Life itself is, not clear, but vivid.
And even the deeper Sciences—those with most of concrete
content, such as History and Psychology,—and also Philosophy,
will always remain outdistanced, not in clearness, but in volume
and vividness of content, by Life wheresoever it is profound.
In Troeltsch's case we must add, on the side of his subject-
matters, the unique depth and vividness, hence the difficulty
as to clearness, of his central interest, Religion. We must add,
on the side of himself, a most rarely alive sense of the special
characteristics of religion and of the different, quite distinct
characteristics of the other depths, ranges and complexes of
human experience and of reality ; and a sense largely new, in
its keen self-consciousness, of the necessary part played in life
generally, and particularly also in religion, by the tension thus
introduced. Add again strong prejudices within this student,
and still stronger prejudices amongst his environment and
audience—prejudices which he very nobly, but only slowly and
partially, throws off, and as to which even his fine courage has
to accommodate, approximate, reconcile, hence somewhat to
obscure, indeed to confuse, the full depth and range of the issues
and admissions. And finally, this man is not a Frenchman,
with a born sense for form, but a German with curiously little
of such a sense even for a German, and who, in each of his
varying moods and growths, tends always to be so emphatic as
to be indeed oppressively clear for *that* point or moment, yet
so as to render more difficult the integration of this his contention
with other parts of his teaching even where this is contemporary.
Take all this together, and you will be prepared for the obscurities
and difficulties, but not, I think—if only you will persevere as
his student—for the bewilderingly rich instructiveness, indeed
the grandly tonic ethical and spiritual training-power, of
Troeltsch.

For now over twenty years, I have learnt quite massively from
Troeltsch, as much where regretfully but firmly I still disagree,
as where, so joyfully, I agreed from the first with all that I am.
Possibly no Englishman, probably no American, knows his mind

and works as intimately as I know them myself. Hence I believe myself to possess some special competence for attempting a description and analysis of his main positions. Nobody less than he himself would wish such an exposition to minimise differences, or not to move on, from our own two selves, to the subject-matter, indeed towards insights and analyses as yet fully neither his nor mine. He considers himself a strong Protestant ; I think he is this in fewer respects than he used to be, or than he thinks himself now still to be. For myself I would wish to be, and I hope I am, a devoted Catholic. Yet just those convictions and habits which, within my own life, I feel to be most centrally Catholic appear to me, ever increasingly, to require the aid precisely of what is most growing, and most rich, in Troeltsch's positive convictions ; and, in return, these convictions seem to me to require for their full protection, expansion and fruitfulness, much of the soil and environment they possess within my own Catholic spiritual life. And if my friend objects that I live with my head in the clouds—that I reason from a Catholicism continuously less apparent in the fully official acts of the Roman Catholic Church, I could, after all, retort, *mutatis mutandis*, in much the same vein, as to Protestantism and *its* contrary, yet very real, difficulties ; especially can I easily show—a point for the most part admitted by himself—how much of precisely what appears in him as his own slow conquest of most fruitful, very difficult insights has been so far anticipated, with any real consistency or depth, in life, temper, analysis and theory, within the various religious and Christian bodies, by the Roman Catholic Church alone.

Two articles in a non-technical magazine cannot attempt to analyse the more than two thousand pages to which conjointly run the Professor's *History of Protestantism* (in *Kultur der Gegenwart*), Second Edition, 1910, his *Social Doctrines of the Christian Churches and Groups*, 1911, and the second volume of his *Collected Works*, 1913 ; let alone many another important article or monograph still awaiting incorporation in further volumes of this collective edition.

These many pages contain much repetition ; they are at times slovenly in style, and the changes introduced into later editions are often unskilfully introduced ; a curiously thin and obtuse,

because unloving spirit spoils, to my own persistent taste, much
of his earlier writings, where these touch Catholicism, as he
defines this complex of religious life, so much richer than,
especially there, he sees it to be ; and, perhaps above all, his
still strongly idealistic philosophy prevents his admirably vivid
apprehensions as to the specific facts, genius and needs of religion
and Christianity from attaining to a fully consistent and persistent,
concrete and comfortable articulation. Yet he nowhere simply
repeats himself ; he is never rhetorical or empty, and can rise,
indeed, to the noblest form wedded to the richest content ; his
additions are always very instructive ; his love for Christianity
is everywhere deeper than his antipathy to Catholicism, indeed
it is that love which, with a growing knowledge of ancient and
especially mediæval Christianity, is increasingly limiting this
antipathy ; and his religious sense is too strong, and his analysis
of it is too keen, for his philosophical idealism not to show
most instructive strains and rents. Certainly no living German
thinker is more sensitively alive to the present prevalence and
the perennial plausibility and ruinousness of Monism in all its
forms ; whilst few, not professedly orthodox Germans have been,
upon the whole, so clear-sighted and courageous concerning
the limitations of Kant, Goethe and Schleiermacher.

I propose in this first paper, to consider his *Fundamental
Concepts of Ethics*, 1902, Second Edition, 1913 (*Ges. Schriften*
II. pp. 552-672) ; and in a second paper, to study his *What
do we mean by the Essence of Christianity?* 1903, Second Edition,
1913 (*Ibid.* pp. 386-451), and especially the conclusion to his
Social Doctrines, 1911, pp. 965-986. These two hundred pages,
all told, contain, I think *in nuce* all the fundamental principles,
strengths and weaknesses of Troeltsch's life-work so far, especially
in all that concerns the constructive interpretation of Theism,
Christianity and the Church, in face of and within our modern
western world.

Now the *Fundamental Problems of Morality*, like so much of
Troeltsch's work, takes the form of a criticism of a particular
author, indeed of a particular work ; yet it equals in range,
and far exceeds in rich fullness and precision, the somewhat
vague suggestions of its title. Its six-score pages constitute an

astonishingly many-sided, wholly live and stimulating treatise
on the special characteristics, forces, difficulties and prospects
of Christianity, and on how to penetrate, utilise, meet and forecast
all these things.

We shall not ourselves be directly occupied with Professor
Wilhelm Hermann and his *Ethics*, thus studied by Troeltsch ;
yet it is well to remember throughout, that Troeltsch is, here,
not starting hares of his own, or beating the air, but is wrestling
with a mind and conviction of rare power and tenacity, and with
a soul unusually full of enthusiastic devotion to Christ ; with a
man, too, highly representative of a very prevalent ingredient of
modern thought, and possessing great influence amongst the
present large class of Germans in search of a faith free from
historical contingencies, metaphysical subtleties, mystical exaltations and priestly oppressions—a combination of Christ and
Kant.   We cannot, thus, fail to strike here, in the positions
criticised by Troeltsch, upon much that is quietly assumed,
or strenuously contended for, by many an English-speaking
contemporary, moved and tried by the difficulties of our present
times.

Let us, then, take briefly Troeltsch's short account of the
starting-point of the past history of the entire enquiry ; and let
us thereupon pass on to a longer consideration of the four main
propositions defended by Troeltsch in this monograph.

1

" Not from a Metaphysic of whatsoever kind, which, by means
of its own concepts, would reveal to us the essence of the world,
do we now-a-days approach the religious problem. But from
the general Ethical Problem of the final values and aims of human
life and action do we reach the religious, metaphysical convictions
enclosed therein ; and from the development of these convictions
do we then, in return, determine the more precise ethical
valuations. Psychological, historical and epistemological ascer-
tainments jointly give us a theory of values ; and in this theory
the metaphysical religious foundations, which underlie it, become
apparent " (*l.c.* p. 553).

He then gives us a short historical retrospect. " The old

Christian Theology paid no systematic attention to Ethics, and nowhere attempted a scientific presentation of them corresponding to those of Religious Metaphysics and of the Dogmas determined by these Metaphysics. From the determination of religious truth the ethical consequences flowed of themselves ; and Ethics could all the more be left to their spontaneous form—to manners and the judgments of the conscience—since Christian Ethics coalesced with the nearly related Stoic and Platonic views in the concept of the Natural Ethical Law, and could, thus, be considered as something fixed by Nature " (p. 554). " When the Catholic Church came to organise her claims and her principles for the direction of all souls, as co-extensive with the entire culture of the time, within her great systems, these systems could not, of course, dispense with an Ethic. But even here Ethics were conceived, in the identification of the Natural Ethical Law with the Aristotelian Ethics, as a complex given independently, which the Church had to accept and only to modify by means of its own higher outlook. The Christian character of Ethics consisted in the subordination of all the ends springing from the Natural Moral Law to the final end of the Church. And this subordination was achieved in the Church's communication of the sacramental forces of grace for the fulfilment of these ethical demands ; in priestly study of the conscience and direction of the soul, which taught the right application of the natural law, and its combination with particular Christian duties in each concrete case ; and, finally, in the manifestation of certain ascetical achievements effected by grace in a quite special manner and degree. Only these last heroic achievements flowed purely and exclusively from the Christian Principle and not from the Natural Law; indeed they completed and exceeded this Law with ascetical and mystical commandments of their own. As, in Dogmatics, the immanental natural metaphysic confronts the revealed super-natural metaphysic, so also, in Ethics, the natural moral law and the special counsels and achievements of grace confront each other, separate indeed from each other within this sinful world and not harmonisable by man, but one and actually harmonious in the Divine Mind Itself. An Ethic of grace, asceticism, contemplation, Divine Love, which springs from the conception of a Supernature and Grace transcending

*F

every creaturely measure, and from the corresponding end of the
creature's participation in the Being of God, is combined with
a natural-philosophical Ethic which follows fom the natural end
of creaturely existence, and which regulates the worldly interests
of Family Life, Society, the State, Economics, Science and Art.
The dualism of the two moralities has its foundation in the
dualism within the Divine Being Itself, which, in the world of
Creation, manifests its Nature, and, in the world of Grace, reveals
its Supernature " (p. 555).

Here I would only refer to the truly masterly account of
the social doctrines of mediæval Catholicism, especially of
St. Thomas, in the *Soziallehren,* as the warmest and wisest
appreciation so far reached by Troeltsch ; and would express
my opinion that, even there, Troeltsch over-simplifies, and only
imperfectly understands or appreciates, the doctrine as to Nature
and Supernature, and its quite unexhausted truth and rich
applicability.

The earlier Protestantism, with and ever since Melanchthon,
also " always, in the first instance, attacks the problem of Ethics
from the side of Dogmatics. Once we have, here, derived from
the Bible (a completely sufficient, completely clear source) our
fundamental view of God, World, Man, Redemption, there flow
from this fixed point the consequences capital for our conception
of Ethics—the doctrines of Conversion, Re-birth, the final
ethical Ideal of Love. And these consequences can then be
applied, by practical experience and by casuistry, to the demands
of Natural Ethics, as these are developed, in connection with
the tradition of the Schools, by philosophers and jurists, out of
the *Lex Naturæ,* and hence also out of the Divine Will. The
contradiction present here, between the Ethics of the utter overcoming of the world and of the love that renounces all resistance
and the this-world Ethics, was certainly felt ; but these strictly
Christian demands were now restricted to the single person,
that is, to private life. The Christian, as a member of public
life, as bearer of an office deriving from the political and economic
system of the Natural Law, has to follow the requirements of
his office, that is of the order of Natural Law permitted by God
together with sin and against sin.   In this way the 'personal'
Ethics are nowhere perilous to the necessities of civilisation.

Ethics here still belong to the domain of the subjective and of the application ; Religion, to the domain of the alone simply objective, to authoritative revelation. To attack the problem of Christianity from the ethical side, had, in these circumstances, no meaning ; and no one here came to think of doing so except the Sectaries who, just because of this endeavour, were contemptuously expelled, as despisers of the Objective Revelation, of Grace as independent of subjective effort, and of the Church as objectively administering these treasures " (*l.c.* pp. 559–560).

The great problems here involved were bound some day to be fully realised, and this their realisation could not fail to change the relations between Ethics and Dogmatics, and hence the general conception of theology. And this realisation and change Troeltsch finds to have been slowly, complicatedly, in great part unconsciously, effected in two largely contradictory stages.

The first stage " reacts against the internecine conflicts of the various Churches and Sects, and seeks a general conception of Religion, which is to include Christianity and is to be based upon Psychology. Religion is here conceived as an essentially practical bearing of the human mind, which indeed contains certain doctrines, as presupposition and as consequence, but which finds its specific legitimation in its practical achievements. And these achievements could, now and at this stage, only be discovered, upon the whole, in certain strengthenings and foundings of Ethics. The result was the closest combination of Ethics and Religion, and the reconstruction of Dogmatics from the basis of Ethics—Ethics conceived here in a predominantly subjective and individualistic manner. Thus Kant and the Kantians consider Ethics (as the necessary, but quite subjective, determinations of the will by the purely practical reason) to be the fundamental science ; whilst Religion is, for them, the addition of the metaphysical guarantees for the victory of the moral order over the phenomenal world and its laws " (p. 564).

But in the second stage " Religion reconquers its independence of Ethics. Prepared by Hamann, Herder, Jacobi, there arose the new epoch-making definition by Schleiermacher, de Wette and Hegel, which found Religion to be distinct both from Ethics and from Metaphysics, as a central self-determination

of the entire personality towards the being and nature of Reality
—as the attainment of a consciousness, a living experience, of
an absolute spiritual content and meaning of existence. Hence
there reappeared an independent, objective determination of
Religion in the conceptions of God and of an elevation of the
soul into the Divine Life." Indeed " also Ethics here find an
objective determination, in the great universally valid ends of
action ; ends which are now found within the nature of reason,
from which they proceed as its necessary fruits. Thus here there
result distinct and specific ends and contents of the State, Society,
Art, Science, the Family, Religion, which severally determine the
will as so many objective values. Religion ceases to be simply a
sanction and guarantee of self-discipline and philanthropy, and
stands as a specific objective value alongside of the other objective values of civilisation. Hence the question here is how the
Christian Ethic, determined as it is by the religious end, constitutes itself under the influence of this end ; and how the
demands which result from this religious end stand with regard
to the demands deriving from the other, the non-religious,
ends " (pp. 565, 566). Troeltsch finds, however, that in Schleiermacher, so largely monistic in his trend and yet, in his later
environment and form, so strongly ecclesiastical, there is so
much abstract unification and æsthetic harmony that " the
tension, extant between action determined by specifically
Christian religious conviction and action determined by the
non-religious ends, ceases to be felt at all " (p. 567).

Yet it is along the general lines of Schleiermacher's Ethics
of Objective Contents and Ends, and not those of Kant's Ethics
of a Formal Universal Validity, that Troeltsch will now, upon the
whole (rightly, I am confident) set to work.

2

Let us, then, now take with care the four chief problems
as faced and met by the system of Ethics proposed to us by
Troeltsch. These are : " the conception of a purely formal, *à priori*
necessity, is it a sufficient basis for Ethics ?" " the Ethics of Jesus,
are they identical with that fundamental moral conception ?"
" does the special, separate character of Christian Ethics reside in

their proffer of a redemptive capacity for moral action?" and, finally, "what is the application of the specifically Christian Ethics to the concrete conditions of life?" I believe Troeltsch to be in substance profoundly right in his answers to the first, second and fourth questions; but seriously inadequate in his reply to the third question. The full originality and richness of Troeltsch's position appears fully disclosed only at the end.

1. As to the first point, Troeltsch admits that Ethics must begin with a general analysis of the Moral, and that thus we reach the conception of an end absolute, necessary, and valuable in itself; although already thus we have to admit a "pleasure," since the agent's recognition of such an *à priori* necessity undoubtedly presupposes his "pleasure" in such a necessity, that is, a sentiment (a sensitiveness) as to ideal values. Also, that the decision as to whether and how an act is really to proceed from such a necessity in the particular cases, is possible only to the ripe ethical conscience, in the form of a judgment offering itself to it as necessarily springing from its moral nature, hence is possible only as an entirely autonomous judgment. And, thirdly, that the essence of Morality consists precisely in the moral disposition—the personal conviction as to the necessity and universal validity of the insight offering itself as moral. Here Troeltsch would only emphasise more clearly and strongly the element of the end, already present here; and would derive the entire system of concepts from the ideally necessary end, with its great bifurcation into the individual and the social ends (p. 617).

But then Troeltsch is promptly faced by the far-reaching fact that "in the reality of the moral life we distinguish between the Subjective Rules which spring entirely from the bearing of the subjects (*e.g.* truthfulness, thoughtfulness, courage; benevolence, justice, loyalty); and the claims, which are ever upon us, to treasure, and to aspire after, the Objective Values (the Family, State, Society, Science, Art, Religion). We certainly recognise also in these latter complexes something valuable, not simply for selfish or sensual reasons, but ideally and objectively; something to be striven for even with the greatest sacrifices. And in these Objective ethical values, we recognise, as in the

Subjective, two sides of both the individual and the social value ; in our devotion to these Objective values we singly acquire a personal worth, which is always closely bound up with our recognition and promotion of the same personal worth in others. Thus only the Subjective and the Objective values, in each case Individual and Social, can conjointly represent the application of the idea of a moral necessity to actual life " (*l.c.* pp. 618, 619).

" Do not object that these Objective Values are the merely natural products of action. For the merely natural processes, which spring simply from physical abilities and needs, or from psychical conditions and instincts, remain a shapeless mass till they are seized by the moral idea of an Ethical Good to be formed upon this natural foundation. Out of the sexual instinct the moral idea thus forms the community of personalities, the Family ; out of the social instinct, the personal community of the State ; out of the craving for food and possessions, the orders of Production and Property ; out of the æsthetic impressions, the work of Art which shows us a higher world shining through the world of sense ; out of curiosity and the need of physical orientation, Science in search of truth to the neglect of every selfish interest ; and out of religious moods and excitations, the conscious and deliberate Religion which organises an entire life for God and with Him. All these ends signify an opposition to natural selfishness, sloth, sensuality, and to the merely given ; they all require, for their achievement, an earnest concentration upon, and devotion to, the object, for the sake of its interior necessary value. They all degenerate when taken simply as pleasures or as outlets to our need for activity. Yet against these ever threatening degenerations the principles of subjective morality would be of no avail ; the only help lies in the recognition that these ends all share the character of the intrinsically necessary, are means for the formation of personality, and hence constitute objective values."

" And especially let us note that also the Religious Element of life belongs, in the first instance, to man's given instincts, and requires, as all the others, to be raised into the sphere where it ceases to be something simply to be enjoyed and possessed, and becomes what it ought to be—the objectively necessary." Yet " Religion is an independent element of life, with its own

sorrows and its own joys, an experience and a temper of soul
which is not artificially produced, but which is lived through
and lived in by man. It stands, in the first instance, as the experience best interpreted by Mysticism, independently by itself,
bound up with Cultus and with Myth. The greater the power
of the Gods becomes, the more does it draw also the legal and
the moral orders under the influence, control, protection of the
Divine. On the other hand, the soul's strivings after religious
values (purity, resignation into God's hands, assimilation to
God) become an imperative which represents the specific
oughtness of Religion " (pp. 618–620).

" Now Ethics, if we attend only to their characteristics of
Universal Validity and Necessity, and to these quite general
foundations for the formation of personality, are naturally, in
principle, without any history, and, in their central features,
are everywhere identical—the differences here concern only
clearness, consistency and strength. The situation is different
as regards the Objective Values; these arise within the labours
of history, and here detach themselves, in the ' heterogony of
ends ' [in the birth of a variety of ends], from merely natural
forms and values. Here the great formations, from the Family
to Religion, have all to be known by means of history. Each of
these values indeed has its own distinct development, which
reveals the specific character of this value and the conditions of
its life and growth. And again the interaction of these several
values possesses also its own history. The end of History, then,
cannot be an Abstract Uniform Idea or reason, but only a Concrete Articulated System of Values; and the question as to the
real articulation of this System of Values becomes thus the central
problem of Ethics."

" And only in this Objective Ethic do we reach the highest
and last, but also the most arduous, problem of Ethics. For in
very truth there does exist an Ethic *sub specie temporis,* and an
Ethic *sub specie æternitatis.* Restrict yourself to purely Formal
Ethic, and you will not notice the contrast, or you will interpret
it wrongly, or will explain it away. Face the complications of
the ethical problems as they battle amidst the Objective Values
of life, and that contrast becomes the most important of all the
facts. Each position here often declares fierce war against the

other, as Immanental and Transcendental Ethics, as Culture and Asceticism. Yet each ever again seeks the other, since either, left to itself, withers and decays. Religion, without reference to the World, narrows and darkens the Ethical, or turns it into some Utopian dream ; Immanental Ethic, without reference to a final, all-englobing, all-determining End, grows flat and aimless " (*l.c.* pp. 623–625).

Throughout this first point I can find only one imperfection —the sense, to my mind ambiguous and shifting, in which the term " nature " is used ; for the rest I take Troeltsch here admirably to see and to state the complex situation as it really is.

2. The second question, as to the identity of the Christian Ethical Ideal with the Kantian formalist Ethic, is a purely historical one, to be decided independently of our own ethical predilections. And taking it thus Troeltsch flatly denies the identity. " It is an extraordinary misconception of the real meaning and spirit of the Gospel, an impossible feat at the stage we have reached in the historical understanding of the New Testament. Not without cause has it been rejected " in the past and the present " by ecclesiastical and by radical spokesmen, from à Kempis and Gottfried Arnold, down to Renan and Nietzsche, Tolstoi and Kierkegaard."

True, what this identification emphasises is a presupposition of the Evangelical Ethic—the spirit of interior liberty and of the need for genuine dispositions which of necessity issue, from the recognition of the End, in an action joyful and assured. This is indeed the soul of the warfare of Jesus against the doctrine of the Pharisees ; the autonomy of Ethics, as the prerequisite of Morality, has probably never, in a popular form, been more vividly insisted on than in the preaching of Jesus.

" Yet this insistence in nowise exhausts the Gospel message. This message does not simply leave each person to do, in each case, what may appear, to his own moral insight, to be necessary and universally valid ; but Jesus points, with the keenest, an all-dominating emphasis, to a concrete and objective Content, End and Value in and for all action."

Already the undoubted superordination in Jesus's preaching of the Kingdom of God, of a community, over the individual, is incapable of derivation from the concept of autonomy ; for the autonomous outlook makes the independent individual the starting-point and centre of the relations within the community. Thus " in the preponderance of the social side we get the expression of the determination of this Ethic by an Objective End, and the connection of this End with a metaphysical, or religious, conviction as to the world. The littleness of the creature in face of the Infinite God, is here united with God's special care for the world as a whole and for all the individuals within it " (p. 629).

" Hence Matt. vii. 12—' Therefore all things whatsoever ye would that men should do to you, do ye even unto them ; for this is the law and the prophets '—cannot possibly constitute the centre of the Ethics of Jesus. Propounded thus as central, this passage would be a great triviality ; and indeed, taken thus, it has always earned the lively applause of Utilitarians and Positivists. The passage, according to the entire spirit of Jesus's preaching and to the context here, can only mean : ' be not hypocrites, demanding of others what you are not prepared to do yourselves.' The *locus classicus* for the temper of Jesus is His answer as to which is the great commandment, Matt. xxii. 37 : ' Thou shalt love the Lord thy God with all thy heart, and with all thy soul, and with all thy mind. This is the first and great commandment. And the second is like unto it, Thou shalt love thy neighbour as thyself. On these two commandments hang all the law and the prophets ' " (p. 630). Indeed simply everywhere in the words and in the spirit of Jesus's preaching appears " this pairing of the two fundamental commandments, and this derivation of their fundamental character from the supreme objective end of God and of a community of all the children of God. The purity of heart and the love here everywhere demanded are a sanctification of the entire person for God and in order to see God. Even where the second fundamental commandment is immediately concerned, all still remains under the religious point of view. We do not here find a love of our neighbour in the humanitarian sense, not, at least, in the first instance. It is the love of God Who has freely given us so much, which is here the motive of the love of the brethren. Even the individual who apparently stands far away, is to feel

the warm breath from the true home of man—and this generosity
will remain a rightful act, even if he do not, in consequence,
turn to God.   For God reigns over the just and the unjust.
Indeed even towards enemies and haters this love must not
expire ; it must effect, by the power of God and by the soul's
insight into the smallness of all human combats, what is impossible to the simply natural man, bounded by his earthly
horizon and with all his little cares looking so important—
it must achieve the disarmament of evil by goodness, or at
least, where the evil will not yield, the lofty serenity of a for-
giving disposition, since most men know not what they do "
(pp. 631, 632).

This specifically religious Ethic, the most consistently perfect
type of religious Ethic based on the prophetic Personalism and
Theism, thus finds the end and motive of action in the Kingdom
of Heaven.   And " this Kingdom of Heaven is, of course, not
the union of men through the common recognition of the law
of autonomy, as planted by God in the human breast—a modern
abstraction entirely foreign to the naïve ancient realism, but
something thoroughly objective, a wonderful Good brought
about exclusively by a great grace and deed of God.   And the
immense concentration of all thought upon this end appears
here in the immediate expectation of this divine deed and grace,
and in the Gospel as simply the call to preparation for this
deed of God.   All this-world considerations and ends have here
become indifferent,—are left far behind and far below by an
Ethic which sees only the End and the Consummation—the
highest and the last aim and end of life " (pp. 634, 635).

" Thus we recognise, in the unlimited sway of the eschatological idea over the evangelical preaching, simply the grandiose
expression of the unique value of the Religious End ; and in the
subjection, inspired by the proximity of the Kingdom, of every
thought to the immediate rule of this religious end, we have
the key to the bearing of the Gospel towards the other objective
values—towards This-World Morality.   This latter morality is,
thus, not combated, but it is put into the background ; we see
here only its dangers and disappointments.   Art and Science in
general are unknown in the circles within which the Gospel
arises, even though the artistic instinct celebrates its naïvest

triumphs in the form of Jesus's parables, and though the scientific search after unity could not fail strongly to be aroused by His concentration upon the thought of God. State and Law are on the downward grade. Work and Property are dangerous, if they go beyond the care for the day. The Gospel loves the poor, as those most needing help, and as the more ready to be loved and to love ; but it neither formulates nor solves any social problems, for the days of Society are numbered and the day of God's Kingdom is at hand. Let us all possess the world as though we possessed it not. But the heralds of this Gospel shall go further—they are to make themselves eunuchs for the kingdom of heaven, and to give all their possessions to the poor ; so that, as shining patterns of a readiness for every sacrifice, they may proclaim the great message through the cities of Israel until He comes " (*l.c.* pp. 635, 636).

" Thus, too, we understand the reality of the analogies between the Ethic of Jesus and every other specifically religious Ethic, which, as such, determines life from the objective religious end, and consequently represses, or even renders indifferent, the this-world ends. The Platonic Ethic, with its methodic elevation of the soul into the world of the alone eternally Abiding and eternally Valid ; the Stoic Ethic, which finds the standard for man's sensible, exterior life in the eternal law of nature—the rule of the Spirit ; the Buddhist Ethic, with its striving after the changeless and impassive Good ; the Mystical Dualisms, and their sharp contrastings of certain mysterious joys of the soul with this our earthly world ; above all, of course, the Prophetical Ethic, with its value of an interior life attained by the individual in union with God : all these convictions, in spite of strong differences, are nearly related to the Christian Ethic, just because they all find the standard for action in an Objective Religious Good. Hence they are all ascetic, rigoristic, super-worldly, transcendent, full of tension towards worldly culture. The Christian Ethic differs from these other Ethics, only as the Christian religious idea differs from *their* religious ideas. Hence the essence of the Christian Ethos does not consist in a contemplative immersion in Being, or in a quietistic denega-tion of the will, but in an active dedication of the will to a God-head overflowingly alive, Which bears within Itself positive

ends for the world and opens up an immense movement for
this same world " (pp. 636, 637).

And, finally, we can thus also answer the most difficult of all
the problems raised by the Christian Ethic—that as to the
precise character of its opposition to the world. Troeltsch himself, indeed, varies considerably on this point at different times,
or even almost simultaneously. But two central convictions are
here and everywhere operative within him—indeed they are
still increasing.

" The historical development which succeeded in rendering
the fundamental ethical convictions of Christianity fruitful
for the work of the world, and which created a civilisation inspired by Christian ideals, has not misunderstood the Gospel,
even though that development itself, in its great complexity,
has not always been properly understood. It is precisely the
specifically Christian element, the personalistic conception of
God, and the optimism in the estimate of the world (which, in
spite of all the dualism concerning the world, is here combined
with that unitary conception of God) from which springs the
perception that the divine action has an end which comprises
and fashions the world, and which assigns to human labour the
task of constituting a community of personalities devoted to
the sanctification of the ends of this world and to making these
ends subserve the full and final end. For the teaching of Jesus
to yield this result it is only necessary that the religious end lose
the vehemence springing from the expectation of its immediate
realisation, and, consequently, its power simply to dissolve
all other pre-occupations. That end may well have been incapable of recognition as the highest and all-dominating end
except under this condition ; but it can continue to be recognised,
even if its realisation is postponed from the immediate to a
distant future. The religious end is indeed continuously renovated by men's concentration upon the image of that classical
beginning when it stood, without a rival, with the power of the
present, before men's hearts. But for the sake of God, the God
of creation, from whom the world and all its good derive, the
world, as soon as it becomes a lasting field for work, must also
be accorded a positive value, and its ends must, as far as possible,
be harmonised with the final end revealed to us by God " (p. 638).

And Troeltsch's second conviction is that something which, as we shall see, even he himself finds difficult to distinguish from the Catholic graduation and distribution of a domestic and an heroic type and degree of morality, constitutes the most adequate solution of the difficulty. He rightly insists, indeed, that, ever thus, we can never, in practice and in this life, attain to more than a relative unification ; yet that " here is a problem from which no one can escape who knows the religious life in its depth, and is prepared to take upon himself its ethical consequences " (p. 639).

" The most specific characteristics of the Ethic of Jesus reside," then, "in the Content of the moral will, and not in the Form; and this Content, far from being something self-evident, constitutes an endless task, giving rise to ever new attempts at its adequate formulation " (p. 639).

I do not see what objection, peculiar to this second proposition of Troeltsch, can validly be raised.

3. The third question is, whether the distinguishing, hence the decisive, character of Christian Ethic lies in its bestowal of power for moral action,—whether it can be considered exclusively as an Ethic of Redemption, whilst the nature of all other Ethics would consist in their not disposing of these redemptive forces, and in thus leaving man a prey to the mere, impotent capacities of his nature.

The answer is found by Troeltsch in the foregoing analysis of Jesus's preaching, a preaching occupied, above all, with the meaning, content and demand of True Justice. " Redemption lies here at the end, at the coming of the Kingdom. But over Jesus's announcement of this proximate future there is diffused such a temper of joy, of certainty of God, of the forgiveness of sins, that His preaching is apprehended as power and life, not as law. This, however, is something very different from that construction of the Christian Ethic which finds the Christian characteristic essentially in the powers here first conferred sufficiently for the execution of the moral law, and which, as against this, conceives the moral demand itself as something universally human " (p. 640).

The combination of a Redemption essentially accomplished in and by Christ and of a universally human Ethic, Troeltsch

finds to appear already in the earliest formation of Christian
ideas—in the Apostolic community and St. Paul. " The Gospel
becomes a faith in Christ and a cultus of Christ. The faithful
venerate, in Jesus, the divine grace, wisdom, revelation made to
man ; and they see in His death, in the sacraments which apply
the fruits of that death, in the out-pouring of the spirit and in
the pneumatic leaders, and, finally, in the official continuators
of the authority of Christ—in the Church—the great foundation
of redemptive grace. All the emphasis is thus shifted, from the
Ethical Content, to the authority of the commands and to the
healing power of the sacraments; whilst that Content appears as
self-evident, and coalesces from every kind of source—Christian,
Jewish, Greek, popular-traditional. We thus get, at last, a trans-
ference of the holiness, from the persons, to the office, the doctrine,
the authority and the sacraments of the Church." Monasticism
and the ideals akin to it now represent, with considerable misconceptions, the still operative influence of the Sermon on the
Mount (pp. 640, 641).

And against this Church-scheme and type, found by him to
reach from St. Paul to Kant, Troeltsch places two other schemes
and types of Christian Ethics. " The Sect-type rejects the
Church and all the dogmas specifically connected with ecclesiasticism, and emphasises, instead, the content of the Christian
Ethics, the Sermon on the Mount, doubtless in a mostly somewhat narrow, literal-legal sense ; and collects small, voluntary
communities of efficiently earnest souls, which manifest themselves as such by adult Baptism. Gentle, retired saints and
violent ethical reformers, firm, exclusive communities and
radical ethical individualists have proceeded from this spirit,
Kierkegaard and Tolstoi have sprung from hence." And " the
Mystical type rejects every external law, and clings to a world-
renouncing filial devotion to God and to a fraternal love that
binds person to person and consumes the intervening selfish
world in its heat. But since the world continues to exist, this
spirit is, now, no more a preparation for the coming, but a
revelation of the present, Kingdom of God—a Kingdom which
slumbers in man and is awakened by Christ's message. This
objective Ethic of the Supreme Good often and easily moves
on into an ascetic *Panentheism* ; so, both within the Roman

Church, as a supplementation to excessive institutional objectivity, and upon Protestant territory, as an independent Christian spiritualism. And where this general mystical spirit abandons the indifference to the world, and inclines to immanental Pantheism, whilst still claiming a real relation to the person and preaching of Jesus, it attains, in our times, to a great prevalence, as with Maeterlinck." " Under the influence of these two groups of the Sect-type and the Mystical type (an influence strengthened by critical research with its discrimination between the historical Jesus, the Pauline Christ, and the Church's God-man), Christian Ethics have, in recent times, been increasingly placed under the influence of Jesus, in lieu of the ethical and dogmatic tradition of the Church (pp. 643, 644).

" If then," Troeltsch concludes this his third question, " the Christian Ethos is not the universally human Ethos, with simply the addition of the forgiveness of sins and the strengthening by grace, these latter things cannot stand in the first and decisive place. The conception of Redemption has to take the second place ; it must prove to be a derivative from the fundamental and first conviction—as to God and the Objective Religious End. And the question then is what, under these conditions, is the significance of Redemption " (*l.c.* pp. 644, 645).

Troeltsch answers here that the Redemption, thus involved in the preaching of the historic Jesus, lies in Faith in God and in Love of God—in this and in nothing else.

Now we have already admitted Troeltsch to be right in discovering the general ethical teaching of Jesus, and its motivation, to be profoundly *sui generis*. And hence we cannot here restrict our Lord's originality to the nature and degree of the Redemption taught and offered by Him. This Redemption must indeed be rooted in that Revelation of the character of God and of man's relations to Him. Nevertheless it is especially over this third position that my dissatisfaction and contrary convictions grow many and definite. But since Troeltsch's fullest, maturest views, on these difficult points, are to be found only in his *Sozial-lehren*, it will be better to adjourn the at all detailed consideration of these matters to my second paper. Here I can only indicate the general outlines of Troeltsch's deeply instructive admissions, and of his no less interesting inconsistencies or non-perceptions.

I note then, here simply in passing, our thinker's full realisation that St. Paul insists strenuously upon the sacramental
principle, and that this principle underlies the entire scheme
of the Johannine writings. Similarly, his noble perception of
how the sacramental and hierarchical principle and practice
arose, not simply from motives of domination, or from an (however involuntary) opposition to, or limitation of, the Christian
spirit, but in order to retain and to perpetuate holiness within
and by Christianity. Again how Troeltsch finds even the most
theocratic Papal claims, from Hildebrand to Cardinal Torquemada, to spring substantially from similar motives and needs,
and how he finds here all " old Catholic " limitations both unjust
as history and inadequate as to practice.

But I also perceive how strangely Troeltsch overlooks the
attitude of the historic Jesus to " brother body," and to physical
symbols and contacts, as occasions and vehicles of spiritual
life ; and how greatly he shrinks from any element of *opus
operatum* in these things, whilst having to admit its unlimited
sway in the gift and coming of the Kingdom as preached by
that same Jesus. Also, how curiously Troeltsch, whilst stumbling
at St. Paul's Christocentrism and Sacramentalism, passes over
all but completely the special, acute intensification of all the
Original Sin conceptions by this same St. Paul, and the fact that
Catholicism, largely from the first, later on more plainly in St.
Thomas, and most clearly at Trent, as against Luther and Calvin,
did not here follow the great Apostle's vehemences. Hence
Troeltsch too much involves *all* traditional ecclesiastical Christianity in these vehemences, whereas they are specially characteristic, not of Catholicism, but of orthodox Protestantism. Again
I perceive how insufficiently he recognises the noble fullness of
insight offered to us all by St. Thomas's assignation of the first
place to the distinction between Nature and Supernature,
in lieu of that between Fallen Nature and Redemption ; and
the same large mind's insistence that, though mere Nature,
however clean, could not reach Supernature, yet such mere
Nature is only what might have existed,—since, in fact, Nature
always was, and still is, variously touched and penetrated by the
prevenient supernatural God ;—it has His salt in its mouth, and
hence thirsts after Him. I perceive, once more, that the psycho-

logy and epistemology of such a " no sacraments " position will not work—they have sprung from extrinsic considerations. I perceive also that, if we insist, as strongly as does Troeltsch, upon the strict necessity for religion, at least amongst mankind at large, of history, worship, cultus of Christ,—if we thus lay a strong emphasis upon the preponderance, in the Christian Ethos, of the Prevenience, the Givenness of God, Christ, Grace, —we accept the Church, and we cannot well reject Sacraments as such.   And all this, finally, leads me to admit the dangers (human nature being what it is in both dispensers and recipients) actually connected with any sacramental system ; and the need of careful discriminations, checks and complements within a large recognition of history and of facts, and of a rich, inclusive organism of life : all this, indeed, follows, but not the rejection of sacraments as such.   Even here, however, Troeltsch still aids us powerfully by his virile penetration of the general position and by the costly sense of reality so characteristic of his sensitively religious soul.

4. The final question asks how the action which springs from the objective religious end of Christianity stands to the action which proceeds from the this-world ends ; and especially how a unitary, harmonious Ethos can ever possibly result from all this variety and clash ? Here, and here especially, do we find Troeltsch great and deep in his fundamental intuitions and advice.

He first replies then : " The problem lies in the fact that the objective ends are characterised by special contents, and hence that we have here a question of Objective Morals, and one that is simply insoluble from the standpoint of Subjective Ethics. The principle of autonomy gives us no aid whatsoever to the solution, nor does the patriarchal category of vocation bring us a single step forward. We have here to do with a relation between objective ends, which, as so many objective ends, require to be thought by us together, and to be brought to the *greatest possible* unity. And the difficulty then lies in that the this-world ends are moral ends possessing the strict character of ethical values, are ends in themselves and necessary for their own sakes, even up to the sacrifice of our natural happiness ; but that they lie in the world and adhere to historical formations which, proceeding from man's physical and psychical nature, dominate his earthly horizon. Contrasted with these this-world ends, the other-world end signifies an entirely different orientation, and a jealous tension towards the competition of the worldly ends." Hence grave complications and strains, and even acute conflicts, have accompanied the attempts at some working compromise and harmonising theory, from the first moment that Christian Ethics began to organise themselves in an enduring world. And as to the modern ethical culture, " its nature consists in maintaining, alongside of the religious end, the this-world ends, and in recognising also these latter ends as ends in themselves. Indeed, just in this combination consist the richness, the breadth and the freedom, but also the painful interior tensions and the difficult problems, of this civilisation. The Christian Ethic here finds Politics, Economics, Technology, Science, Art, Æsthetics, in full operative existence as so many independent ends, each possessed of its own logic and going its own way, and leaving to that Ethic at most the possibility of coming to an understanding and of a regulation, but not of a reconstruction proceeding independently from itself " (*l.c.* pp. 654, 655).

And next Troeltsch insists that this costly recognition will not arise, or at least will not persist, within us, except we possess the insight that " morality is, for us men, at the first, nothing unitary but something manifold and with many fissures ; man grows up with a plurality of moral ends, the unification of which is his problem and not his starting-point. This multiplicity can be further determined as the contrast between two poles, both embedded within man's nature, from which proceed the two chief types of ends, the religious and the this-worldly. It is the polarity of religious and of humane morality, neither of which can be missed without moral damage, yet which, all the same, refuse to be brought to a common formula. Upon this polarity reposes the richness of our life, and also its difficulty ; but from it also there ever arises anew the ardent endeavour to find some unification " (pp. 657, 658).

And a further point is here clear to Troeltsch : " This unification will always have to be effected from the side of the ethico-religious idea. True, there exists a morality which eliminates the religious end, and bases itself upon this-world ends alone ;

which, in lieu of real religion, is content with a mere general belief in a world-order that, somehow, regulates the spiritual ends of nature. But thus—as we can trace in Goethe, in Socialism, in the Spinozist Ethic—the competition between the various ends is more than ever left open, and this, without aim or standard. And especially do such non-religious ends and strivings fail, as experience shows, to satisfy the deepest requirements of man."

" These this-world ends indeed present themselves as ends in themselves, but they do not contain the Ultimate which alone satisfies our hunger after a last, unitary, all-embracing objective value. Hence, when taken as though ultimate, these non-religious ends either make men superficial, thus checking their moral striving ; or restless, in a never ceasing search after higher ends." Nietzsche, Anatole France are here examples. (pp. 658, 659.) " The religious end, on the contrary, contains what is lacking in the this-world ends ; for it springs from the soul's relation to the Eternal and Infinite, from what alone contains the final meaning of all things, from the sphere of the Unconditional, the Absolute, the Simple,—in its highest Christian form, from the soul's self-dedication to a holy living God, Who, whilst containing within Himself the source and meaning of all spiritual-personal life, proposes to this life, as its highest task, the full elaboration and elevation of its personality to a communion with His will " (l.c. pp. 658, 659).

And Troeltsch points to history as showing a double current and influence at work between the two kinds of ends. " Only where the this-world ends had already proved their insufficiency —as in Palestine and in the ancient Græco-Roman world generally —have the Christian Ethics exercised their fullest appeal. And, conversely, Christianity has filled the this-world ends with a far mightier, deeper life than they ever possessed before, and has, nevertheless, made any return to the old pagan self-limitation of the soul to these ends and to nature an impossibility or an affectation for us " (pp. 660–661).

Once more, Troeltsch finds that " the synthesis we are here seeking will have to be, not a doctrine with absolutely fixed lines, but a practical distribution of the predominance, here of the one, there of the other end, according to the individual and natural capacities of the several souls, which cannot, by any ethical training, be brought to a complete equality. Thus there will be groups : some will more exclusively devote themselves to the religious end—in the clerical calling, in missionary work, in nursing the sick, in a contemplative renunciation of the world ; others will, according to their several gifts, inclinations, circumstances, devote themselves more especially to the humane ends—the State, Law, Economics, Science, Art— where the service of these causes even demands the subordination of the worker's personal Christianity to the necessities of his special field of work. The influences across and back will equalise, for the whole, the one-sidedness of the parts, and will keep each group under the influence of the others." The several ages, also, of the same soul will similarly, upon the whole, constitute stages of growth moving from a preponderance of the this-world ends to a preponderance of the that-world end and value. " From first to last, indeed, the final end should be placed and be kept before the soul ; yet a certain liberty and range should be left for both ends and forms, so that continually, and with as great ease as possible, there may result the deepening of the humane ends by Christian Ethics, and the humanising of the Christian end—so that life, within the humane ends, may, simultaneously, be a service of God ; and that the service of God may, simultaneously, transfigure the world " (*l.c.* pp. 664, 655).

Troeltsch fully realises that all this " approximates to that Catholic doctrine which, at the zenith of mediæval thinking, disposed Nature and Supernature as a succession of steps in the becoming of the personality, and conceived finite man to mount from the first to the second ; and which, moreover, distributed a predominance of this-world morality and a predominance of superworldly morality amongst different persons, according to their several dispositions and gifts." He even finds, precisely because of this, in Catholic Ethics " a mobility and capacity for adaptation and for various shadings which Protestant Ethics, with their equalisation of the moral demand, and their individualisation of it in the civil vocation alone, have not possessed." And he shows how " where Protestantism outgrew this *bourgeois* narrowness, and coalesced with the New Humanism,

its genuine ethical categories became lost, and the new ones had
no room for the " profoundly necessary " tension between God
and the world, as we can trace in Herder, Schleiermacher and
Goethe " (pp. 667, 668).

And finally Troeltsch insists that " this entire dualism lies
deeply embedded in the metaphysical constitution of man ;
the contrast apparent within his motives is but one of the effects
of his general double position : he fronts both the Finite-Sensible
and the Infinite-Supersensible. And this dualism can be sur-
mounted at all only within the becoming of history and within
the becoming of the individual. True, even after man's complete self-dedication, here on earth, to the final, the religious
end, he will still, in his life and motives, have to experience the
doubleness of his motivation. But since this doubleness has a
metaphysical reason, it can only find a metaphysical resolution ;
and hence the final solution appears here as a life after death "
(l.c. pp. 665, 666).

In my second paper I hope to show Troeltsch again fuller,
deeper, richer than he can here be found. And meanwhile I
would conclude with a little simile that brings out, perhaps,
the point to which I think both he and I would wish this short
study to converge.

Is there a more nobly characteristic modern building, so
ethereal-looking and yet so strong, than is the Paris Eiffel Tower ?
Whence its strength ? Storms have come and gone, hurricanes
may beat against it ; it has stood and will stand. It breaks not,
because it bends ; it sinks not, because it sways. It yields as
much as five feet in any direction, this grand steel whip, elastic
in its live resilience. So also does our frail-seeming soul-life
persist, midst storms and hurricanes of temptation and of trial,
by means of its range from pole to pole, of the sensible, spatial-
temporal (almost to philistinism), and of the spiritual, super-
spatial and super-temporal, Eternal (almost to fanaticism). Thus
rich and not rigid it can, in its little measure, participate in the
utterly harmonious, utterly peaceful power and fruitfulness of
the Unmoving Energy, the Ever Living God.

II

Reality of mind, sense of what really is and what really matters, insight into the actual, driving forces of this our difficult, rich human life and task and end : how rare are these entrancingly noble things ! Perhaps my previous study has already given the reader some experience of such reality of mind, as it works, massively alive, in the *Fundamental Problems of Ethics* of Professor Troeltsch. Here I now want to penetrate into further, even more manysided, instances of such awakeness, whilst reserving for the penultimate division of this last paper the consideration of a certain abstractive, attenuating temper and current that, perhaps everywhere, more or less misfits and hampers this great soul's noble religious realism.

Only one point shall first be taken from the monograph *What is meant by " the Essence of Christianity "* ? (1903 ; *Gesammelte Schriften*, vol. II., 1913). And then five groups of questions shall be studied, partly in an order of my own, from the monumental work *The Social Doctrines of the Christian Churches and Groups*, 1912.

Among the six characters which Troeltsch finds to be involved in the idea and method of " the Essence of Christianity," that of " ' the Essence ' as Criticism " is particularly important when brought to the following application.

" As soon as we go beyond history of the purely empirical, inductive kind, and venture upon such high matters as the determination of the Essence, we cannot continue to cling to the ethically indifferent point of view of the mere understanding of the interconnections,—to the mere measuring of so many happenings by an immanental impulse of development. We have, at this point, to recognise that all the values which proceed within the human spirit from a feeling of their necessity, are everywhere more or less opposed by negation—by an isolating, disintegrating self-seeking, by crude, animal instincts, by a sloth and luxuriousness which refuse to be dislodged, by a dullness of apprehension which drags down all things to pettiness, or, at the least, by a commonness busy with turning them into coarse objects of sense. Whosoever combines, with the conception of the Essence in history, the conviction of a value and an end springing from an ideal necessitation, cannot fail simultaneously to admit the operative existence of radical evil. At all events, we cannot ignore this evil when we come face to face with the great systems of ethico-religious life. Monism, whether of the more materialist or of the more spiritualist kind, is indeed sufficiently questionable also in other provinces of thought; but on the territory of history it is an incredible delusion, for it contradicts every unprejudiced impression of the actual working of life, and is directly refuted by that bit of history which each one of us knows well, since each one of us lives it—our own personal experience."

" The determination of the Essence thus involves a criticism of all that has proceeded from the dullness and vulgarity, the passion and shortsightedness, the stupidity and malice, the indifference and worldly cunning of mankind : theology cannot evade the reproach of a moralising conception of history. Much as such a conception should be forbidden to touch the details, where a causal explanation of the various connections is in place —for the whole, and at the end, this ethical conception is simply unavoidable. Indeed, a general insight into the Essence is sought, after all, only in order to secure a sound judgment as to what is essential, whence we can, not only ignore what is unessential, but also condemn what is contrary to the Essence."

" And from hence light accrues to a conception which, in many ways, confuses the determination of the Essence—the conception of ' the necessary.' Necessity, in the psychological-causal sense, is one thing ; necessity, in the teleological and ethical sense, is another thing. Psychological-causal necessity concerns empirical inductive history ; and such ' necessity ' never means more than the linking of an event to certain forces which lay at the back of it. The various possibilities with which man, whilst he is in action, reckons as with so many undeniably extant alternatives, have no place in such empirical inductive history, where the effect which actually occurred is attributed to the motives which have been proved the strongest precisely by the result which they have here produced. Thus the psycho-logical-causal ' necessity ' reached by this explanation is not

co-extensive with the teleological-ethical necessity which invites
the decision of the man who deliberates, for his coming action,
as to what is the consequence of an idea demanded by this idea
itself. Only the latter kind of necessity is in debate when we
speak of the ' necessary ' development and elaboration of a
principle ; and, for the estimation of necessity in this sense,
only an interior conviction and personal decision can furnish
the test and solution " (*Ges. Schr.* II. pp. 409–411).

I take this distinction to be as important as its application
is difficult. But I cannot help finding here two excesses in
Troeltsch's own position.

When that virile thinker " Ideal " Ward reached his last
earthly years, he came to see clearly, I remember, how, in his
feeling and his writing, he had been too prone to "unspeakably,"
" incredibly," and the like. So here, as often with Ward when
pressed back to his last entrenchments, Troeltsch, after his quiet,
complex yet converging arguments and thinkings, appears
finally reduced to a vehement judgment of an apparently quite
subjective and inherently problematic kind. He thus, I think,
does his actual convictions some real injustice, since I take him
to hold that if such judgments inevitably contain an element
of risk and daring, yet also the previous training, experience,
insight are all necessary to it ; and, again, that the risk and
danger are, in reality, necessary here, only because, through
our human sensible-rational, temporal-spatial conditions of
apprehension and our many passions and self-involvements,
we never can *hic et nunc* hold all our achieved, still less all our
possible experience and evidence fully present and luminous
before us, at least not in far-reaching and deep-going questions
such as these. We have thus, here and now (by an act rendered
possible and rational through all we possess and know and are),
to exceed, and thus to complete, the evidence here and now
before us—an evidence which, in itself and in the long run, is
sufficient for these our convictions and decisions.

And, again, Troeltsch finds that such a critical judgment concerning the Essence of Christianity as is here propounded by
himself, is possible only to Protestantism, with its strong appeal
to the individual judgment and sincerity. I believe this would
be true, were the judgment a " purely personal " affair, such as

some of Troeltsch's words and antitheses suggest it to be. But if, intrinsically and at its best, we have here something " personal " rather in the sense of the deepest and most fruitful syntheses or hypotheses of Science, then Catholicism, at its deepest, not only is capable of such judgments, but it is, in some important respects, better furnished for the—in any case very difficult—task than is Protestantism. For these scientific syntheses or hypotheses no less require all the great facts that went before them, and a wide experience and generous appreciation of these facts, than they need intuition and courage fully to penetrate, indeed to exceed these facts, and thus to see more in them than ever before. And the Church-type at its best (*i.e.* Catholicism at its best) possesses a longer, wider and more many-sided experience of the religious facts and capabilities than does any other type or group. Only if all seeking after, and adhering to, methods and standards special to the several subject-matters to be studied, experienced, penetrated and awakened by the human mind and soul ; only if all such dispositions, as is sometimes implied, were to be tabooed as " subjectivism " or " private judgment " : only then would Catholicism be really debarred from the judgments concerning the " Essence " as (I submit) these judgments actually have to be. But then we are still a long way from such a Catholicism, which would, in very truth, become an Idol in a desert,—a Church thus vigorous in the destruction of its own supports, stimulations and subject-matters.

It is not easy to furnish a short yet useful account and criticism of Troeltsch's *Soziallehren*, with its nearly thousand pages, its bewildering variety of topics, and the range and delicacy of competence it so strikingly reveals. And all this is here subservient to certain few, closely interdependent, central convictions and conclusions. And again these self-commitments are reached only across surging seas of the strongest feeling and closest net-works of objective complication. And then, too, as I must attempt to show in my penultimate section, there is a relic, a shadow or echo, of Subjectivism frequently, perhaps always, haunting the outskirts of Troeltsch's convictions, or rather of their formulations, which—I believe more than anything else—prevents his religious reader from settling down with perfect peace and buoyancy under the influence and guidance of this large strong mind and soul.

I must regretfully ignore the instructive autobiographic Preface, and the dry but important Introduction, with its fruitful distinction between the *sociological* scheme and action developed by the three types of religion (Church, Sect, Mysticism) within their own organisations, and the *social* idea and attitude developed by them with respect to the non-religious organisations of life. And even from the three gigantic Chapters composing the body of the work I can but take certain culminating points of the last two chapters. The wonderfully close-knit and rich Conclusion shall furnish my final translations and suggestions.

1

The very great " Mediæval Catholicism " Chapter is, in the first instance, busy with the full expression of the Church-type ; let us here fix upon three passages.

1. As to the Problem, Troeltsch describes how " the ancient Church indeed organised itself with a full, firm sociological articulation ; but its social attitude—its attitude towards the State and Society—was a curiously mixed thing—partly a recognition, as of entities sheltered by the Natural Law ; partly a theocratic subjugation and utilisation ; partly a propping of the powers of the State, when these had become insufficient for their purpose ; partly a rejection of the State and Society in general, expressed in the theory of the sinfulness of everything founded by the relative Natural Law, and in the practice of the renunciation of the world. A Christian civilisation possessed of an interior unity existed neither in fact nor in principle ; the whole idea was foreign to antiquity. And the decisive difference between the Middle Ages and Antiquity consists precisely in the possession, by the Middle Ages, of such an ideal—in their practice and still more in theory ; indeed even in official Catholicism of our own day this ideal, with some adaptations to the modern world, is still active in all its social doctrines " (pp. 178, 179).

And Troeltsch cogently insists :

" The significance of the question of how at all, and in what way, this ideal and solution could arise in the Middle Ages," and only then, " fails to be duly estimated by all those who ascribe already to the Ancient Church, or even to Christianity generally, such a striving after a unified Christian civilisation." Yet, in reality " for Stoicism and Platonism, and still more for Christianity, a doctrine of society and civilisation based upon the values of the free personality in its union with God and of the universal communion of mankind, offered the greatest difficulties ; and Christianity, in particular, produced indeed a mighty, purely religious organisation, and ordered within it the conditions of its members' lives in tolerable conformity with its own principles, but," during its first eight centuries, the Church in this its organisation " was hostile to the world at large—it failed to discover any bond and link between itself and the complexes outside. The Middle Ages, however, lived to see the development of the Church to a social entity inclusive both of the sociological circle of religion itself, and of the politico-social formations also, and which thus realised, in its own way, what had haunted Plato, in his *Republic* as the true end of a single state—the rule of the wise and of the friends of God over an organic, many-levelled social entity, and what the Stoic Cosmopolis had sought —the share of all men in an ethical universal kingdom " (pp. 181, 182).

2. As to the contrast between the Ancient Christian and the Mediæval Christian positions concerning man's nature, place, destination Troeltsch is deeply instructive.

" The decisive point here is the conception, peculiar to the Middle Ages, of what is Christian as supernatural, or rather the full elaboration of the consequences involved in the idea of the Supernatural. The Supernatural here is not only present in the miracle of the God-Man, of the Church and of the Sacraments,—in the great " complex " miracle of man's redemption from out of the world corrupted by original sin ; it has no longer, as in the Ancient Church, an essentially apologetic significance. But the Supernatural now unfolds itself as an autonomous logical, religious and ethical principle. The creature, even the perfect creature, is only natural—possessed of natural laws and ends ; God alone is supernatural. And accordingly, the essence of Christian Supernaturalism consists in its elevation of the creature, above this creature's co-natural limitations, to God's own supernature, to participation in His nature. The mediation necessary here lies thus, no longer, as in the Ancient Church, between two kinds (respectively perfect and relative) of the one sole Natural Law, but between Natural Law in general and Supernature generally; and especially all Ethics and Social Philosophy now rest, in the last resort, upon the mediation between Nature (perfect or imperfect) and Supernature. The Decalogue, in reality, is not yet the Christian Ethic, and the Natural Law, identical with the Decalogue, stands, to the specifically Christian Ethic, to the *Nova Lex*, as near and as far as precisely does the Decalogue. ' Biblical ' now means revealed, but not necessarily Christian ; for the Bible represents, for Aquinas, a process of development moving through universal history and possessed of varying stages. The Decalogue persists in the legislation of Christ, but as a stage preliminary to the Christian Ethic and as an instruction in the exterior application of the new motives springing from this Ethic. The formula, on the other hand, for the specifically Christian Moral Law is the Augustinian formula of the love of God, as the highest and absolute, the entirely simple, moral end,—an end which contains the demand of the love of God in the stricter sense (through self-sanctification, self-denial and contemplation), and the demand of the love of our neighbour (through the active relating of all to God, the active inter-connecting of all in God, and the most intimate mutual self-sacrifice for God). We have thus a self-love in God, which loves not the natural self, but the self united to God ; and a brotherly love in God, which loves not the natural fellow-man, but the brother in God. This Ethic (a mystical interpretation of the Evangelical preaching) forms an unmistakably strong contrast to the this-world Ethic of the Natural Law, Aristotle, the Decalogue and natural prosperity ; but this cannot fail to be the case, given the entire fundamental character of the Christian Ethic. This same contrast indeed appeared also, clearly enough, in the life of mediæval society, —in the relations between Church and State, between laymen, monks and priests ; and was still at work within the ethical demands made upon even the simplest layman " (pp. 263–265).

Has Aquinas, on the ample questions here discussed, been

anywhere penetrated as delicately and deeply, as generously
and justly, as is done here, in these noble sections of a truly
great book ?

2

And yet the culmination of interest and power is reached by
the *Soziallehren,* where also the Sect-type, and later on where
the third and last type, the Mystical, appear at their fullest
on the stage of history, and where, with their contrasting
strengths and defects and their tough vitality and far-reaching
operation and use, they bring into full relief the abiding truth
and meaning of the Church-type, together with the character
and range of their own types. Let us attend first to the Sect-
type.

1. The main historical origins and stages of this Sect-type
appear to be as follows. Paulinism already prepared the orientation of Christianity towards conservatism ; yet already alongside
of Paulinism there existed a radicalism which was indifferent,
or even hostile, to the world—so in the communism of love of
the primitive community, and in the chiliastic-apocalyptic rejection of the world. Similarly, alongside of the social development
of the ancient Church which continued the Pauline conservatism,
the radicalism persisted in the Montanist and Donatist sects
and (at least as regards extension and importance) especially in
Monasticism—the latter influencing various Fathers of the Fourth
Century in their teaching as to an original communism and
equality (p. 359). The first clear emergence of the problem is in
A.D. 393–420, in the conflict between St. Augustine's sacramental
hierarchical conception of the Church and the Donatists ; but
its decisive appearance follows only upon the completion of the
Church concept in the reform of Pope Gregory VII., A.D. 1073–
1085, although, here especially, the antagonistic popular excite-
ment was largely pushed into the formation of separate sects
by the intensely rigorous Church authorities themselves—so
especially with the Waldensians (pp. 367 ; 388, 389 ; 403 n.).

2. The all-important point for Troeltsch here is that " both
the Church-type and the Sect-type lie in the consequence of
the Gospel, and only conjointly do they exhaust the range of
the sociological effects and the social consequences of this same

Gospel. The Church, assuredly, is not a simple defection from the Gospel, however much it may (at first sight) appear to be so in the contrast between its hierarchy and sacraments and the preaching of Jesus. For where the Gospel is, in the first instance, apprehended as a Gift, a Grace, where, in the picture which faith forms of Christ, it appears as a Divine Institution, where the interior liberty of the spirit (distinct from all human making and organising) is experienced as the meaning of Jesus, and where His grand indifference to worldly things is correspondingly apprehended as an interior independence from, together with an exterior use of, these things : there men will consider the establishment of the Church as the normal continuation and transformation of the Gospel. At the same time, the Church, by its emphatic universalism, preserves the fundamental impulse of the evangelical preaching ; but that preaching had committed all detailed questions, concerning the possibility and execution of the mission, to the wonderful coming of the Kingdom, whereas a Church, working in the duration of the world, had to organise and order, and so to make its compromises."

" Nevertheless, the Sect also is not simply a defection—a mere lopsided, crippling misgrowth of the elements of religious life already exhaustively furnished by the Church ; but it is an immediate continuation of certain evangelical convictions. The radical individualism and love reaches its full recognition only in the Sect ; only the Sect instinctively construes the entire community from thence, and attains, precisely through this radicalism of love, an immense firmness in its subjective-interior bond, in lieu of any merely external appurtenance to an institution. Thus the Sect clings to the original radicalism of the ideal and to its sharp contrast to the world, and abides by the demand of personal performance as persistently fundamental. This performance the Sect also can apprehend as the work of grace ; but in this grace, it emphasises the subjective realisation and effect, not the objective assuredness and presence."

" The preaching of Jesus, which looks forward to the coming end and the Kingdom, which collects and unites determined confessors, and which bids the brusquest adieu to the world and its children, goes in the direction of the Sect. The faith of the apostles, which looks back upon the miracle of redemption

and of the person of Christ and which lives in the powers of its
heavenly master : this faith which leans upon something achieved
and objective, in which it unites its faithful and allows them
to rest, proceeds in the direction of the Church. Thus the New
Testament aids in the formation both of the Church and of the
Sect ; it has done so from the first. But the Church had the
start and the great mission into the wide world. And only when
the objectification of the Church had " under Hildebrand " been
severely completed, did the tendency which forms Sects react
once again, and indeed in a union and persistence greater than
ever before, against this excessive objectification " (pp. 375–377).

3. Troeltsch delicately apprehends the wide-ranging effects
of this Sect-reaction.

" The institution by the Sect of the absolute law of God and
Nature as the sole authority, and the consequent removal of
the entire conception of steps and development, involve the most
far-reaching consequences,—consequences not perceived by the
(mostly very simple) theology of the Sects. Here the intention
and law of God are expressed, without a shadow of ambiguity,
in the Bible and in the voice of pure Nature alone ; there is no
need for any complicated doctrine as to this law. The moral
demand proceeds to all men alike ; there is no need of a graduation of perfection, according to various vocations. Creation
does not descend through various stages down to materiality,
nor does creation thence mount again through steps, as though
a great work of art, from Nature up to Grace and Supernature.
But creation places mankind immediately before the task of the
realisation of its ideal, and this ideal is here without the character
of a mystical supernature, of the elevation of man's essence above
itself. . . . And since such mystical beatitude, as the crown of
the system of stages, falls all but entirely away for the Sects, the
conception of Law " (which, in the Catholic system, was but one
of the two determinations for God, alongside with that of Substance) " now takes up an all-dominating position. God's being
and will are His natural and revealed Law ; the Bible is the Law-
book of revelation, identical with the Law-book of Nature. Thus,
in lieu of the institution of Grace and Redemption, the conception of Law becomes the centre of the Sect theology "
(pp. 380–382).

4. To these deeply stimulating analyses and positions I would attach three criticisms of my own.

My first regret has been already expressed in connection with Troeltsch's earlier and shorter *Grundprobleme*, but recurs again here with respect to his later, very long work, and concerns his non-perception that sensible contacts, vehicles and symbols, that the principle and rudiments of sacraments, are already present in the spirit and practice of Jesus. I will return to this objection presently in conjunction with my third dissatisfaction, a dissatisfaction so fundamental and general as to be better reserved for discussion till just before the end and my last expression of deep gratitude for all that Troeltsch has brought us.

But my second objection is specially in place just here. I find, then, that even the very generous measure in which Troeltsch recognises already within the preaching of Jesus conceptions and impulses making for the Church, does not, in the greater part of his book, reach to the fullness of the facts. For it is now thoroughly acknowledged by all the best historical workers that the direct central subject of Jesus's preaching was the Kingdom, and its Proximate Coming. This Kingdom was presented in this preaching emphatically as a pure gift, a sheer *opus operatum* of God ; men can prepare themselves for it, and can determine the character of its effect upon themselves ; but they do not produce it, they do not constitute it.—And again, neither Jesus Himself nor His Apostles are, it is true, of priestly families, and there is no marked formal ordination of them ; yet it is Jesus, in His humanity, who calls and trains and sends out these special Twelve,—not any and everyone is treated as free to put himself forward to preach on the strength of some purely interior call. In these two fundamental points, then, the teaching and practice of Jesus demonstrably initiate the objectivity of the Church and the special calls to the clerical office ; we have here sheer historical facts and not interpretations (however legitimate and part-constitutive of religion) such as, for the most part at least, Troeltsch takes these points to be. Thus the chief characteristic of the central doctrine of Jesus emphasises Givenness, Object, Church, not Activity, Subject, Sect ; and the prominent feature of the organising action of Jesus is certainly not simply an acceptance of souls all equally

and secretly inspired, but a calling of some few men, by Him,
the Man, God, from out of the crowd of mankind, even from out
of the crowd of elementary or secret believers.

3

Troeltsch has most effectively located the detailed studies
of his three types of Christianity : that of the Church, in the
High Middle Ages ; that of the Sect, in the first instance immediately after the High Middle Ages, hence still in the Middle
Ages ; and that of Mysticism, after the Protestant Churches and
Sects. For he thus examines each type at the time of its own
fullest articulation and strongest influence, and of its most vivid
contrast with the other types. We must now consider the part
which, in this book thus late, for the first time studies fully
the Mystical type,—the great pages 850–877.

1. " Mysticism, in the widest sense, is nothing but the insistence upon immediacy, interiority, presence of religious
experience. It presupposes the objectification of religious life
in Rites, Myths or Dogmas, and is either a reaction against such
objectifications which it attempts to put back into the living
process, or a supplementation of the traditional cults by a personal and vital excitation. Mysticism is thus always something
secondary and intentionally reflective, although this deliberately
produced condition is conjoined with a quite contrary immediacy
of the feeling itself. It thus always contains some degree of
paradox, an antithesis to the masses and their average. Hence
the primitive religious act and life, for which the event and its
expression are simply identical, is never mystical. But the liveli-
ness of the religious sense, when face to face with objectified
religion, easily and often assumes mystical characteristics,—
enthusiastic or even orgiastic exaltation, vision or hallucination,
religious subjectivism and spiritualism, concentration upon the
purely interior and only emotionally apprehensible. Such
visions, indeed, are almost always only expansions and interpretations of the common faith, as with the pneumatic gifts of
the early Christians and with the countless visions and prophecies
of mediæval recluses and saints. But this mystical sense can
also create a passionate realism of intercourse with the Godhead,

*G

where the erotic side of human nature often plays a great rôle. And again such immediacy of feeling loves to fly beyond the sensible-finite world by a spiritualism which treats it as indifferent or ignores it, or which by ascetical mortification moves it away into the distance. Thus Mysticism is open to the incursions both of a spiritualistic Pantheism and of a radical Dualism of flesh and spirit, of time and eternity ; and, in connection therewith, to the suggestions of an Asceticism destructive of all things finite or of a Libertinism treating them all as indifferent."

2. " Now Mysticism, in these various forms, is a phenomenon general in all the religious territories, and is (or was) highly developed especially in India and Persia, in Greece, Asia Minor, Syria. And, naturally, it did not remain foreign to the primitive Christian movement, but in part sprang also from it, in part was brought into it from without and eagerly appropriated there."

" To this Mysticism belong the so-called enthusiasm of the primitive Christians, a large part of the gifts of the Spirit, the speaking with tongues, exorcism, the pneumatic activity. But especially does also Paul himself belong to it—Paul in his mystical orientation which stood in a continuous tension (not, however, experienced by himself as such) with his Church conviction. Paul took over the Christ-cultus of the primitive community as already objectified in its outlines in worship and organisation. But he gave further aliveness to this religion by means of a profound and passionate mysticism, which consequently also utilises the ancient terminology of the heathen mysteries. Here alone lay his religious originality as against the primitive community, and thus only did his anti-Jewish universalism become a workable, effective enterprise. Thus the Lord's Supper, the centre of the new Cultus, became with him a mystical union of substances, Baptism became a real dying and arising with Christ. Thus Christ became for him a new life-sphere of a supersensible kind, in which the believer lives, feels, and thinks, and becomes a new, pneumatic creature. Thus all mere ceremonial and tradition became an element of this world, and Christ after the flesh was known no more. And thus again the Israelitish history of redemption was allegorised into a drama immediately applicable to the Christian believers, and the Christian community became the spiritual body of Christ."

" Here, in the primitive Christian enthusiasm and in the Pauline Mysticism as to Christ, lie the inexhaustible sources of a Christian Mysticism. In the Fourth Gospel this Mysticism has already become self-possessed and adjusted to the historical and objective ; yet here especially it has produced or found its characteristic terms—flesh, spirit ; darkness, light ; allegory, letter. And thus, through the New Testament, Mysticism (of the pneumatic and Pauline kind) has become a permanent power which always anew awakens and articulates similar needs, especially in periods of criticism of tradition, of religious lassitude and of religious reform."

3. " In primitive Christianity, in the New Testament itself, then, lie the germs of the Church, given with the conception of Grace and of the completed institution for the salvation of the world. And in it lie the germs of the Sect, which reveres its Master's Sermon on the Mount as its moral Law, continues His expectation of the Kingdom about to descend upon earth, and collects the pure and holy into a community tarrying for Christ's return. But in it lie also the germs of a Mysticism for which all that passes is but a symbol ; all that is sensible-earthly, but a limitation ; all cultus, but a means of substantial union ; all faith, but an immediate transplantation into the invisible life of God and Christ " (pp. 850–852).

4. We cannot here follow Troeltsch in all his fine study of " Mysticism in the narrower, technical sense of the word, where it becomes a religious philosophy," and where, unlike its New Testament kinds, it can take up a position of deliberate independence, of open denial, or of allegorising evaporation of concrete religion. Yet also this technical kind can still require and serve historical, institutional religion, as in the Dominican cognitive Mysticism, in the Franciscan Mysticism of the affections and the will, and in the more generally philosophical Mysticism of the theologians of the Ancient Church. All these mysticisms more or less require Christian history, and more or less maintain ethical personality. Especially is Troeltsch moved by the conception of the indwelling of Christ : " Thus was the cleavage overcome between Past and Present, Doctrine and Practice ;

thus did mediæval devotion to Christ strike the water of life
from out of the rock of the Byzantine dogma " (pp. 856–858).

5. As to the Sociological peculiarities of Mysticism, where
(as in the various forms of Christian Spiritualism) it is more or
other than sheer enthusiasm, and finds its basis in the doctrine
of the permanent, equable divine spark in the human soul, we
learn :

" Mysticism is a radical individualism very different from
that of the Sect. The Sect differentiates individuals against the
world, by conscious contrast and ethical rigorism ; unites them
in a community resting upon a willed association and growing
under disciplinary control ; binds them to the example and
authority of Christ ; and intensifies the individualism precisely
through its inclusion within such a community and cultus. But
Mysticism insists upon a relation, not between man and man,
but of man to God ; and reduces everything historical, authoritative, cultual to a mere stimulant, which (in strictness) it can do
without. As long as such a Mysticism or Spiritualism remains
Christian, the Bible and the historical figure of Christ still play
an important rôle, yet never with a power sufficient to produce a
firmly-knit community. Thus we do not here find, as we find
in the Sect, a community which possesses an activity and a confession of faith of its own—a community which is continuously
reconstituted from the interaction of the individual wills, but
we are given here a parallelism of religious spontaneities conjoined only by the divine life-ground from which they spring,
by the common disposition of love, and by the union in the free,
invisible work of the divine spirit. In so far as this Mysticism
is founded solely upon faith and feeling, it exceeds the individualism even of the most individualistic of the Sects ; yet
this mystical individualism is, on the other hand, much weaker
than is that of those Sects, because of its tendency to quietude
and abandonment and to the exercise of works of love only from
case to case " (pp. 864, 865).

And as to their Social aims, " where such Mystics form groups
they do not intend them, sect-like, to replace the great invisible
Church or to interfere with God's own work of spreading the
spirit, but simply as familiar circles for the edification of souls.
The Mystics have thus not nearly as much inclination to separate

from the Church as have the Sects " (p. 868). " Of themselves
these Mystics cultivate only the individual believer and the
interests of his particular soul ; and though they simultaneously
believe, and sometimes strongly emphasise, the universal communion of spirits and of love, yet Church and religious organisation " are for them " concessions to human weakness, without
interior necessity and divinity." And " towards Politics and
Economics the indifference and helplessness are complete ;
only sexual and family ethics are here studied, and indeed with
great penetration " (pp. 940, 941 ; 864).

I will take my criticisms of Troeltsch on the Mystical Type
in connection with the most fundamental and general of my
dissatisfactions in the following separate section.

4

The translations given in these papers from Troeltsch have
deliberately softened or omitted one paradoxical peculiarity
which, like a contrary surface-current, runs along much of his
thinking and feeling, since, in such mere extracts, I could not
otherwise sufficiently render what I am confident is his fundamental vision and volition. For the same Troeltsch who so persistently emphasises the need and the reality of certain historical
facts, of community, cultus, organisation, and who, still deeper
down, so vividly sees and describes religion as an experience
and affirmation of trans-subjective, more-than-human fact and
reality, as metaphysical and ontological or nothing, is also
strangely thin, abstract, hypothetic, indeed subjectivist in
many of his favourite terms and connotations. " Thought,"
" thoughts," " thinking," the mind's spontaneity," " mental
creations " ; " the Christian legend," " the religious myth " :
I have mostly translated the former terms with " apprehension,"
" conviction," " perceptions," etc., and have hardly given a
passage containing the latter expressions.

1. Now Troeltsch, rightly I believe, considers Protestantism
in the first instance to have been, as a matter of fact, whether
rightly or wrongly, " a reduction " of all religion " to what
it held can alone be an object of faith, trust, disposition,—
viz., to a thought—the thought of God, derived from the

Apostolic presentation of Christ, as the Holy Gracious Will which forgives us our sins and thus lifts us to a higher life. And this thought includes, in addition, only what can render it certain for the sinner,—the insight into God's self-revelation in the Logos," as " the assurance afforded to us men of God's sin-remitting love " (pp. 439, 440).

And when, much later on in history, Kant appears, I believe Troeltsch, with practically all historians, is right in finding in him very specially " the philosopher of Protestantism "—a Protestantism, however, representing a much greater retreat of religion upon thought and the subject than was that of Luther.

2. Now doubtless not only Luther but Kant also intended thus to find certainty concerning God within their own souls, and so to escape that lapse into doubt and self-delusion which they considered to attach to all seeking of such assurance in social traditions and external proofs and practices. Yet the modern idealist philosophy, as first clearly formulated (between Luther's time and the time of Kant) by Descartes in his fundamental principle, was so eager to make sure of this kind of interiority and sincerity, that it started, not from the concrete fact, viz., a mind thinking *something*, and from the analysis of this ultimate trinity in unity (the subject, the thinking, and the object), but from that pure abstraction—thinking, or thought, or a thinking of a thought ; and, from this unreal starting-point, this philosophy strove to reach that now quite problematical thing, the object. Hume had no difficulty, from such premises, in reaching the purest Scepticism. And although Kant, the greatest of Hume's opponents, profoundly advanced Ethics and the Theory of Knowledge, especially in his formulations of the problems, and though his intention was throughout to ground Theism upon unshakable foundations, yet his actual influence, especially in the Neo-Kantian interpretation, has been, upon the whole, hardly less agnostic than that of Hume himself. For take Kant, not from his moral but from his epistemological side, not from the two last *Critiques* but from the first, not in this or that of his (at least three) different theories of knowledge, but according to his predominant mood, or along the line of least resistance, and you will find that here man knows nothing really of the real nature of anything, although (strangely enough) he *does* know,

so certainly as to be above discussion, that the reality of everything is always utterly different from what this thing appears
to be.

3. No living thinker has so much as Troeltsch insisted upon
the sense of Givenness and of Otherness, as characteristic of
all genuine religion ; and no one has better analysed and described this evidential character of all religion, or has more
clearly shown how only the acceptance of this evidence as true
and final brings firmness, interconnection and sufficient rationality into our life as a whole, and depth into all its parts. It is
indeed the very vividness and massiveness of this religious sense
which brings the sympathising reader to a quick and keen
bewilderment, or to a painful arrest and benumbedness of feeling,
when the same Troeltsch attempts the philosophical formulation of this his religious sense. For in his philosophical formulation Troeltsch clings to a more or less Kantian Idealism, which
is not always, indeed perhaps never quite clearly, restricted to
its rich, almost Realist stage. Indeed at times he writes as
though this Idealism, even taken thus in general, were almost
an abiding new presentation of Christianity. Thus the religious
Troeltsch continually propels and warms us religiously, but
the philosophical Troeltsch often, at the same time, draws us
back and chills us philosophically, indeed also religiously, since,
after all, man's soul is not a man-of-war divided into so many
water-tight compartments. Again, where the religious Troeltsch
speaks, Religion requires history, indeed Christianity is held
actually to retain a nucleus of critically established happenings,
and permanently to need such a nucleus as essential to its own
persistence. And these happenings are thus treasured, because
they are in their depths far more than they seem on the surface
— because they contain and transmit religious realities and
powers. Yet when the philosophical Troeltsch speaks, these real
happenings and their real, religious contents dwindle to such
windy subjectivities as the Christian " legend," indeed even
the Christian " myth." Again Christianity, for Troeltsch the
believer, exercises its finest and farthest reaching influence as
a special kind of Mysticism. Yet for Troeltsch, as thinker, the
original religious fact and experience of the fact are always
unmystical, and Mysticism is always dependent upon, and is

secondary to, this unmystical fact and experience. Nor does
such supervening Mysticism distil and express from out of
that original fact and experience their real though latent meaning
and virtue; but the Mystical apprehension is here simply a
" creation of the religious spontaneity." Further, according to
Troeltsch, the original, unmystical religious fact and experience
arise, in all their greatest, world-moving instances, amongst
the socially humble and educationally elementary classes and
individuals, thus affording us the spectacle of " power made
perfect in infirmity." Yet Troeltsch the thinker does not, by
this, simply mean that these classes and individuals are given or
attain, and that they irradiate, a finer and fuller insight into what
is than do the other, more sophisticated and more sceptical
mortals of the middle and upper classes. It is merely that these
lower-class men approve themselves to be specially rich in " myth-
constructing capacity." And finally Troeltsch, especially the
religious Troeltsch, insists that man is never without, that he
cannot, even if he would, get rid of, the impression that realities
not himself directly impinge upon and penetrate himself,
realities which are (thus and so far) really known to him, though
known only in part, and in that part largely obscurely. Man
thus finds his entire nature to be awakened by the various
realities distinct from and independent of itself; he finds that
his awakened senses awaken his reason and his spirit; and he
finds that this generally awake condition of his nature calls forth
within his spirit a painful consciousness of the finitude and con-
tingency of it all, a sense of a contrasting Other, Infinite, Intrinsic
and Abiding. Yet for Troeltsch the thinker, our own mind
appears often to be what alone we incontestably start with, and
any reality, distinct from the mind's consciousness of itself, is
but an inference of this mind from this its consciousness and
requires proof as to its trans-subjective validity; the belief in
the need of sense-stimulation for the awakening of the mind
and of the soul, is, in religion, sheer " magic-mongering ";
and the sense of the Contrasting Other comes late and upon
reflection, in the mystical reaction against the early and child-
like anthropomorphism of the Heavenly Father. In a word,
here, everywhere, Religion proclaims and demands trans-subjective, more than human Reality; and here, everywhere,

Philosophy never gets clearly beyond a subjectivism incapable of consistent certainty even as regards the minimum on which all human certainty and action (even where these are previous to religion or more superficial than religion) are demonstrably built.

It is thus Troeltsch himself who, more even by his intensely alive religious sense than by his many acute criticisms of Kantianism, makes us thirst for a fully thought-out, self-consistent Critical Realism. Everywhere such a Realism would assume or announce that thought, primarily and normally, never stands alone, and never is thought of thought, but always thought of a reality distinct from this thinking of it; that the activity of the human mind and soul, as known to us in this life, always more or less requires sense-stimulation, and that superstition here lies as truly in denying as in exaggerating this need; that our knowledge is always an incomplete knowledge yet a knowledge of reality—since the objects really reveal, in various degrees, their real nature; that the primary qualities of material objects are trans-subjectively real, and that the instinctive recognition of this reality plays an important part also in the religious habits and certainties of the soul; that the mystical type of religion is indeed secondary and reflective in so far as it seeks and sees *all things* as immediately present, but that the original religious fact and experience of religion already always contains *an element* of immediacy. Thus, for our Lord's consciousness, God was immediately present; God's Kingdom, its advent upon earth, was proximate, but not simply present.

With some such a philosophy would disappear, from out of Troeltsch's noble writings, that disturbing, numbing counter-current certainly present in them now.

And such a philosophy need, in no sense or degree, contravene Troeltsch's most precious resolve " not to recognise any specially theological, still less any specially Christian, methods of study " (*Soziallehren*, p. ix.). For such a philosophy would be adopted only because it had been found more adequate to the analysis and elucidation of the facts of human consciousness and knowledge, of physical science, and of religion; and because philosophy, to remain truly such, has to be the sensitively docile interpreter of actual life and reality, not their harshly doctrinaire explainer-away. And such a philosophy, once adopted, would have carefully to guard against any wholesale conclusions, and any niggardliness of admiration and docility towards the profound gains in method, perception, facts brought us by the Critical Idealism. Careful research, severe criticism, daring hypothesis, independence from aught but the laws and tests found to be obstinately intrinsic to the respective ranges and levels of study, will be as needful as ever ; but all will now move within a frank recognition of Givenness, of Otherness, of Reality. Our minds will now range from the Givenness of the pebble and the star to the Givenness of the lichen, of the bee and bird, on to the immensely greater Givenness of the human spirit, and (contrasting with, yet sustaining, all such Givennesses and their numberless given, real inter-relations) the primary, absolute Givenness and Reality of God.

5

But let us go back to learn some final lessons from Troeltsch in his rousing summary of some of his rich gains, and finish this very imperfect study of Troeltsch's conceptions of Christianity, its specific Genius and Capacities, with some analysis of the conclusion to his *Soziallehren*, probably the most reasoned and best balanced piece in the entire great work. We thus can end on a nobly prophetic, splendidly sober, ideally realist, humanely Christian, unconquered and unconquerable note of faith in the perennial need, because truth and fact, of religion, and of its great Origin, Object and End.

I will, here, concentrate upon the author's deeper, religious conclusions ; upon his practical suggestions ; and upon his final outlook (pp. 978–986).

1. The religious conclusions strive to emphasise the abiding ethical values contained in the many-coloured Christian social doctrines : I do not see how they could be made more movingly deep and true. " The Christian Ethos alone," as against many a more showy, more easy faith or fancy, " possesses, in virtue of its personalistic Theism, a conviction of personality and individuality rooted in a Metaphysic, and lifted above destruction

from any and all the Naturalisms and Pessimisms. Only the
personality which arises, out of man, to beyond man in his
range as a merely natural product — a personality achieved
through a union of his will and deepest being with God—this
alone is raised above the finite and alone can defy it. Without
this support, every individualism evaporates into thin air."

And again : " the Christian Ethos alone, in virtue of its
conviction of a Divine Love which attends to all souls and
which unites them all, possesses a truly unshakable," a sound
" Socialism. Only in the medium of the Divine do those conflicts
and exclusivenesses disappear, which belong to man as a natural
product and which shape his natural existence ; only here do
the associations formed by coercion, physical need, sex-instinct,
work, organisation attain a connection superior to them all
and indestructible, because now metaphysical."

Again : " only the Christian Ethos resolves the problem of
equality and inequality, since it neither glorifies violence and
accident, in the sense of a Nietzschian cult of breed, nor out-
rages the patent facts of life by a doctrinaire equalitarianism.
It first recognises the fundamental difference in the social positions, the powers and gifts of men, as a condition established by
the inscrutable will of God, and then transforms this condition,
by the interior upbuilding of the personality and the development of the sense of mutual obligation, into an ethical cosmos."

" The Christian Ethos, through its estimation of personality
and its love, produces what no social organisation, be it ever so
just and rational, can ever entirely do without, since everywhere
there always remain incalculable sufferings, needs and maladies
—claims upon disinterested caritative help. This helpfulness
has, as a matter of sheer fact, sprung from the Christian spirit,
and only through this spirit can it persist."

And finally, " the Christian Ethos alone places a goal before
the eyes of us all who have to live and struggle through our
difficult social existence,—a goal which lies beyond all the
relativities of the earthly life, and, compared with which, everything else represents only approximate values. The conviction
of the Divine Kingdom of the future, which is but faith in the
final realisation of the Absolute, in whatever way we may conceive this realisation, does not, as short-sighted opponents

maintain, deprive the world, and the life in the world of their value; but it makes the soul strong, throughout its various stages of progression, in the certainty of a last absolute sense and aim for human toil. It thus raises the soul above the world without denying it." Only through this, the deepest insight of all Christian asceticism, do " all social utopias become superfluous ; and the impossibility, always preached anew by experience, of a full understanding and a full execution of the ideal, need not then throw back the seeker into that scepticism which so easily springs precisely from an earnest veracity, and which is everywhere invading the finer spirits of our times. The Beyond is, in very truth, the power of our Now and Here " (pp. 978, 979).

2. And then he gives us four pregnant positions with regard to the propagation and organisation of these religious forces. " The religious life, upon reaching the stage of spiritual religion, requires an organisation distinct from the simply natural articulations of society. Without a community, organisation and cultus, Christianity is incapable of propagation and fruitfulness."

" Amongst the forms of organisation, the Church-type is superior to the Sect-type and to Mysticism. It is the Church which alone fully retains the characteristic of religion as essentially Salvation and Grace ; which renders the presence of Grace independent of the performances of individuals ; which is able to embrace the most diverse stages of spiritual ripeness and Christianisation, and which, hence, is alone fit to harbour a popular religion within the inevitable graduation of its members."

" The Church-type, precisely because of the tension within it between pure Christianity and adaptation to the world, has had a most varied history " and is, in these our times, in a condition of change and in a situation of great perplexity. " Without compulsion, a lasting, uniform, indivisible Church body is inconceivable ; and compulsion again is inconceivable without the aid of the State. And, indeed in times of a general naïf belief, such a compulsion has no harmful or irreligious consequences."

" But," finally, " just because of its connection with the unbroken unity of the general life and outlook of large groups of peoples, the unbroken Church-type is interiorly appropriate to such times alone. For at other times, what is a matter of course for the general outlook tallies no more with what is a matter of course for the Church. Compulsion is then no longer the preservation of the whole from isolated disturbances, but a violation of the movements of the larger life as it actually is." And Troeltsch considers the future unification and cohesion of Protestantism as possible only " on the supposition that the Churches, created though they have been in part by state-enforced conformity, may become homes in which henceforth a variety of Christian spirits will find room to dwell and act." " The Home which was constructed by compulsion and un-shrinking uniformitarianism can thus be inhabited by finer and especially by very various spirits, who then, it is true, will have carefully to guard a mutual toleration within certain wide limits." " The spirit of the Church-type would thus be here maintained in its grand conviction of an historical substance of life common to all, a substance which, in the various smaller religious groups and declarations, would be expressed, a part in this group, a part in that group, and would thus be kept from stagnation. We thus retain the sense of a common faith and the consciousness of heredity, as ' a minimum of the Church ' " (pp. 980–983).

3. And the valedictory warning is, surely, supremely impressive in its virile sobriety :

" If the present social situation is to be mastered by Christian principles, thoughts will be necessary which have not yet been thought and which will correspond to this new situation, as the older forms corresponded to the older situations. These thoughts will have to be drawn from the interior spontaneity of the Christian idea and not exclusively from the New Testament, as indeed has always been the case with the great Christian social forms of the past. And they will have the fate in store for all the creations of the religious-ethical idea : they will render indispensable services and will develop the profoundest forces ; but they will never fully realise their specific ideal intention within the range of our terrestrial conflicts."

" As little as any other power in this our world will they create the Kingdom of God on earth, as a completed social ethical organism : every idea will still be met by brutal facts, every upward development by interior and exterior checks. There exists no absolute Christian Ethic, still awaiting its first discovery; but only an overcoming of the changing situations of the world, as also the earlier Christian Ethic was not an absolute Christian Ethic, but only such an overcoming, in its own way. There exists also no absolute ethical transformation of material nature or of human nature, but only a wrestling with them both. Only doctrinaire idealists or religious fanatics can fail to recognise these facts. Faith is indeed the very sinews of the battle of life, but life does in very deed remain a battle ever renewed along ever new fronts. For every threatening abyss that is closed a new one yawns before us. The old truth remains true : the Kingdom of God is within us. But we must let our light shine before men in confident and ceaseless labour, that they may see our works and may praise our heavenly Father. The final ends of all humanity lie hidden within His hands " (pp. 985, 986).

Entire peoples clash in arms, gigantic industrial struggles pulse across continents and oceans, immense physical discoveries and inventions almost annihilate time and space. Yet engrossing, and deeply important (also and especially in their help or hindrance to our moral and spiritual upbuilding and faith) as are these wild, vast, fleeting things all around us, it is not they, but it is this upbuilding and this faith, it is the ultimate Realities which they touch, which indeed penetrate and occasion them, that are the greater and the greatest things experienced by man. And even simply as the utterances of one who, amidst the amazing distractions of our times, steadily perceives and proclaims this abiding pre-eminence of religion, Troeltsch's writings stand amongst the most impressive, because most circumspect and veracious, testimonies to the indestructible need and conviction that the human mind and conscience, still, at bottom, can find rest alone in God, its home.

7

WHAT DO WE MEAN BY HEAVEN?
AND WHAT DO WE MEAN BY HELL?[1]

SOME sixty years after our Lord's death upon the Cross, one of the deepest of Jewish religious writers, yet one who, even then, knew not the historic Jesus, or reached not in Him the Christ, wrote the so-called Fourth Book of Ezra. And there God, in the person of the Angel, says to Ezra : " Just as the husband-man sows much seed in the ground, and yet not all the seeds which were sown shall be saved in due season ; so also they that are sown in the world shall not all be saved." And Ezra answers : " The husbandman's seed, if it come not up, perishes ; but the son of man, who has been fashioned with thine own hands like thine own image . . . hast thou likened him to the seed of the husbandman ? " And God in His reply assures Ezra : " Thou comest far short of being able to love my creation more than I." These very facts, problems, difficulties remain with us still ; and we have to face them in this article. Yet many other points as to the After Life must be passed over by us—such as the reasons for holding any immortality of man's soul or personality at all. I will simply assume throughout the discussion that our two questions are asked by men who are already convinced of the reality of some kind of After Life ; and who, besides, accept the historic reality and the character of Jesus and the trend and implications of His teaching. I take our questioners to accept all these religious facts as true and as the deepest revelation and test of true religion, especially as these facts appear in the Synoptic Gospels, as they have awakened, directed and purified the spiritual needs and hunger of the most inclusive Christian souls, and as they have, in return,

[1] An Address delivered to the Religious Thought Society of London in February, 1917. Reprinted from the *Church Quarterly Review*, April, 1917.

been articulated and expanded by these same souls. All this, then, shall be for us here the true type and test of the fuller and fullest spiritual apprehension of our questions and of the answers to them.

Nevertheless, to be at all clear and fruitful concerning the two great subjects here confronted, I must, first, describe shortly the method which I believe alone capable of furnishing solid and sober results ; and I must, secondly and as shortly, eliminate certain peripheral problems which, if left uneliminated, would give our direct subject-matters, and our conclusions concerning them, an appearance which I do not believe them intrinsically to possess. Our direct subject-matters again will require some general considerations before we can articulate our ultimate proposals. I will group all I have to say within five sections— two introductory and three containing the direct effort.

I

It is most understandable, yet none the less regrettable for us who approach the After Life problems from within religion and for religion, that two attitudes and activities of mind, as to these very problems, frequently attract—distract—the soul whilst still religiously unsettled, and (I believe in practically all cases) gravely arrest or deflect its still dim and groping religious insight. The first of these attitudes concerns the content of the Future Life ; the second concerns the evidences for a Future Life. By the first attitude, the Future Life is desired and conceived as simply a prolongation of this our earthly life, less its pain and (usually) its grossness. In this way of course, and only in this way, can we men fully picture a Future Life at all—it thus is just merely a continuation of this life, with all within it that is attractive to our average tastes in our average moments. And by the second attitude we seek the evidence for the reality of this continuance in intimations which are somehow to be gained from the very persons, thus still thoroughly their old selves, who are now living in the Beyond. And these two attitudes usually go together.

It is certainly, at first sight, very remarkable that the fantastic

abnormality of the form and method, which characterises all
animistic and spiritualist practices, should habitually yield so
less than a normal, so shrunken, banal, and boring a content.
Yet such a method cannot fail to reach no further than this very
little distance.

The simple fact, assuredly, is that the soul, *qua* religious, has
no interest in just simple unending existence, of no matter
what kind or of a merely natural kind—an existence with God
at most as the dim background to a vivid experience of its own
unending natural existence. The specifically religious desire
of Immortality begins, not with Immortality, but with God;
it rests upon God; and it ends in God. The religious soul
does not seek, find or assume its own Immortality; and thereupon seek, find, or assume God. But it seeks, finds, experiences,
and loves God; and because of God, and of this, its very real
though still very imperfect, intercourse with God—because of
these experiences which lie right within the noblest joys, fears,
hopes, necessities, certainties which emerge within any and
every field of its life here below—it finds, rather than seeks,
Immortality of a certain kind. The very slow but solidly sure,
the very sober but severely spiritual, growth of the belief in
Immortality amongst the Jews, a belief fully endorsed and
greatly developed by our Lord, was entirely thus—not from
Immortality of no matter what kind to God, but from God to a
special kind of Immortality. Especially does Christ always keep
God and the Kingdom of God central, as the beginning and end
of all, and the Immortality peripheral, as but the extension and
full establishment of the soul's supernatural union with, and
of its supernatural activity towards, God and man.

And let us carefully note: such a method does not leave us
empty of any vivid and experienced content for our conception
of the Future Life. Quite the contrary: for no experiences are
so real, none, in a way, are so well understood by the experiencing
soul, as are its supernatural experiences. By supernatural we
here mean nothing preternatural, nothing even essentially
miraculous, nothing that men, who are at all complete according
to man's supernatural call and awakeness, cannot, or do not,
experience. We mean, on the contrary, acts, experiences,
necessities which, though distinct, not only from all evil but

also from all simply natural goodness, are nevertheless acts, experiences, necessities found scattered about amongst the specific qualities and ends of nature. And these acts, experiences, necessities are such that men at large, in their nobler and noblest moments, cannot help saluting and revering them. And, again, this Supernaturalness does not concern Goodness alone, but also Truth and Beauty. God is the Fountain and the Fullness, the Origin and the End, the ultimate Measure of every kind and degree, as much of Beauty and of Truth as of Goodness. Hence wheresoever there are acts, experiences, necessities of sheer self-surrender, in the deepest search and work within the visible and temporal, the contingent and relative, to the Invisible, the Eternal, and the Unconditional: wheresoever such self-surrender is from those temporalities, apprehended as such, to these Eternities, accepted, adored as such : there is the Super-natural. Walter Bagehot, in his great study of Bishop Butler, finds two kinds of religion—that which looks out upon the world, especially the starlit heavens, and finds there God in their beauty; and that which looks within upon the human soul itself, especially the conscience, and finds here God in its sublimity; Bagehot calls the former Natural, the latter Supernatural. But I plead here for a conviction which finds the Natural (including a certain Natural Religion) in the looking within, and in the acceptance of, conscience, as well as in the looking outwards, and in the belief in beauty ; and which, again, finds the Super-natural—Supernatural Religion—within both these same move-ments and materials. So long as either movement and conviction is primarily busy with the beauty, the truth or the goodness simply in their particular forms, and only vaguely or derivatively assumes or implies their unconditional claim upon the soul, you have Nature. So soon as either movement and conviction attains to a central occupation with the Abidingness, the Non-contingency, of the Beauty, the Truth or the Goodness thus partially revealed and to a recognition of their right to the unlimited service of the observer, you have Supernature.

We have thus to discriminate, not simply between Evil and Good, but also between Good and Good—between Natural Good and Supernatural Good. Both these Goods come from God ; both are operative—in different proportions and in greatly different degrees and ways—in all normal, adult and awake human beings; and each, as we shall see, variously requires the other, and variously participates in Heaven itself.

The morality of honest barter, of moderate living; the requirements of the counting-house, the law-courts, the State; Confucius, Bentham: such moralities, institutions, persons, in their general and positive trend and in their prevalent acceptance, are assuredly good and necessary, but they are natural. Such moralities, institutions, persons, we may wish to last for ever; but they do not, of themselves, suggest or require the heightened consciousness, the closer and closest intercourse with God, the reaching, in Him, of the ultimate, living Beauty, Truth and Goodness, which the religious soul seeks when it seeks Immortal Life. And let us note—it is not the absence of any explicitly religious reference that stamps these "natural" things and persons as only naturally good. The reference, in such persons, if not to God or to a God, then at least to their consciences, is fairly constant; yet we cannot well count all that is thus referred as supernatural. And the reference in Judaism and Unitarianism to God is continual, and undoubtedly constitutes even the average of these positions as, at the least, Natural Religions. Yet it can fairly be maintained that the reference is here largely dry and distant, and is then to God rather as the supreme rule and reward of average earthly honesty, decency and justice, than as the deepest meaning and the final assuagement of the soul's thirst for more and other than these things.

For assuredly there are certain other acts, dispositions, strivings, of individual souls, and there are certain other ideals and best achievements of certain institutions, which essentially transcend the character, standard and instruments of the Naturally Good. The deepest of the Jewish Psalms, the Seer whose vision of the Suffering Servant of Jehovah is incorporated in the Book of Isaiah, the serenely self-oblivious prayer of Stephen, the deacon, for his enemies whilst they stone him to death; above all, Christ's entire life and work, crowned by the forgiveness of His crucifiers even as He hangs upon the Cross, are the great and the greatest, the most fully explicit, instances of the Supernaturally Good. But indeed, off and on, here and there, sooner

or later, we can find, within the larger human groups and during
the longer human periods, some lives, some acts, not all different
to those acts and lives — at least some touches, some desires
for some such lives and some such acts. And if such acts or
desires never and nowhere occurred within an entire race of
men or within an entire age of the world, then that race and that
age would, already by this alone, stand revealed as less than what
man actually is—a being natural in his constitution yet variously
solicited and sustained by supernatural influences, requirements,
helps and aims. The Christian Church, at all times in its indestructible ideal, and indeed always in its fullest and fairest
fruits, has been and abides the special training ground, home, and
inspirer of this supernatural spirit. Our Lord's Beatitudes are
its classical expression, and the Feast of All Saints is the peren-
nially touching commemoration of its countless manifestations
in every age, clime, race, and religious environment.

Now the specifically religious desire for Immortality is a
desire, not only for the continuance of such supernatural acts
and dispositions, and for the continuance of the soul, in so far
as thus acting and disposed, but for the final establishment of
the soul in a world of powers, acts and persons truly adequate
to such supernaturalness. Here below, this our visible world
of time and space suffices for the naturally good acts and the
naturally good soul. Heaven is not a necessary environment
for not cheating in the sale of peas or potatoes, for not smashing
street lamps, for not telling calumnies against one's wife or
brother. But only Heaven furnishes the adequate environment
for the elevation and expansion of spirit of a Damian, when he,
here below, devoted himself to sure leprosy for the sake of his
outcast fellow-creatures ; of a Joan of Arc, when, in the France
of her day, she reaped her short earthly success and her swiftly
following witch's death ; or of the average trooper on the
Birkenhead going down, without moving, at attention, with the
women and children being saved alive before his eyes in those
boats where he was deliberately refusing to take a place at the
cost of others, many of whom had no special claim upon himself. Indeed all of us have ourselves witnessed, or have learnt
from eye-witnesses, deeds or dispositions of a similar quality.
Humanity will never, universally or permanently, treat such acts

as folly, or indeed as anything less than the very flower of life. Yet to claim that the Trades Union, or a Political or Social Party, or the State, should or could, or ever wisely will, require such things, or directly work for them, is assuredly quixotic. Such a demand or hope can only lead to a dangerous Utopia, followed by a not less dangerous reaction. Thus such heroic goodness points to a Beyond, as indeed does all philosophical research, all scientific work, all artistic effort—whensoever these endeavours penetrate deeper than a certain superficial and conventional level. All such heroic, self-oblivious search and reception of Truth and Beauty, as possessing the right to such self-surrender, appear as special divine gifts rather than as mere human efforts, as glimpses of realities which, for their adequate environment and apprehension, require, not this world and this life, but another life and another world.

II

We have so far spoken as though Heaven and Hell were the sole, not only ultimate, but also immediate, alternatives for every man moved by, and called to, Supernature ; and, still more, we have let it appear as though the call of the human race in general to such Supernature involved, of necessity, the call of every individual belonging to that race, to this same Supernature. We must now make some important distinctions in both these positions—for we cannot, if we do hold a Heaven and a Hell in the full sense of the terms, escape, I am confident, from acceptance of some kind of Purgatory, and of some kind of Limbo.

As concerns the supernaturally awakened souls, we cannot, surely, conceive the majority of these to be, when they die, immediately fit for Heaven, even if they be not really fit for Hell. Yet we are often reminded of certain spiritual facts which seem to rule out any intermediate state. Thus we are told that it is not Christian, nor even deeply religious in general, to think of man as ever truly owing his salvation to his own merits ; he can, in strictness, owe such salvation only to the generosity and gift of God—indeed the very power to merit at all is a pure

grace of God—as pure as is man's creation. Conformably with
this it is insisted that the commencement, the continuation, the
crowning of any soul's supernatural life, is through and through
rendered possible only by God and His grace ; and that it never
becomes actual without the active aid of the same God and grace.
Thus all supernaturally awakened souls, however free from sin,
whether original or actual, we may suppose them, attain (at
least on one ground entirely common to them all—their original
nothingness) to Heaven through God's gift and mercy. To this
is added the further contention that this gift and mercy is specially abundant in the case of those supernaturally awakened souls
which die with sinful or imperfect habits and attachments still
clinging to them, and which, nevertheless, attain to Heaven.
And it is then asked, if all this be really so, what need there is
of an Intermediate State at all.

The answer surely is that we who are still on this side of the
veil, have direct and real knowledge of the manner in which
God's grace and mercy operate, even though in this life only ;
and that, in this life, these gifts usually obey certain general
laws of their own. We are able roughly to follow some of the
main outlines of these orderings by God Himself of God's own
generosities and gifts. We see how, in this our earthly time at
least, every impure thought, untrue word or cruel act, every
cowardly shrinking from the usually costly docility to our own
best insight and special grace, relax or stain, or harden or deflect,
our own inclinations, habits, and acts, even more certainly than
they similarly affect our influences and achievements in the
world at large. We note how even sincere, and fairly deep,
repentance for any one evil action, no more removes all such
inward effects of this action than it removes all the outward
effects of the same action. Thus I regret certain acts of gambling,
I even cease to gamble ; but this does not, of necessity, eradicate
certain inclinations to gamble fully willed by me before and half
willed by me still ; it does not eliminate the entire gambling
habit, any more than it restores to my bank, or to my creditor
friends, the moneys I have gambled away from them. My
repentance, at any degree of depth, will be a grace of God
through Christ to me ; yet this repentance and grace, unless it
be of the deepest kind—an act of Pure Love as it was with the

Good Thief on Calvary on Good Friday—will still leave me with variously imperfect habits and inclinations. These habits and inclinations, again, will be rectified within me, by the grace of God and Christ ; but this grace will, in most cases, work slowly within innumerable new acts of mine, acts contrary in character to those old habits, and within a long self-discipline which now, step by step, retraces the previous long self-dissipation of the soul. Purgatory is thus, so far at least, a sheer fact for the soul in its relation to God during this life. But it is not reasonable to assume a radical change or supersession of so fundamental a spiritual law at the death of the body, except under the constraint of some very definite and unanswerable reason. Such a reason is not forthcoming. And hence I can find no serious ground to deny the reality of a similar Purgatory for the same soul in face of the same God in the other life. And if Purgatory exists also in the Beyond, then most of the supernaturally called souls will presumably go, at death, not to Hell, nor, in the first instance, to Heaven, but, first of all, to Purgatory.

As concerns mankind at large, we have certain general facts of human existence and of life in general, and certain ordinary teachings of theologians, which appear to indicate that many, possibly most, individual human souls do not attain to the supernatural call, choice, and consequences—that Heaven or Hell can be as little their actual final end, as Purgatory can be their immediate destination. Three large considerations seem to show that this is actually the case in the realm of human souls ; that it is in full parallel with other ranges and stages of observable life ; and that it is in no wise cruel or unjust.

This position appears to state an actual fact. For the majority of human beings (if we take the life of the soul to begin at the moment of the conception of the corresponding body) die before they attain the age of reason. If we take seriously even the fundamental lines, the general trend, of the Christian outlook, we must reject all reincarnation schemes ; and we must require, as the ordinary prerequisite for the supernatural call of any individual soul, the mental and volitional awakeness of this soul. True, the doctrine and practice of Infant Baptism raise a difficulty here. But Infant Baptism admittedly reaches only a small minority of the cases in question, if the human soul is infused into its corresponding body at the moment of this body's conception ; and if, of the human beings who attain to birth at all, much the greater number of those dying in infancy die without Baptism. And again, Baptism is held to extend to the infant the spiritual life of the Christian Church at large, and this spiritual life in the Church at large is, at the time of the baptism of the spiritually slumbering infant, possessed and practised by souls mentally and volitionally awake. And finally, the effects of such Baptism, if the infant dies in infancy, are different in degree from the effects of this same Baptism, if this baptised soul attains to maturity. Theologians have, since many a day, admitted that unbaptised infants live in the Beyond a life of natural happiness—a sort of prolongation of the happiness of children here below, less their physical sufferings, and less any supernatural experiences which may be traceable in most of them from about seven years of age onwards. Thus souls that depart this life as infants, though they be unbaptised, do not go to Hell. But souls that pass into the Beyond as infants, if they be baptised, attain indeed to Heaven, yet to a far lesser degree of the supernatural beatitude than do souls which have struggled long and much in and for the supernatural life here below, and which have died substantially fit for Heaven at last, even though they be in need of a long Purgatory first.

Some such position is also alone parallel to the facts observable in all the other ranges and levels of life known to us in any detail. Thus all wheat-seeds, all lily bulbs, all acorns contain the elementary materials and structures of richly fruitful wheat-plants, exquisitely tinted blossoms, and broad-spreading oak trees ; their respective species are intended to reach, and actually do reach, in some fortunate representatives, this consummation : yet of these individual seeds, bulbs, acorns, not one in a hundred, or even less, attains to this full end of its species. So again with insects, fishes, birds, mammals : the proportion of individuals that actually attain to the full development, ideally intended for each and all, is astonishingly small. Thus, from the smallest moss or lichen up to man, we find everywhere, even though in a lesser and lesser degree, the distinction between the carefulness as to the type and species, and the apparently careless profusion as to the individual incorporations of the type. And hence life, in its manifold degrees and kinds, witnesses distinctly against any belief that mankind, and mankind alone within the world of creatures well known to us, reaches, in every individual man, the fullness of its natural and supernatural call. } *supernat. call*

And finally, the position here defended cannot justly be charged with imputing cruelty or injustice to God. For the souls that attain only to natural felicity have, *ex hypothesi*, never known the solicitations of the supernatural; all their actual, or even latent individual consciousness and needs are fulfilled within their own special kind and degree—a thing thoroughly possible, if, as we have already contended, Nature and Supernature are not one and the same call and condition, but two. Thus these souls are not the less fully happy because other human souls hunger and thirst after a higher and deeper, a different life; or because these other souls are satiated with a correspondingly different happiness. A man with much salt in his mouth requires much more drink to slake his thirst than does the man who has never tasted salt; the thirst of the man untouched by salt is slaked by a small glassful of water, the thirst of the man aroused by salt is not appeased by less liquid than a bucketful. And if we take the difference between the two classes of souls objectively, we find that the two calls and ends are largely balanced by the fact that the supernatural call and end usually involves spiritual struggles, sacrifices, dangers, profound alternatives, whilst the natural call and end is always devoid of all supernatural pains and perils.

III

We stand now before the problem of Heaven and Hell properly so called, the final supernatural alternatives of the supernaturally awakened soul. Yet, here again, we must first clear away three very prevalent objections and misapprehensions. Let us move from the more general to the more particular difficulties.

First and foremost, then, we have to confront the opinion, increasingly prevalent in Western Europe since the beginning of the eighteenth century, one which now pervades fairly all the non-religious, and even much of the religious, thought of

H

our day—that the conception of Heaven is, in substance, beautiful, or at least true, or at the very least harmless ; but that any and every conception of Hell is essentially hideous, or at all events unreasonable, or at the very least most dangerous and noxious. Thus serious scholars attempt to prove that our Lord's utterances as to Hell are all due to misconceptions of His disciples, or even to amplifications by writers who had not heard His words ; or, again, that these utterances, if really proceeding from our Lord Himself, only continue, without any special verification or emphasis, certain already prevalent opinions— that they have no organic connexion with the roots of His revelation and message. Thus, too, otherwise helpful religious philosophers reduce Hell to a long Purgatory, or simply to a rhetorical or emotional expression (perceived or not perceived by our Lord Himself to be only such) for a correct and indeed noble sense of the intrinsic difference between right and wrong and of the correspondingly intrinsic differences between the respective consequences of right and of wrong—differences which are really outside of time and space, but which can only be described, at all vividly, in temporal and spatial pictures. The net result of all such teachings (quite apart from the still more prevalent and insidious Pantheistic tendencies of our time) is at the least to emphasise the conviction of Mother Julian of Norwich that " all will be well," whilst the teaching of Christ and of His Church will nevertheless turn out to have been true ; or, more boldly, to welcome back, as alone satisfactory, the notions, not of Origen himself, but of some Origenists, as to the eventual Restitution of All Things—of all souls; or, again, quite generally, to treat as a barbarous, impertinent irruption into our superior insight and humanity, not only the applications and details, but the very substance, of the convictions of Tertullian, St. Augustine and Dante. What can we adduce against such a denial?

We must first of all remember our discrimination—that the question concerning the final destination of man, as such, is not identical with the question concerning the final condition of particular human beings. Hence it is quite beside the mark to bring up the cases of little children, of idiots, of pure savages. We must also not forget that there need be no real question of

Hell even for the majority of the supernaturally awakened souls, if there actually exists a state and process of purgation in the Beyond, as there undoubtedly exists such a state and process here. Yet these provisos do not eliminate the real possibility of Hell, as the general rule, wheresoever is a real possibility of Heaven ; they leave Heaven and Hell as a generally inter-related couple.

We must next try vividly to realise the fact that it is not Hell which is so much more difficult to believe in than is Heaven ; but that it is the entire specifically spiritual conception of man, of his deepest self, which is difficult, as contrasted with the naturalistic view of these same things. The purely naturalistic view of man conceives him as a mere superior animal, which projects its own largely fantastic wishes on to the void or the unknown, and which then fishes them back as objective realities distinct from itself their true creator. And this view is the more plausible, the more quickly statable, the more vividly picturable, the alone readily transmittable, view. But then, the view has all these qualities, precisely because it stops short at the surface-impressions of things, and remains utterly inadequate to all the deeper and deepest implications, requirements and ends of knowledge in general, and of art, ethics, philosophy and religion in particular. Yet as soon as we hold the difference between various kinds of human acts and dispositions to be always potentially, and often actually, of essential, of ultimate, of more than simply social, simply human importance, we are insisting upon values and realities that essentially transcend space and even time. Every at all noble, every even tolerably adequate, outlook always possesses some such more than merely empirical, simply contingent, or purely material and mechanical character. Plato, the Stoics, Plotinus possess this outlook, although in very different degrees ; it ruled the Western world, during the Christian Middle Ages ; and, after the largely negative rationality of most of the Renaissance, it gave its note of pathetic distinction and splendour to the great spirit of Spinoza, gravely cramped by Pantheism though it was in its speculation. In Kant it again reappears in a more theistic setting, and with the deep perception of that deep fact—radical evil—of man's frequent declaring, willing and doing what he well knows to be false

and bad, but pleasant ; in Schopenhauer it relieves the general
pessimistic oppression with glimpses of a Beauty abiding and
all-sustaining. And now, in these our times, we are again coming,
in different lands and from different experiences and starting-
points, to schemes really adequate, indeed deeply friendly, to
this Transcendence present in all our nobler aspirations, acts and
ends. Thus every profound search after, or belief in, the fundamental truth or essential beauty or satisfying goodness of anything—when we press it duly home and sincerely and delicately
analyse it—overflows the ordinary, superficially obvious, requirements of man's knowledge, action, life. In each case we get
a scheme that looks too big and too ambitious for us little men,
and that involves alternatives too wide and deep for the average
moments of the average mortal.

We have then, for our purpose, only to ask whether the
alternatives—Heaven, Hell—are like or are unlike these ultimate
implications of man's deepest needs and aspirations, elevations
and falls. And the answer will assuredly be : " They are not
unlike, but like."

We shall, I believe, be driven to such a general conclusion,
if and when we dwell upon our memories of men we have known
at all well and long and in sufficient numbers, even though
these men may have belonged to classes and callings least
supernaturally attempered at a first appearance. Thus I look
back to my eight friends, the horse bus drivers, in a northern
suburb of London. There was their patriarch, Johnnie D., of
the grey top hat, so humorously irritated by " them Belgiums,"
when these white Flemish horses answered so languidly to his
whip. " Don't you ever trust an 'orse dealer," he advised me,
" all 'orse dealers is rogues. Ought to know : me own father was
an 'orse dealer." There was William D., who would dare his
conductor there and then to tell how many shoulders and legs
of mutton were passing when droves of sheep passed by ; and
who bred canaries in his spare time. " Me eldest lad sings that
beautiful in the Wesleyan Chapel choir. Sorry he will not take
to the slaughterin'—me own line at first. Strange, for he's that
fond o' animals." There was the Scotchman R. " See this 'and
o' mine ? Writes a beautiful 'and—always did. Got all the
prizes at school. Always steady, lad and man." And there was

Travel.

the red-haired young Orange Irishman William S., impulsive, improvident, humorous, humble, sweet. " Look at that Salvation Army old saint there ; 'ave known 'im established above all sin and fallin' exactly sixteen times." " I sits on this box up to midnight, Sir, these foggy November nights, I drinks lots o' beer—it lies that 'eavy, cold, cold upon me chest ; Doctor says it'll ruin me." I saw him dying in a little, quiet room. " Is there anything you want, S. ? " " Nothing, Sir : they've kindly found a mangle for me wife, and the children is all took by good people. And yet—yes, there *is* a thing I miss ; I wish that here, from me bed, I could hear the old bus go by."

The lethargic white old " Belgiums " have long since ceased to drag the heavy old bus up that hill—their bones lie some-where utterly forgotten. Johnnie D. himself has gone, I know ; perhaps also the whilom slaughterer and the self-complacent steady Scotchman have already followed Johnnie, so thoroughly English in character, and the touching, drinking Irishman. Yet even during those years when these men so much refreshed me with their spontaneity, sincerity and simplicity, and still more now when I look back upon what I learnt from these my friends, I saw and felt, I see and feel, that not a little of the supernatural was working variously, indirectly, hiddenly, yet most really, also here. " *Non omnis moriar,*" wrote the polished Horace, thinking only of his poetry ; they have not, they could not, altogether die—not their works, but they, their own selves—these my humble, humorous fellows, touched, sweetened, widened, deepened, as they were, by our common supernatural call and lot, so far beyond their own power to articulate even what they already were, still less what at times they longed to become.

And we must finally consider the character of our Lord's outlook as a whole. As to this point, we not only find certain texts in the Synoptic Gospels which directly teach Hell and which put it in simple parallel with Heaven ; but (an even more conclusive fact) we can clearly trace, throughout our Lord's teachings, the keen conviction, and the austere inculcation of the conviction, that the spiritual life is a great, all-important alternative and choice—a choice once for all, with consequences final and immense. The entire *texture* and implications of

Jesus's outlook require such choice within this one earthly life
on the part of supernaturally awakened souls, and such abidingness of the results of this their choice. " What does it profit a
man if he gain the whole world and suffer the loss of his own
soul ? "—is but an example of what runs (as implication, allusion,
pathos, entreaty, menace), throughout the whole of our Lord's
teaching in proportion as, especially in its second stage, this
teaching is continuously busy with man's supernatural call and
the strenuous conditions and severe consequences of this call.

Only two serious objections can, I believe, be raised against
this contention that our Lord Himself unequivocally taught the
doctrine of fundamental alternatives and abiding consequences.
The one objection is derived from an analysis and grouping of
the Synoptic texts, the other is drawn from the doctrine of St.
Paul.

As to the Synoptists, such serious scholars as the late Dr. H. J.
Holtzmann and many others distinguish between a series of
very simple sayings and parables, which reproduce our Lord's
direct teachings, and the great or complicated pictures and
similes, which are so many developments, by the primitive
Christian community and writers, of certain elements or adumbrations of our Lord's own doctrine. And only in these latter
pictures—such as Christ the King separating the sheep from
the goats at the Last Judgment (St. Matt. xxv. 31–46)—do
these scholars find any direct parallel contrast between the saved
and the lost, and any explicit insistence upon the abidingness
of the condition of the lost as balancing the abidingness of the
condition of the saved. Nevertheless, even the passages thus still
accepted as fully primitive are, I submit, quite sufficient for our
purpose ; since, interpreted otherwise than as involving the
conviction of abiding consequences, these sayings, so assuredly
strenuous and austere, lose all their specific point and poignancy.
Thus we are still told of " the Father which seeth in secret,
who shall reward openly "—who will forgive, or who will not
forgive, men's trespasses against Himself, according as men
forgive, or do not forgive, their fellow-men's trespasses against
themselves (St. Matt. vi. 4, 6, 18 ; vi. 14, 15). We are still
warned " Fear not them which kill the body, but are not able
to kill the soul ; but rather fear him which is able to destroy

both soul and body in hell " (St. Matt. x. 20). We still hear the solemn woes pronounced against the unbelieving cities—of the great straits that await them at the Day of Judgment (St. Matt. xi. 21–24 ; xxiii. 37, 38). Jesus still insists that He has come to divide a man from his father, and a daughter from her mother, and that only " he that loseth his life for my sake shall find it " (St. Matt. xi. 35–39) ; and, again, that at the Day of Judgment, " two shall be in the field " or " grinding at the mill "—" one shall be taken and the other left " (St. Matt. xxv. 40, 41). He still exhorts us to cut off hand or foot, or to pluck out an eye, rather than be cast with both our hands or feet or eyes into Hell (St. Mark ix. 43–48). He still proclaims that " he that is not with me is against me " (St. Matt. xii. 30) ; and He still declares that there exists a sin against the Spirit of God which cannot be forgiven (St. Luke xii. 10 and the parallels). And we have still the parables of the Two Houses built respectively on the rock and on the sand, and resulting respectively in persistent safety and in utter ruin ; of the Unjust Steward ; of the Talents ; of the Men at the Door asking admittance, when it is too late, from the master of the house (St. Luke xiii. 24–30) ; and of the Wise and Foolish Virgins. All these parables teach the same lesson and possess the same implications. And indeed Hell and its endlessness appear, explicitly and repeatedly, in these parables, as they also do in the corresponding series of sayings.[1]

As to St. Paul, it is true that we have, in the magnificent chapter fifteen of the First Epistle to the Corinthians, an account of the resurrection followed by an unending condition, which appears to say nothing as to the fate of unfaithful human souls, and which, indeed, contains passages that have been repeatedly interpreted in the sense of a Final Restitution of All Things, such as was held by some Origenists. Yet every close and careful analysis of this chapter and of St. Paul's other long and highly technical doctrinal expositions shows clearly that nothing is said here as to the fate of human sinners, simply because St. Paul is busy here with our Lord's resurrection, and with the fate of those human souls which have faithfully conformed themselves to His life. Indeed, in such severely speculative passages St. Paul

---

[1] See H. J. Holtzmann, *Lehrbuch der Neutestamentlichen Theologie*, edition 1911, vol. i., pp. 392–95.

does not apparently hold a resurrection of the wicked, nor a subsequent life, whether temporary or unending, for such persons, at all. The just have, during their earthly life, chosen in favour of the Spirit and the Body; and hence they live, and are raised to full life, for ever, with and through these powers—the ever living Spirit and the ever vivifiable Body. The wicked have chosen in favour of the Psyche (the Animal Soul) and the Flesh ; and hence they die altogether, with these essentially deadly and mortal powers. Hence, even if this be the sense of these speculative passages, St. Paul continues here the doctrine of Abiding Consequences ; only that the wicked here appear simply to cease to exist, as against the good who expand into the full life. Indeed St. Paul, when he is not thus developing a severely antithetic speculation, largely (as such) his own, speaks on this point, as he does also on other points, in close resemblance to our Lord's own sayings. For he declares that " we must all appear," or " be made manifest," " before the Judgment-seat of Christ, that everyone may receive the things done in his body —according to that he hath done, whether it be good or bad " (2 Cor. v. 10). And in that very chapter fifteen of the First to the Corinthians, Christ, at the end, " puts down all rule and all authority and power " (v. 24)—doubtless, hostile spirits, which are thus not changed in their willings, but are simply overruled and rendered innocuous henceforth. And assuredly the finish here " that God may be all in all " (v. 28), refers to the relations between Christ with His Saints and God the Father, and has nothing to do with any question as to God's presence and operation elsewhere. Thus this chapter no more teaches the Restitution of All Things, than this doctrine is meant by the terms *palingenesia* (" new birth ") of St. Matt. xix. 28, or *apokatastasis panton* (" restitution of all things ") of Acts iii. 21, passages which merely signify the restoration of the full divine order at the end of the world—an order which includes the subjection, but not the salvation, of the godless.

Thus we confront the impressive fact that throughout the New Testament there is nowhere a denial or ignoring, but there is everywhere an affirmation or implication, of man's life here below as a choice between immense alternatives furnished with corresponding abiding consequences.

Primitive Buddhism could not have existed without the conviction of the dizzying " Wheel of Life," as the starting-point
of that creed ; or without *Nirvana*, as the goal of the same creed :
and Wheel and *Nirvana* each there postulate the other ; only
together do they constitute that Buddhism. But Christianity,
whether primitive or in any conceivable form which may still
leave it essentially Christian, could not coexist with the conviction
of the " Wheel of Life "—with any reincarnation scheme ; or
with a *Nirvana* of any kind. For here, instead of a passive
resignation and despair, is an active choice and hope ; and this
because here, instead of an utterly flowing and chaotic Nature
and of the soul fascinated by all this flow and chaos, there is an
abiding, a wise and loving God behind Nature, itself seen as
largely a cosmos, and there is, in front of this Nature, the
persistence, self-identity, personality of the individual soul.

We must then retain choice and alternative as at the very
centre of the Christian outlook—at least as regards supernaturally awake souls. Yet we must equally guard this alternative
against a certain exclusiveness and against a certain excess.

We must guard against excluding all Nature from Heaven.
Man, without a certain amount of Nature as his substratum,
would cease to be a creature at all, and would be God ; and man
without a certain amount of his own human nature would cease
to be a man at all, and would be really an angel or some other
non-human creature. And yet it is certain that man is to save
or to lose his soul, to be in Heaven or in Hell, assuredly not as
God, yet also not as angel, but as man. We certainly do not
know precisely how much of the Nature of man will be thus
preserved, and with what expansions, perfectionings, utilisations.
Indeed the general questions as to how a disembodied soul can,
as such, experience anything or can act at all ; or, again, how
it can refashion a body sufficiently spiritual to be serviceable
there, and yet sufficiently material to be at all identical with its
former body *here*, are full of difficulties. Yet we can easily show
that the entire Christian outlook requires such a preservation
of a certain substratum of Nature, and indeed some kind and
degree of resurrection of the body. For Nature, in this outlook,
is, as to its essentials, good in and for itself ; and it is still better
in and for Supernature. " Grace does not abolish Nature, but

*H

perfects it " is the fundamental axiom of all the teaching of
Aquinas. And hence, as leavened bread cannot exist without the
meal, or salt water without the salt ; this particular bread, without this its particular meal, and this particular salt water, without
this its particular salt : so neither can supernaturalised man exist
without human nature ; this particular man, without this his
particular Nature. Thus in Heaven each soul will retain the
essentials of its particular Nature, expanded, completed, elevated
by its particular Supernature, as this Supernature has now and
there found its final form and fullness. And thus again, there will
not, indeed, exist in Heaven husbands and wives, parents and
children, brothers and sisters, and the other sweet relationships
of earth, just simply as such, and merely because they existed
upon earth. And yet not one of these, or of any other naturally
good, relationships, but will continue substantially in Heaven,
in so far as this relationship has become the essential natural
material of our supernatural life here on earth, and in so far as
it thus requires to continue as the essential natural substratum
of our full supernatural life in Heaven. Hence, if truly transfigured by grace already here, these relationships can and will
continue, in their substance, fully and finally transfigured,
there. And thus the sweetness of Nature, the severity of the
Choice, and the serenity of Heaven all appear very really each
to fit the other.

And we must guard against a certain excess of contrast. Evil,
and the evil effects of Evil, are, indeed, not the mere absence
of Good and of the good effects of Good ; Evil is in truth a
force and positive—it is an actual perversion, and not an abolition,
of the efficacious will. Yet Evil and its effects are not as fully
and concentratedly evil, as Good and its effects are full and concentrated. If this were false, Manichæism would be true, and
Evil would fully balance Good. According to all Theism, and
especially all Christianity, the Good, if not sheerly all-powerful,
is, at the least, more powerful for good than is the Evil for evil.
No doubt, the absolute parallelism of form present in certain
of our Lord's declarations concerning Heaven and Hell, as these
are given in St. Mark and St. Matthew, and as they operate in
practically all the popular echoes and expansions of these declarations ever since their utterance, would, if pressed, rule out this

discrimination; yet such a discrimination cannot otherwise be seriously refuted from any sensitively Christian premisis. We shall thus indeed admit an Evil and a Suffering in the Lost, in correspondence to the respective Good and Happiness of the Saved; but we shall carefully guard against finding that Evil and Suffering to be as full and as concentrated as is this Good and Happiness.

IV

We are at last face to face with the special subject-matter of our quest. And we must, consequently, attempt to find and to describe the characteristics of our deepest experiences; and, in each instance, to contrast the fully willed and bliss-bringing acceptance, and the full refusal, with its pain and contraction, of this our profoundest call.

Our deepest spiritual experiences appear always to possess some or all of four qualities. And the contrasted effects, as respectively within the right disposition and the wrong disposition, seem to be as follows :

1) In our deepest moments here below, our experiences are least changeful and most constant; they are, in those moments, least successive and most nearly simultaneous. They thus come nearest to the character of God, and to an apprehension of that character. God is Pure Eternity, Sheer Simultaneity; the animal man is almost Pure Succession, indeed all but mere change; the spiritual man is, in proportion to his spirituality, More or Less Simultaneous.

We have every reason, then, to hold that these experiences, and their differences, apply also to the supernaturally awakened souls in the Beyond. The saved spirits will thus, according to the degree of their supernatural call and of their supernatural establishment within it, be quasi-simultaneous in their intelligence, feeling, volition, acts, effectuations. This their life will, at any one moment of its slow succession, be too rich and varied to require much succession for the unravelling of its capacities and acts. Indeed, this richness will be actually the richer for this quasi-simultaneity of its contents and gains; since thus the many connexions and contrasts between these many things will be very largely present together with the things themselves.

The lost spirits will persist, according to the degree of their permanent self-willed defection from their supernatural call, in the all but mere changingness, scatteredness, distractedness, variously characteristic of their self-elected earthly life. And owing to their past experience of the opposite conditions, and to their (still extant although diminished) consciousness of the supernatural call, they will feel the unsatisfactoriness of this their permanent non-recollection more than they felt it upon earth.

In our deepest moments here below, again, our greatest expansion and delight arises from our sense of contact, more or less close and vivid, with Realities not ourselves; in such moments we not simply reach truth—something abstract, something which we predominantly refer to the already developed tests and standard of our own minds—but Reality, some deeply concrete and living thing which enlarges our experiences of fact and indeed our thus experiencing souls themselves.

We have then, again, every reason to hold that these experiences, and their contrasted differences, will persist, greatly heightened, in the Beyond. The saved spirits will thus, according to the degree of their supernatural call and of their supernatural establishment, be supported, environed, penetrated by the Supreme Reality and by the keenest sense of this Reality. This sense of God,—of God as distinct from, previous to, independent of, our apprehension of Him—of God as self-revealing and self-giving, will evoke continuous acts and habits—an entire state—of a responsive self-givingness in the soul itself. The great Divine Ecstasy will evoke and be met by the little human ecstasy. Not primarily, this, a self-consciousness of the soul, with a more or less dim or even hypothetic reference to, or assumption of, God derivatively attached thereto; but the sense of God and of the joy in Him, central and supreme, and the sense of the self, chiefly as of the channel for, the recipient of, and the response to, all this Divine Reality, Joy and Life.

The lost spirits will persist, according to the degree of their permanent self-willed defection from their supernatural call, in the varyingly all but complete self-centredness and sub-

jectivity of their self-elected earthly life. But now they will feel,
far more fully than they ever felt on earth, the stuntedness, the
self-mutilation, the imprisonment involved in this their endless
self-occupation and jealous evasion of all reality not simply their
own selves.

3) In our deepest moments, once more, we reach the fullest
sense of our membership of the social human organism, of our
possessing a fruitful action upon it precisely because of this
our glad acceptance of our special little place within the great
family of the thinkers, workers, sufferers, achievers amongst our
fellows in the long past and in the wide present. We have, then,
no reason to doubt that, in the Beyond, these experiences and
their contrasted differences will obtain—and in still greater
measure.

The saved spirits, then, will receive, exercise, enjoy, aid, and
complete a richly various, deep and tender, social life with
fellow souls. And as the intercourse of these spirits with God
is not simply mental or abstractly contemplative, but quite as
much emotional, volitional, active, efficacious ; so also this their
intercourse with the fellow souls is mental, emotional, volitional,
active, efficacious. And the quasi-simultaneity, and the deep
sense of and delight in realities, which we have already found so
strongly to characterise these saved spirits, will doubtless penetrate and enrich this their social joy. For thus they will profoundly perceive, feel and will themselves as just parts, special
parts, of this great social whole ; and they will profoundly see, feel
and will themselves, as greatly surpassed in sanctity by innumerable other souls. The joy in the rich interconnexion and various
supplementation between these countlessly different souls, and
the joy in reality—realities other and far fuller than themselves,
will thus add to the bliss and the fruitfulness, outwards and
inwards, which spring from the social experience and activity
of the saved.

The lost spirits will persist, according to the degree of their
permanent defection, in their claimfulness and envious self-
isolation, in their niggardly pain at the sight or thought of the
unmatchable greatness and goodness of other souls. But now
the disharmony of all this with their own past better experiences
and their own still present sense of the supernatural call, becomes

more fully and more unintermittently conscious within them than it was wont to be in them on earth.

4) suffering in all joy And lastly, our deepest moments are assuredly often, perhaps always, shot through, in their very joy, with suffering—even though this suffering be only the birth-pangs of a fuller spiritual life and fruitfulness. Our profoundest happiness here below always possesses something of the heroic; and the heroic appears impossible without obscurity met by faith, pain borne by patience, risk and loss faced and transformed by the magic of self-immolation. Thus our fullest nobility and its unique joys appear as though, after all, reserved for this our earth alone. But not so.

The saved spirits in the Beyond will doubtless no further know suffering and pain, temptation and risk and fall, within themselves, such as we poor little men now know them upon earth. And yet it is not difficult to find, within the deepest characteristics of the human soul even upon earth and the most certain and most dominant conditions of the Other Life, operative causes for the continuance in Heaven itself of the essentials in the nobility furnished by devoted suffering and self-sacrifice here below. For the saved spirits in the Beyond indeed see God as He is— but this doubtless only in so far as their finite natures, indefinitely raised and expanded by Supernature though they be, can do so. What they see is indeed the very Reality of God; what they feel and will, and what they act with and for, is in very truth this Reality itself. Nevertheless, they are not themselves Gods; they are finite, God is infinite; they are more or less successive, God is purely simultaneous; they exist through Him, He is self-existent; and thus contrastedly in many other ways. And yet it is God, as He is in Himself, and not as He is only partially seen by them, whom these spirits desire to comprehend, to love, to will and to serve. Hence, even in Heaven, there remains, for the saved soul, room and the need to transcend itself, to lose itself, that it may truly find itself. Here is an act possessed of an element of genuine darkness, of real tension, succeeded by an accession of further light and wider expansion. St. Catherine of Genoa, from her own spiritual experiences, vividly conceived and finely pictured, in the souls destined to Purgatory, their joyous acceptance of, their freely willed plunge into, this intrinsi-

cally necessary bath of purgation ; and their escape, by means
of this pain, from the now far greater suffering produced within
them by their clear perception of the stains and disharmonies
still present in their own souls. Such souls thus taste an ever-
increasing bliss and peace within their ever-decreasing pain,
whilst those impurities and hardenings are slowly, surely, suffer-
ingly yet serenely, purified, softened and willed away. We can,
mutatis mutandis, similarly picture to ourselves the soul's acts
in confrontation of God, even in Heaven, as, in a sense, plunges,
away from the quite clear yet limited vision, into a wider, but
at first dimmer, experience of the great Reality. And thus such
plunges of the soul there into God, and the somewhat similar
goings-out there of the same soul to its fellow souls (whom also
it will hardly see as completely as it wills to love and serve, and
to learn from them) are the equivalents there of men's heroic
plunges here away from sin and self, or from quite clear sense-
impressions and pictures of the visible world into the suffering
and sacrifice which accompany the fidelity to the instincts and
intuitions (as yet relatively obscure) of a fuller love and service
of God and men.

The lost souls are left to the pain of stainedness and self-
contraction ; they do not attain to, since they do not really will,
the suffering of purification and expansive harmonisation. For
man, once he is supernaturally awakened, cannot escape pain ;
he can only choose between the pain of fruitful growth, expansion,
tension—the throes of spiritual parturition,—the pangs of the
wide-open welcome to the pressing inflow of the fuller life, and
the aches of fruitless stunting, contraction, relaxation, the dull
and dreary, or the angry and reckless, drifting in bitter-sweet
unfaithful or immoral feelings, acts, habits, which, thus indulged,
bring ever-increasing spiritual blindness, volitional paralysis and
a living death. Only in Heaven and in Hell is the will finally
determined as between the solicitations of the pain within the
joy of the right, and of the pleasure within the dreariness of the
wrong. Yet even in Heaven there is a certain analogue to the
genuine cost in the real gain traceable within the deepest acts
of the human soul whilst here on earth. And hence, correspondingly, the very pains of Hell consist largely in the perception by the lost soul of how unattainable is that fruitful suffering

which would furnish the one escape from the fruitless pangs now actually endured.

Let us conclude all with four general reflexions as to Hell, and two anecdotes in illustration of Heaven.

As to Hell. It will be well for us, as concerns the question quite generally, to realise with fullness and vividness how inadequate is the prevalent easy-going, slipshod thinking, feeling and living with regard to our free will and responsibility, our moral weakness and the reality of sin. Only those profoundly awake to, and earnest about, these great facts have any right to be counted as opinions in the question of Abiding Consequences. And again it will be useful for us clearly to note how pantheistic is the general outlook of the more notable deniers of this Abidingness. It was, of course, inevitable that a John Scotus Erigena, for whom God was the sole substance and man's sin a mere nonentity, should have refused to deduce any unending effects from the behaviour of men. It was equally inevitable that such a violently naturalistic Pantheist as Giordano Bruno should ceaselessly revile every notion of accountability and of sin—still more so, then, of Heaven and Hell. It was similarly inevitable that Spinoza's pantheistic system should, as such, have left no logical room or justification for that great soul's intuitions concerning the costliness, the rarity, the priceless worth of the true, ethical and spiritual life ; hence that even Spinoza's influence should be deadly to any belief in any objective personal survival and any other-world Heaven or Hell. And it was inevitable again that Schleiermacher, so predominantly æsthetic and pantheistic, should have laboured hard to eliminate all belief in the abidingness of evil—evil being too little real for him at all times for this thin and shadowy thing to be likely, in his opinion, to last throughout all time. We will not, then, follow in the wake of such men. But if we walk, instead, in the footsteps of definite and sensitive Theists we shall find that the doctrine of Abiding Consequences can, at the least, not be treated lightly—the possibility of its substantial truth will persistently demand a serious, pensive consideration.

It is true that by any and every acceptance of this doctrine, we allow that God's will or God's power does not, or cannot,

effect, within the realm of human souls, its own entire triumph
—a triumph which evidently consists in the subjectively free and
objectively right self-determination of all awakened human souls.
And we cannot escape this difficulty by holding such partial
failure to spring directly from any libertarian scheme as
such. For St. Augustine teaches admirably that " it is a great
liberty to be able not to sin ; it is the greatest liberty to be
unable to sin "—a doctrine which must be true, unless God
is not free. Thus we can only say that even the possibility
of sin arises, not from the freedom of the will as such, but,
on the contrary, from the imperfection of the freedom ; and
that there are doubtless reasons, connected with the power
of God or with His knowledge (concerning what will, upon the
whole, produce a maximum of a certain kind of spiritual happiness), why He chose, or permitted, the existing scheme of imperfect liberty amongst human souls. After all, it is not as though
man could possess his *special* pathos, power, patience and peace
without this, his actual, imperfection of liberty : these things,
assuredly, all stand and fall together. And thus we can boldly
affirm that man would, indeed, be a higher creature were Hell
impossible for him ; he would be something further, but he
would also, throughout, be something different—man would
no more be man.

And as to the essentials of Hell, I like to remember what a
cultivated, experienced Roman Catholic cleric insisted upon to
me, namely, the importance of the distinction between the
essence of the doctrine of Hell and the various images and interpretations given to this essence : that the essence lies assuredly,
above all, in the unendingness. Hence even the most terrible
of the descriptions in Dante's *Inferno* could be held literally,
and yet, if the sufferings there described were considered eventu-
ally to cease altogether, Hell would thereby be denied in its
very root. And contrariwise, a man might be at a loss to find
any really appropriate definitions, or more than popular images,
for the sufferings of Hell ; he might even fail to reach a clear
belief in more than an unending, though not necessarily very
active, disharmony and unappeased longing in the Lost ; and
yet he would still be holding the essence of the faith in Hell.

And as regards Hell in view of men's ignorances, errors,

denials in matters of religion, there is a quaternity of most certain facts and principles which we ought never to forget. Men are as genuinely responsible, they can as really sin gravely and can as truly end with Hell, by their deliberate thinkings as by their deliberate feelings, willings, or visible acts. The deepest of all sins are precisely sins of thought, self-idolisation and arrogant revolt against the truth as perceived by the soul in its depths. Men can, however, in countless degrees and ways, be excusably ignorant, or invincibly prejudiced, concerning various facts of religion and certain laws of the spiritual life ; this, however, far more easily and more permanently with respect to the historical facts and the contingent institutions, such even as Jesus Christ and the Catholic Church, than with regard to the metaphysical, non-contingent fact and presence of God. It is well known that the Roman Catholic Church itself is clearly on the side of such breadth as regards Christ and the Church, and appears strict only as concerns God. Men can, however, be without any gift or training for the correct analysis or theory of their own actual deepest convictions, even as to their faith in God. Hence it matters not so much what a man thinks he thinks, as what he thinks in actual reality. And men, especially men of this very numerous unanalytic, untheoretic kind, can claim much patience in such times of transition seemingly in everything, as have been the last hundred and fifty years in our Western Europe. Such persons are greatly overimpressed as to the range and depth of our real discoveries and final revolutions, and are thus bewildered as to the ultimate facts and laws of the spiritual life, facts and laws which persist substantially as they were.

Certain great New Testament texts appear conjointly to cover all these four contentions. To men in general, and on all subjects, Christ declares that " out of the heart proceed evil thoughts," alongside of acts as heinous as murders, adulteries, blasphemies; and again that " every idle word that men shall speak "—assuredly, then, also every idle thought that men shall think—they shall give account thereof at the Judgment (St. Matt. xv. 19; xii. 36). To the (doubtless many) men who are not aware that they are actually serving Christ in their heroic service of their suffering fellow-creatures, to men, then, who presumably do not at all know the historic Jesus or who do not perceive Him to be the Christ, Christ the King says at the Judgment " Come, ye blessed of my Father, inherit the Kingdom prepared for you from the foundation of the world. Inasmuch as ye have done these things unto the least of these my brethren, ye have done it unto me " (St. Matt. xxv. 34–40). As to the governors, priests, soldiers, who have actually crucified Him, Christ prays upon His cross, " Father, forgive them, for they know not what they do " (St. Luke xxiii. 34). And as to the sceptical, superstitious and restlessly curious men of letters—men so vague and doubtful as to the nature of God Himself, as to have erected an altar inscribed " To the Unknown God "—St. Paul declares : " Whom ye ignorantly worship, Him declare I unto you " (Acts xvii. 23).

And as to Heaven. A good and simple, yet somewhat dry and conventional Roman Catholic priest, a worker for many years among souls, told me one day, in a South of England town, of the sudden revelation of heights and depths of holiness that had just enveloped and enlarged his head and heart. He had been called, a few nights before, to a small pot-house in the outskirts of this largely fashionable town. And there, in a dreary little garret, lay, stricken down with sudden double pneumonia, an Irish young woman, twenty-eight years of age, doomed to die within an hour or two. A large fringe covered her forehead, and all the other externals were those of an average barmaid who had, at a public bar, served half-tipsy, coarsely-joking men, for some ten years or more. And she was still full of physical energy—of the physical craving for physical existence. Yet, as soon as she began to pour out her last and general confession, my informant felt, so he told me, a lively impulse to arise and to cast himself on the ground before her. For there, in her intention, lay one of the simple, strong, sweet saints of God at his feet. She told how deeply she desired to become as pure as possible for this grand grace, this glorious privilege, so full of peace, of now abandoning her still young, vividly pulsing life, of placing it utterly within the hands of the God, of the Christ whom she loved so much, and who loved her so much more ; that this great gift, she humbly felt, would bring the grace of its full acceptance with it, and might help her to aid, with God and Christ, the souls she loved so truly, the souls He loved so far more deeply than ever she herself could love them.

And she died soon after in a perfect rapture of joy—in a joy overflowing, utterly sweetening all the mighty bitter floods of her pain. Now *that* is Supernatural.

A young friend, now bravely at Red Cross work in France, told me how, in her little, then sleepy English country town, a retired elderly sergeant, who had fought through the Boer War, and who was now a quite average working man, told her the following experience of his own. He was riding in the Transvaal, during that strenuous campaign, with a small troop of cavalry along a road between two British posts. A Boer post in ambush fired upon the troop—he himself was hit and slid off his horse ; the rest effected their escape to the near-by post, whence they would bring him help. All galloped off thus, except a quite young lieutenant of ancient lineage, luxurious nurture, and, doubtless, largely inarticulate intelligence and conviction— an Eton lad, come straight out to the War. The lieutenant sprang from his horse, clasped the wounded man in his arms, and, as the Boers renewed their fire, shielded the sergeant with his body. The volley took its effect on the young man ; a great gush of his blood streamed over his elderly charge. The sergeant saw that his rescuer was dying. " Oh, how sad," he said, " that you, just starting on a brilliant long life, should die thus for and instead of me—an elderly man of no special outlook or importance ! " The lieutenant turned a beaming countenance upon him : " Sad ? What could be better ! " he exclaimed, and fell back dead. *That*, again, is supernatural.

And in both cases, the first with the explicit religious reference, the second with no such (at least spoken) explication—in every at all similar case—the roots, justifications and implications, at all adequate to such acts and dispositions, are the Eternity, Reality, Sociality, and Self-giving Love which, original and fully active in God, are shared in a measure by man, when thus supernaturally touched and supernaturally responsive—a little here below already ; more completely and securely, indeed for ever, in Heaven.

III

PAPERS ON THE CHURCH AND CATHOLICISM

8

THE ESSENTIALS OF CATHOLICISM [1]

IT would be possible to treat this subject in one of three ways :
1. Historically, as to where, when, how and why the term and
idea of Catholicism arose, grew, was lived, and opposed. 2. Con-
troversially or negatively, by examining the chief forms of real
or supposed anti-Catholicism. 3. By exhibiting the obvious
characteristics of some one religious body now extant, or a substance common to more than one body. But there are objections
to all three ways—the first would be too long, the second would
obscure the positive character of Catholicism, the last would be
too exclusive.

I propose, instead of any such one unbroken way and advance,
to make various plunges, from different starting-points and sides,
more or less *in medias res,* and down to the roots and foundations
of the Catholic conviction ; and yet to make these plunges all
converge towards the elucidation of one *complex of characteristics*
ever present in all fuller spiritual and religious life. I thus hope
vividly to indicate, by the aid of such facts and experiences, the
characteristics rightly termed Catholic which are implied and
required by all such fuller life, and to make us grasp and feel
the essential conditions, the dangers, the necessity, and the
greatness of such Catholicism.

These plunges shall be three, and shall each deal with some
recent book or discussion : 1. The *Origin and Essence of
Catholicism,* Göttingen, 1911, by the Lutheran, Rudolf Sohm,
a German lay canonist. 2. The Letters of Mgr. Luigi Puecher
Passavalli, an Italian ecclesiastic of strong anti-Curialist views,
published in Milan in 1911. 3. Articles in *La Semaine Sociale de
Bordeaux*—a French lay philosopher's studies (Paris, 1909–10).

[1] An Address to a Gathering of Young Men at Liddon House, London, in May,
1913. Reprinted from the *Liddon House Occasional Paper* for July, 1913.

I

Professor Sohm's Dissertation—the detailed historical correctness or incorrectness of which does not concern us here—raises a deeply interesting question, and meets it in a strikingly simple and noble manner. He insists upon how great a mystery the appearance of a full-blown Catholic Church, already in the middle of the second Christian century, remains for the outlook of those scholars—still the all but totality of the German Protestant workers —who *will* make this conception and fact, of a single Universal Church, to result from the amalgamation of countless local Churches, previously independent of each other in theory and in practice, or from the usurpation by some one Church amongst these local Churches over against its fellow-Churches. And Sohm accounts for the apparent strange suddenness of this huge *fait accompli*, by maintaining that, from the first, " where ' two or three ' were assembled in the Spirit of Christ, *there* was, in the religious sense, the Church—always the same Church, the same Christendom, Ecclesia, life of humanity through Christ with God. The community of Christians in its local grouping is nothing as a local complex (*Grösse*), for as a local complex it is religiously worthless. This community is all that it is, only as the expression, the visible appearance, of an *œcumenical* community, of the *religious* complex (*Grösse*) of *universal* (as Ignatius has it, of ' Catholic ') Christendom. This community is Church, Catholic Church, not Congregation. . . . Hence, even in one and the same place, there can exist many Churches. For the smallest assembly of Christians is religiously equivalent to the greatest." Thus the whole was previous to the parts, or from the first was operative within the parts, and constituted them ; it was not subsequent to the parts, and a mere sum-total of them.

There *was* indeed, according to Sohm, a change—a *profound* change, indeed deterioration, but not as regards the Catholicism, the unity and universality of the Church. The change was, simply, from one universal, grace-impelled, purely voluntary body, to one universal, legalist, compulsory body.

Whatever may be objected against this view, it brings out

admirably, I think, what it is that attracts, and what it is that repels, the deeper religious modern mind, in the general doctrines and habits offered to it, under the one term " Catholicism."

And yet there is one all-pervading constituent in Sohm's position which is, indeed, most intelligible, as a reaction against great contrary dangers, excesses and abuses, yet which, nevertheless, militates against certain essential characteristics of a full and balanced Catholicism,—characteristics, at bottom, as necessary to it, and as attractive to the deeper religious modern mind, as are the unity and universality so finely apprehended by him. Everywhere we can trace in Sohm's mind the operation of the antinomy : spirit of liberty, of religion, of Christ, then (in precisely the same proportion) no legal forms or concepts, however intermittent and rudimentary ; or legal forms and concepts, then (precisely so far) no spirit of liberty, of religion, of Christ. " It is *impossible*," he says, " that the Church, in the religious sense, can form a unity otherwise than by means of God, of faith, of the Spirit ; that is, the Church *cannot* form a unity otherwise than religiously. It *cannot* be, at the same time, a legal, that is a corporative, unity."

The Invisible Church thus *excludes* the Visible Church ; and the Visible Church *excludes* the Invisible Church. The very essence of Roman, *i.e.*, of false Catholicism, consists, according to Sohm, in the sheer identification of the Invisible with the Visible Church ; and the essence of Lutheran, *i.e.*, of true Catholicism, consists, again according to Sohm, in the mutual exclusiveness of the Invisible and the Visible Church.

Yet Sohm himself has to make many damaging admissions, as that " in primitive Christianity generally no distinction was made between Christendom and the People of God, the Ecclesia, present only for the eye of faith " ; and again, " already long before Luther the idea existed of an invisible Church of the predestined " (pp. 12 and 24).

Surely already this much suggests that Primitive Christians instinctively assumed *some* ordinary, indeed necessary, interconnection between the Invisible as a whole and the Visible as a whole, and that the reason why Sohm has to come so low down as Luther to find the first complete, formal and fundamental, mutual exclusion of each by the other, is that, in this matter, there

exists no such radical antagonism between Primitive Christianity
and early Catholic, indeed Mediæval Christianity, as Sohm tries
to find. Undoubtedly, as he himself indicates, certain Curialist
theologians of the Renaissance and Reformation times, *e.g.*,
Cardinal Torquemada, *did* attempt to elaborate and to impose
a system of sheer identification of the Visible and the Invisible
Church ; and this *is* in contradiction with Primitive Christianity.
But so is Luther's insistence upon the mutual exclusion obtaining
between the Visible and the Invisible Church.

Nothing indeed is more certain than that Roman Catholicism
remains to this hour, even in its strictest official definitions, hostile
to, and assuredly incompatible with, such a sheer identification of the Visible and the Invisible Church. What otherwise
is, *e.g.*, the meaning of the doctrine of Invincible Ignorance,
or of the fallibility of all excommunications, or the still most
orthodox principle : " there are many members of the Visible
Church who are not members of the Invisible Church, and there
are many members of the Invisible Church who are not members
of the Visible Church " ? Two principles and no more underlie,
I think, all the Roman definitions in this matter :

1. The Invisible, as a whole, is related to, is awakened by,
and can and should (and does) variously permeate, the Visible as
a whole—not only in the case of the Roman Catholic Church,
or of Christianity generally, but, in their respective lesser degrees
and other ways, also in the case of Judaism, and of the other
religions. And

2. So little is the Invisible as a whole unrelated to the Visible
as a whole, that the full and balanced, the typical growth in
religious depth and fruitfulness is *not* a growth away from the
stimulations, occasions, concomitants, vehicles and expressions
of sense, and away from the frank admission of their operation,
but, contrariwise, is a growth by means of, and into, an ever
richer and wider sensible material, and into an ever wiser and
more articulate placing, understanding and spiritualising of such
means. Certainly Christianity is irreducibly *incarnational*; and
this its Incarnationalism is already half misunderstood, or half
suppressed, if it is taken to mean only a spirituality which, already
fully possessed by souls outside of, and prior to, all sense stimulations and visible vehicles and forms, is then simply expressed

and handed on in such purely spiritual ways. No: some such stimulations, vehicles and forms are (upon the whole and in the long run) as truly required fully to awaken the religious life as they are to express it and to transmit it, when already fully awakened. Such celebrated cases as the deaf-mute-blind girls, Laura Bridgeman and Rose Kellerman, indicate, plainly enough, that man's soul, whilst united to the body, remains, in the first instance, unawake even to God and to itself, until the psychic life is aroused by sense stimulation, by the effective impact of the sensible and visible upon man's mind and soul.

But indeed—in spite of George Fox and many another noble would-be Pure Interiorist — a simply invisible Church and Religion does not exist amongst men. Fox and his friends are steeped in images and convictions that have grown up amongst, that have been handed down by, concrete, historical men, and concrete, historical institutions and cultual acts. The " Universal Reason," " the Word," " the Inner Light," " the Universal Brotherhood," " the Bread of Life," are all based upon some two thousand years of Jewish and Christian Church experience, articulated in part by centuries of Greek philosophical thought.

What remains true is that the Invisible is the central — is the heart of religion ; that the Visible can be so taken as to choke the Invisible ; that there are, amongst those who see too exclusively the Visible, fanatics who would declare the Invisible to be coterminous and identical with the Visible, just as, amongst those who too exclusively apprehend the Invisible and the intolerableness of the foregoing abuse, there are enthusiasts so little aware of the history and implications of their convictions and of the constitution of our common human nature, as to seek an impossible and unchristian (because unincarnative and unhistorical) simplification — an Invisible achieved outside of all contact with the Visible.

Fortunately, however, both Curialist and Quaker find themselves in a world, and are actually moved and determined by experiences and conceptions, much richer than the formal explicit theory or analysis of either party apprehends or fathoms ; and they are thus prevented, both from without and from within, from making too large, i.e., too disastrous, an experiment of that which, in their formulated positions, is excessive and exclusive—hence, not Catholic.

II

The Capuchin Archbishop Passavalli is, as we find him in his letters, stronger in spiritual insight than in philosophical analysis and theory, or than in balance and completeness of outlook. Thus his rejection of the definitions of the Vatican Council concerning Infallibility and the universal direct Magisterium of the Pope, as incapable of reasonable supplementation or interpretation; his apparent inability to perceive the permanent greatness and fruitfulness of *some* voluntary self-commitment to life-long continence on the part of the clergy; above all his later acceptance of a doctrine of successive earthly lives for human souls, surely indicate, in increasing degrees, a certain lack of balance and coherence. Nevertheless, three interconnected chief difficulties, dangers, abuses, that dog the steps of every largely institutional religion *within the range of religion itself,* are most vividly revealed in this striking correspondence; and any argument in favour of Catholicism (if conceived and rightly conceived, as, of necessity, including a similar institutionalism) will have to meet the objections involved in such revelations.

Monsignor Passavalli's first experience and conviction, then, concerns the profound attachment of Churchmen, especially of the Roman Curia, to temporal power, temporal riches, temporal prestige as such, and the irreconcilably unchristian, anti-Christian character of such attachment. He thirsts for the Church's " detachment from temporal possessions, and from all affairs extraneous to the Apostolic ministry—a detachment which, to my mind," he adds, " ought to be inexorable and abiding." He laments that " the experience that I have acquired, during many years, of the *personnel* of the Pontifical Curia has produced in me an unconquerable conviction that *never, never,* to the very end of the world, will they consent to renounce Temporal Power—they will utilise every means (at one time public at another secret, at one time more violent at another less so) to repossess themselves of that Power at any and every price." And he speaks of " this anti-national and anti-Christian influence."

The Archbishop's second conviction regards the large place actually assigned by Providence to the layman in the Church, —how God can and does use laymen to awaken priests as well as laymen to the Christian, the twice-born temper, and to the need of a continual renovation of their own souls and of alertness to the work of God—to the seekings after Him in the great world outside. And also this conviction is pierced by sad experience—of how there is no recognised position or action of such a directly spiritual kind left to the layman in the Roman Church of to-day.

And thirdly Monsignor Passavalli has the keen sense of how it is the Church's duty to welcome any and every religious light and grace manifesting itself outside of her visible bounds ; and yet how predominant has been, and is, amongst ecclesiastics, the contrary spirit—a spirit of suspicious, angry, oppressive monopoly.

Now the three difficulties and abuses, thus insisted on, are very real, very widespread, very deep. Yet it will be sufficient for our purpose if I briefly point out that they all three are so little the result of a well-understood and genuine Catholicism, as to be, in reality, direct contradictions of it and to become impossible in proportion to the prevalence of such a Catholicism.

For Catholicism is essentially a twice-born temper, a moving indeed into the visible and sublunar ; yet this, in order to raise this visible and sublunar to the invisible and transcendent, in order that, by such work and contact, Catholicism may itself awaken (more and more fully) to its own twice-born character, and in order again to move back and away from all the finite and temporal, to God the Infinite and Eternal. Thus, in proportion as the soul is truly Catholic, it will turn away with disgust from what, when taken as simply the final and full end, ever degrades and kills the soul.

Catholicism, again, is essentially organic—the social body it aims at building up is constituted by the several groups of men, down indeed to the individual souls; and to these groups and individuals it gives their special, characteristic functions and delicate, irreplaceable interactions. Only such a conception, as it is magnificently pictured by St. Paul, is truly Catholic. A monopoly of all influence—a monopoly also of consultation, preparation, application—by the Clergy is as uncatholic as is every attempt to have no Clergy, no official heads, administrators, teachers and formulators, and no hierarchical subordination. In both cases we get impoverishment; whereas Catholicism is essentially balance, inclusiveness, richness.

And finally, Catholicism, in its deepest affinities and in its widest self-commitments, has always held and persistently holds the doctrine of stages of religious light, life and love, and of Christ in the Church as appealing to, and answered by, God in the World. The solemn, and utterly final, inclusion of the entire Jewish Old Testament in the Catholic Canon of Scripture, the large utilisation and incorporation of Greek Platonic philosophy in the Fourth Gospel, in the works of Justin Martyr and Clement of Alexandria, on to even larger absorptions of Proclus by the Pseudo-Areopagite and of Aristotle by Aquinas, — the very accusation of Paganising so frequently brought against the Official Church, all prove this recognition of stages, or at least they all tend in this direction. At this point no more is required than that the full implications of this conduct, and above all that the generosity involved in the deepest and most delicate Christian spirit, should persistently be realised and instinctively be applied.

It is, however, easy and common to seek after an insufficient and uncatholic escape from this third grievance. We most of us appear still haunted by the, surely artificial, alternative which has so largely, more or less from the first, predominated amongst orthodox theologians : that " God's grace and truth are given either within (and by means of) the Roman Catholic, or within some other Christian Church, or within all the Christian Churches ; or such grace and truth is given entirely outside of, quite unconnected with, any and every organisation, history, cult, directly by God Himself." Yet nothing, on the contrary, is more obvious, at least to historically trained minds now, than that actual life cries aloud for the doctrine of Cardinal Juan de Lugo—the Spanish Jesuit who taught theology in Rome from 1621 to 1641, who teaches in his *de Fide,* that the members of

the various Christian bodies or sects, of the Jewish and Mohammedan communities, and of the heathen philosophical schools
(he is thinking especially of the Græco-Roman ones), who achieve
their salvation, do so, as a rule, simply by the action of the grace
of God which aids their good faith instinctively to concentrate
itself upon, and to practise, those elements in the worship and
teaching of their respective sect, communion, school which are
true and good and originally revealed by God.

This principle is distinctly more Catholic than is the other
view which would make the salvation of such souls something
entirely extraneous to such institutionalism as may environ them ;
indeed this principle is profoundly Catholic, is alone fully
Catholic. For we thus admit indeed *some* light and life and love,
some helps and heroisms, everywhere and at all times, whilst we
equally insist upon endless diversities and degrees and stages
of illumination, awakening, and love. And, above all, we insist
that outside the Roman Catholic Church, or even outside any
other Christian Body, indeed beyond the pale of Christianity
and Judaism altogether, man, as a general rule, is still saved
(in so far as he is saved at all) never indeed by his own, or by
other men's efforts and labours alone, yet also not by an absolutely naked and utterly separate action upon his individual
mind and will by God alone ; that he is saved, here also, by God
working with and in and through the senses of this soul's body,
the powers of this soul's mind and will, and the varyingly rich
or poor history, society, institutions which (during centuries
or millenniums before this soul's existence and throughout our
most various humankind now around it) have experienced,
articulated, and transmitted, and are at this moment more or
less mediating, the touch, the light, the food of God. Thus only
do we get a fully Catholic, because an organic, an incarnational
conception, not only of the Catholic Church or even of Christianity, but, in their various seekings and stages, of every sort of
religion, indeed of all spiritual life at all.

III

The French philosopher, whose articles were collected together under the title of *Catholicisme Social et le Monophorisme*, insists upon, and carefully develops, the doctrine of St. Augustine, the least naturalistic of the Fathers, in his great exclamation : "fecisti nos ad Te, et inquietum est cor nostrum donec requiescat in Te." And this development fully reveals the profoundly Catholic, alone Catholic, doctrine that "the state of 'pure nature' might, without doubt, have existed, but that, in fact, it does not exist, and that, in fact, it never has existed." And he concludes—I slightly modify the grouping and range of his nomenclature—"In the recent controversies we have, only too often, thought that only two alternatives are extant : on the one hand, the *Immanentism* so justly condemned by the Church, which makes the entire religious and Christian development to spring from below and from the obscure depths of the human conscience ; and on the other hand a doctrine which, from horror of that Immanentism, perceives nought except the gift from without, the revelation formulated from above,—authority addressing itself to a pure receptivity and a passive obedience." Nevertheless "the thesis according to which all, in Christianity, comes from without, *extrinsecus*, from *afference*, is no less inexact than the thesis according to which all comes from within, from *efference*. These false or incomplete doctrines—of simple *afference* or of simple *efference*—we might call two kinds of *monophorism*; and to such *monophorisms* we must oppose and prefer the doctrine of the double contribution—afference *and* efference." Thus everywhere, within human souls, is there an unrest—a demand, which, at deepest, are of grace and divine, and which are met and satisfied by graces, revelations from without,—a supply. Thus the Jew, indeed the Moslem, the Brahmin, the Buddhist, even the Agnostic and the sincere Atheist, are being secretly solicited by grace within themselves to love and to practise whatsoever is good and true within their present community or position, and, in various degrees, to welcome, and to move on into, the fuller light and self-discovery offered to them from the greater fullness outside of themselves in the world of other souls and of other institutions.

And yet, even thus, we have not yet articulated, still less, resolved, the final twin difficulty of religion, which is thus put by Professor Troeltsch in his *Gesammelte Schriften*, Vol. II., 1913. ' The difficulty " (concerning the relations between religion, especially Christianity, and the other complexes of life), " lies in this, that the *this-world ends* of our life bear the strict character of moral ends—of ends claiming to be sought for their own sakes, up to the sacrifice of our natural happiness —but that they lie within this world and depend upon certain historical complexes which spring from the physical and psychical nature of man and which dominate his earthly horizon. In face of these ends, the *super-world end* signifies an entirely different orientatation and a jealous tension against the competition of those this-world ends. This state of things has obtained since a Christian Ethic began to make some kind of home for itself in this visible world, and it is this state of things which called forth the heavy crises of ancient Christendom. The revolt of Montanism and the repugnance to science are the clearest symptoms of those crises. Later on, a compromise was formed, which persisted till the arising of the free modern national civilisations. But since then there has arisen the modern culture, partly under the influence of the classical world, now liberated from ecclesiastical tutelage, partly out of special and original struggles. The specific character of this culture consists precisely in maintaining, alongside of the religious end, the this-world ends, and in recognising these latter ends as ends in themselves. And just in this combination consist the richness, the breadth and the freedom, but also the painful interior tensions and the difficult problems of this civilisation. Politics, Sociology, Sexual Ethics, Technology, Science, Art, Æsthetics : they all go their own way, and construct independently their own ideals from out of their own several conditions of existence and their own historical developments. The Christian Ethic finds these several disciplines all fully extant as independent ends, each with its own logic and autonomous action upon real life, and as objects of so many specific sciences ; and it possesses, with regard to them, at most the means of accommodation and of regulation, but not of a construction proceeding independently from itself." " It is simply impossible to treat these ends and their pursuit as

I

mere natural forms of existence. As we have to recognise, in Christian Ethics, the rule of an objective other-world religious end, so also must we recognise frankly and fully, in these ends of civilisation, this-world moral ends of a strictly objective character."

Let us note here, three things, and with them conclude our entire study.

There can, to-day less than ever, be any question of abandoning this magnificent sense of the Transcendent and Infinite, and of the Immanent and Redemptive Light, Life, Love, God ; of levelling down to sheer naturalism—that dreary impossibility, or even simply to the once-born stage of religion. We must have the Real God, and we must have the Real Christ, the Real Church. We require, then, not Agnosticism, not non-religious Ethic, not even Unitarianism, not Quakerism. We must have Catholicism, God in man, and man conscious of sin and sorrow ; nature in grace, and grace in nature ; the Infinite and Spaceless in Time and Space ; spirit in the body—the body, the stimulator and spring-board, the material and training ground, of spirit. And whatever may be the obscurities, complications, difficulties of the enterprise, we simply must persist in it—we must strive to awaken and utilise every stage and range of genuine life, with its special characteristics, in its right place and degree, for the calling into full action of all the rest. But such an insistent, pertinacious *organic* trend is Catholicism.

And next, this Catholicism, with a most delicate, difficult alertness and selflessness, will have to be truly *incarnational*— that is, it will have to recognise, respect, love, and protect continually, not only the less full and less articulate stages of grace, in the other religions and in all they possess of what is true, but it will have to recognise, respect, love and protect also the non-religious levels and complexes of life, as also coming from God, as occasions, materials, stimulations, necessary for us men towards the development of our complete humanity, and especially also of our religion. There must at no time be any question of eliminating or weakening the transcendental, other-world, God-ward, recollective movement ; it, on the contrary, will have, as keenly and penetratingly as ever, to be the great sheet-anchor of our souls and the great root of the self-identity of the

Catholic religion and of its world-conquering peace. We shall only, in our other movement—in the out-going, the world-ward, the incarnational movement, have, far more keenly than men were able to realise in the past, to be attentive, active, observant, hospitable, there also—not merely with the sense of doing good, or with the wish directly to find or to introduce religious facts and categories, but especially with the conviction that these various stages and ranges, each and all, come from God, possess their own immanent laws and conditions of existence and growth, and deserve our love and service in this their nature and development. We shall feel sure that they will, in the long run, benefit (often in the most unexpected but most real ways) regions of life apparently far apart from them, and especially will aid religion, the deepest life of all. And in so doing we shall be Catholic, that is rich—more rich, in the world-ward movement, than men could be in the past : what a gain for mankind and for Catholicism !

And lastly, our Catholicism will, owing to this its greater awakeness, this its increased delicacy and sensitiveness of interior organisation and incarnationalism, acquire a great increase in the probing character of the Cross, of purification, of tension, contradiction, suspense,—since these will now be found more fully also in precisely what it loves most—in the evidences and symmetry of theology, and in the ready and assured application of religion itself. For not only has the religious man now, in one of his two necessary movements of soul, to be, and to keep himself, awake to ranges and complexes of life and reality dominated by laws and affinities other than those obtaining in religion. But, if he is not a Pietist but a Catholic, he will have to continue to utilise, to appeal to, strictly to require, history, philosophy, sociology, art for religion itself : yet he will have, in appealing to them, and in so far as he thus appeals, to abide, not by the tests of religion, still less by any impatience of his own, but simply by the proofs special to these several complexes of reality and knowledge.

Let us vividly realise that, although Catholicism has held and taught a considerable number of religious truths as so many factual happenings, yet that it has ever so taught them—thus, as factual happenings,—not on the ground of intuition but of historical evidence—*i.e.*, it has, for its historical element, always appealed to historical documents. <u>And indeed an abiding nucleus of factual happenings is essential to Catholicism, as Christian, as incarnational.</u> But Catholicism—its essence which we are here studying—is directly bound up only with the persistent existence of some such nucleus, and with the persistent openness of the historical appeal and the real cogency of the historical proofs ; whereas Catholicism in its essence is only indirectly, only conditionally, bound up with the factual character of all and every truth long held to be not only a spiritual truth but also a factual happening. And though the great central figure— Our Lord, and the main outlines of His life and teaching, death and apparitions—require, for the integrity of Catholicism, to be not only spiritual truths but factual happenings, it does not follow that the same is necessarily the case with every truth and doctrine concerning Him. Certainly the Descent into Hell is now conceived, by all educated Christians, in spite of their continuous acceptance of its truth and importance,—it stands in the Apostles' Creed,—not in the directly, simply factual way in which it was understood in early times. As I take the relations between the Visible and the Invisible Church, so also do I take the relations between the Factual and the Doctrinal to be neither relations of sheer co-extension nor, still less, relations of even possible sheer antagonism or sheer mutual exclusion. On the contrary : *some*, a very real, an operative, <u>relation exists between the Visible and the Invisible Church, and between the Factual and the Doctrinal.</u> And indeed we know that actual life persists in furnishing us with the basis for such a double conviction ;— that is, we know that *some* amount of Visible Organisation and of Factual Happening remains, and persists in connection with Invisible Reality in both cases, beyond reasonable challenge to this hour. Above all, we know that God exists and that He will continue to operate within those other complexes—history, philosophy, art, as well as within the deepest of all complexes, religion.

It is God we believe in, it is God we trust. Without His reality, and without faith in His reality, the world around us and within us is confusion and dismay. But God *is*—the all-pervading sustainer, the initiator of all light and life and love. And

Catholicism apprehends, lives, and loves Him thus—universal, but in different stages and degrees ; simple, but in overflowing richness; and the Supreme Reality, but self-limited and divinely respectful of the liberty given by Himself even when and where such liberty is used against Him. God slowly levels upwards, and Catholicism affirms, loves, encourages these various levels and their slow purification and elevation by and towards God, their one origin and universal home.

9

THE
CONVICTIONS COMMON TO CATHOLICISM AND PROTESTANTISM [1]

It is an honour for a convinced Roman Catholic student to be asked to speak in the company of highly distinguished Protestant scholars, concerning the positions and implications of the Catholic doctrines, when these doctrines are confronted with those of the Protestant outlook. I propose, first, to indicate the chief difficulties of my task, the range and method I propose to give to it, and certain points which I shall assume throughout. I will next describe the convictions common in the past to Catholicism and Protestantism. And I will conclude with the points which I believe to be in process of acceptance for the future.

I

The difficulties of my task, even were a long volume allotted to it, are many and profound, for it is notorious that Protestantism, as such, has always been *fissiparous*—a spirit or principle or doctrine prolific, among other things, of divisions down almost to so many individual minds. Hence it is well-nigh impossible, for either Protestant or Catholic, to reach a definition or delimitation of Protestantism acceptable to all Protestants ; and, indeed, for one's own mind, the diversities even among the larger and more permanent groupings and currents that claim the title raise perplexing questions as to what varieties, to the right or to the left, still belong to Protestantism.

[1] An Article written by invitation for the then approaching fourth centenary of the Protestant Reformation. Reprinted from the *Homiletic Review* of New York, September, 1917.

I take the great successive variations of Protestantism to be four. The first stage, daring and inexperienced, yet deeply instructive, is chiefly represented by Luther during his first three years of protest (1517–20); but it is better to extend it beyond the Anabaptist catastrophe of Münster (1534, 1535) to the religious peace of Augsburg (1555), indeed to about 1560 —the deaths of Melanchthon and Calvin, and the approbation of the Jesuits. The second stage yields a century and a half of mostly conservative consolidation, during which large parts of the practice and convictions of the old Church are bit by bit resumed; but generally with only a heightened denunciation of Rome, and certainly with little consciousness of the provenance of these resumptions. The third stage covers the eighteenth century, with its levelling down and emptying out of the religious conviction and life. And the fourth, last period, still in progress, approximately begins with Kant, continues as the Romantic movement and the Idealist philosophy, and (in spite of the profoundly Naturalistic reaction in the Europe of the middle of the last century) represents, upon the whole increasingly, a deeply-lying historic and eirenic sense—a struggle after a due comprehension of man's entire past, and of the positions of each man's present adversaries. Here I shall take practically only the first stage and the last.

As to the simultaneous diversities, we have to decide whether all, or which, are to be included in our conception of Protestantism. It is obvious that the great organised bodies of Lutheranism and Calvinism, the latter including Zwinglianism, form the staple of Protestantism. Again, roughly one-half of Anglicanism is, historically, Protestant, indeed Calvinist. But are the Anabaptists Protestants? And, still more, are the Socinians such? If the essence of Protestantism consist in protestation, the Socinians will be more thorough Protestants than any High-church Lutheran or Anglican can ever possibly be. Even the purely Immanentist conception of religion, which empties it of every non-human objective content, appeals, through such able representatives as Dr. Paul Natorp, to sayings of Luther and to one whole side of the Protestant movement, as proving its right to figure as the residuary legatee of Protestantism.

I believe it will be more equitable and more fruitful to measure Protestantism not simply, or even primarily, by the range of its protests or negations, but to accept, as largely operative, the obviously sincere intention of Luther, and of Calvin, and even of Zwingli, to abide by the Christian Church and creeds of the first five centuries. We thus eliminate the Immanentist movement as a whole, and we take the Socinian movement as primarily an emphasising and development, not of Protestantism, but of the colder and more purely intellectual elements of the Renaissance current. And the Anabaptist movement, and various other sects and groups not belonging to one of the great church organisations, we shall take as largely Protestant, although, in considerable part, they are a continuation or revival of late mediæval movements.

On the side of the Roman Catholic Church we need hardly attend to the simultaneous variations, since these, whatever their depth and range, are always held (where the appurtenance to the Church is seriously recognised) as diversities well within one great common life and training-school ; but the chief successive developments, which it can variously claim or admit as its own, require undoubtedly to be borne in mind. I take them to be eight.

The first period, of the New Testament and the Apostolic Fathers, reaches to about A.D. 160 ; the second, of the apologists, Fathers, and great councils, to about A.D. 500 ; and the third period, the welter of the Teutonic migrations, ends the Old World with the coronation of Charlemagne in A.D. 800.

The fourth period, in action to about A.D. 1240, in speculation largely up to 1274, indeed up to 1300—the Middle Ages at their best—achieves a differentiation, and yet a connexion and equilibrium, between the State and the Church, reason and faith, liberty and authority, this world and the next. And the fifth period, up to about A.D. 1500, dissolves the mediæval synthesis by the apparently overwhelming triumph of the claims to direct universal, spiritual-temporal sovereignty of various of these later popes, and the ominously rapid development of an opposition even to the abidingly central, spiritual truth and rights of the Church. These two centuries achieve the divorce, in many Christian minds, between reason and faith, State and Church, liberty and authority. Occam, the English Franciscan, is probably the most typical representative of this universal disintegration, philosophical scepticism, and sheer volitional religion.

The sixth period inaugurates the modern era, from the revolution of Protestantism up to the eighteenth century, and is dominated by the Council of Trent—a period less rich, generous, and spontaneous than the early Middle Ages, yet which nobly eliminated, once for all, the danger of Roman Catholic enslavement to the Occamist conception. The seventh period, the eighteenth century, is, for Roman Catholicism as well as for Protestantism, largely a time of stagnation and decline ; while the eighth period, in which we still live, shows a remarkable renaissance of Catholic principles also among the finest Protestant minds, often where these minds still consider themselves irreconcilably anti-Roman.

Of these eight periods I will bear in mind especially the first, the New Testament period ; the fourth and fifth—the great early and the decadent late Middle Ages ; and the eighth, our own storm-tossed age.

I will assume four points throughout what follows. First, the Reformation was (largely for its leaders, and still more largely for their immediate recruits) a *revolution*. We may think the movement to have been inevitable ; but a revolution, and not simply a reform, it most undoubtedly was. And if it really was a just and wise and generous revolution it was indeed a white raven—a most rare exception among such upheavals. Secondly, within the limits indicated above, Protestantism was a religious, a Christian movement. The great Benedictines of the Congregation of St. Maur, the chief founders of modern historical science, always called Protestants " our separated brethren " ; I will treat them here as such. Thirdly, Protestantism (at least incidentally, in the long run, and conjointly with other forces) brought considerable and very necessary liberation from certain downright abuses, excesses, or one-sidednesses in the latter Middle-Age practice and outlook, especially in two directions. The magnificent efforts of the Popes during the earlier Middle Ages, for the liberty of the Church, as the organism for the abiding life, in face of the State, as the organisation for the temporal life, were succeeded by

*I

the policies of an Innocent IV. and Boniface VIII., which largely ignored, or directly subordinated, the really different rights specific to the State. The flagrant abuses of the " provisions," the oppressions of the Inquisition, the sometimes nobly used but always mixedly operative deposing power, and similar complications, appeared to many minds as ineradicable except by a full breach with the papal power. And in science and scholarship, turned chiefly earthward by the Renaissance, a wider patience and welcome for things new and strange, than was often accorded by those churchmen who remained definitely religious, had become necessary, unless the non-religious side of life was to be gravely crippled, and religion itself was, indirectly, to lose much of its vigour and appeal. But fourthly, nothing of all this decides whether Protestantism itself brings us a truly adequate conception and practice of these difficult matters ; and, still less, whether Protestantism itself constitutes a truly deeper religion, or has succeeded in capturing for itself the richness and resourcefulness of the old faith. Certainly the Lutheran and Anglican general reduction of the Church to a mere department of the State is a sorry dereliction of an essential attribute of developed religion ; while Protestant bibliolatry has actually much hampered, first, geology and, later, Biblical criticism. And as to the depth and delicacy, wisdom and passion, of religion itself, there assuredly still or again exist not a few religiously ripe Protestants, who instinctively perceive how large is the store of these dearest of treasures, of a quite specific, unique, quality, which remain, still uncaptured, in the hands of the Roman Catholic Church.

II

I take the points common in the past to Catholicism and Protestantism (taken within the limits fixed above) to be six. First, the essential Givenness of Religion. This characteristic was perceived, even one-sidedly, by the Early Great Protestant Leaders, especially by Luther and Calvin. Religion is here felt intensely as the work of God and as the witness of His presence and spirit. Secondly, this givenness appears in the Society of

Believers, or at least of the predestined—the particular soul is awakened within, or into, or by, this pre-existing society. The mystical, indeed the subconscious, element is thus apprehended here, and gives fundamental significance to infant baptism, and to its tenacious retention by Luther and Calvin. Thirdly, there is the keen sense of the Historical, concrete, contingent, unique Character of the Jewish-Christian Revelation. This is especially marked in Luther's even excessive insistence upon the necessity of knowledge of the historic Christ, and in Calvin's emphasis on the covenant character of religion.

The Protestant Non-Conformists in part contribute the following three, largely contrary, common points. (1) Religion is a Work of Man—a deliberate, lifelong, methodical renunciation and self-discipline. It is thus not only a gift and a faith, but also an effort and a labour. This is doubtless the deepest meaning of the insistence upon adult baptism. The fully conscious, deliberately ascetical element of Christianity, its detachment from the world, appears here with force and vehemence, even though mostly without any sense of affinity to the Catholic, monastic celibate ideal, and, indeed, mostly with an angry prejudice against this form of asceticism. (2) Man even in his present earthly condition can, through God's grace, attain in this work on himself to a Real, not an imputed, Sanctity, and can so attain as a special manifestation of God's power (which thus achieves more than any covering up of sinfulness) and of God's truthfulness (Who cannot consider the soul holy which still harbours aught that is unholy). Of the early Protestant sects only the varieties and individuals of a pre-Reformation spiritual descent appear to have held views of this kind ; but later on these positions were systematically developed, even alongside of other doctrines of an intensely Puritan and anti-Roman kind, by the Society of Friends, and, less picturesquely, but here associated with teachings of a more or less Catholic kind, by John Wesley and a considerable proportion of his followers. And (3) the Church is Free ; the Visible Society of Believers is distinct from, and independent of, the State. Luther soon ceased to perceive this point ; Calvin aimed at it to the end, but largely indirectly ; Anglicans did not widely apprehend it until the times of King Charles I. But the Protestant Non-Conformist

Bodies, especially the Anabaptists and Baptists, and the Independents (Congregationalists), have nobly and costingly held this essential conviction from the first, though mostly with an ever keener antagonism to all Episcopal, and especially Papal, Church Government, as but a still more oppressive intrusion of (at bottom) State power within the domain of the religious conscience.

Thus we have three points common to the Church-type of Protestantism and Catholicism as world-seeking, as the religious society which mingles with and moulds the non-religious associations of human life, and practises the maximum of that *attachment* which all religious souls must practise a little ; and three points common to the Sect-type and the same Catholicism as world-fleeing, as a school of solitude, wherein single heroic souls learn to practise a maximum of that *detachment* which all religious souls must practise a little.

III

Now the unchecked effect in the direction of an approximation to Catholicism, which is certainly involved in the above six Catholic positions at work in Protestantism, will be attained only by the full and widespread acceptance of certain further common points, which are now assuredly in process of recognition, largely newly among Protestants and in part afresh or more consciously among Catholics.

First, Luther's own later account (1530 onward) of his own earlier monastic experiences and of the teachings and spirit of the religious orders and official church of his Protestant days (1505–17) is predominantly a legend. Denifle's *Luther und Lutherthum* (1904–9), in spite of its unpleasing polemical vehemence and of its weak imputations of conscious untruthfulness, has undoubtedly proved this up to the hilt. But if so, even so largely fair-minded an account as Dr. T. M. Lindsay's *History of the Reformation* (1907) still falls short of the fullness of the facts. For Lindsay still follows Luther's own later account of his own earlier self, and thus retains the figure of the early Luther who then probed the depths of Jewish legalism and popish, monastic self-righteousness, and whose sensitively Christian soul then ended its self-torture only when it discovered, entirely alone, the meaning of " the justice of God " as proclaimed by St. Paul. And Lindsay still only praises the domestic, popular religion and hymns of the mediæval Church, as part sources of Luther's discoveries as to the absolute need of grace and the prevenience of grace, and as to the measure of Christian perfection consisting simply in the love of God and the love of man. Against all this, the traditional Protestant presentation, Denifle gives countless quotations from letters by, and descriptions of, Luther during his convent days ; from the rules and office-books of the Augustinian Eremites of Luther's time and monastery, and from some sixty prominent doctors of the Church from about A.D. 370 to 1474 and on to Luther as official Augustinian lecturer himself, which demonstrate the contrary on each count. No, and again no; these last mediæval times were not bereft of deeply spiritual and Christian official teaching in church and convent, and justice now requires that we all frankly admit this simple fact, which, after all, need not break the heart of anyone.

Secondly, it is strange and pathetic, to any modern Biblical scholar, to note Luther's unawareness of the contrast between the Synoptic Gospels and St. Paul. Even his *Liberty of a Christian Man* (1520), deservedly held to be the mellowest of his Protestant writings, quotes St. Paul as against the three Synoptists in a proportion of (roughly) ten to one ; and even these few Synoptic quotations do not touch the points raised by the severe antithesis between faith and works so dear to St. Paul, in his systematic polemical mood—an antithesis so little present in the Synoptists. Luther thus forgets (and only thus *can* forget) how Jesus first advises the rich young man to keep all the Commandments, and then, assured that they had been kept, recommends the youth, if he would be perfect, to go and sell all things and follow Jesus—that he will thus have treasure in Heaven. Here are Luther's three bugbears all together : good works, works of supererogation, merit and reward—three detestable, specifically Jewish notions, yet somehow notions prominent in the actual words of Jesus. And so, again, Luther can forget, and does forget, the movement characteristic of our Lord in appointing the apostles. It is Our Lord Himself, the One, who here picks out certain twelve, and appoints one of them the head. It is to these twelve, and not to any and every Christian, that He says : " He that heareth you heareth me, and he that despiseth you despiseth me." The universal priesthood of all believers is doubtless, in some sense, true. But in the Synoptics Our Lord confers certain intrinsic powers only upon a few ; the fruits, but not the roots, are to be shared by all. And, finally, the act of conversion appears in the Synoptics as an active turning on the part of the soul, as is the case throughout the great Hebrew prophets. The true translation is not " Unless ye be converted," but " Unless ye turn." Of course, all such human activity appears as anticipated, rendered possible, and sustained by God's action. But the one action does not exclude the other ; and Luther has here also still further emphasised a point in St. Paul which assuredly requires no such heightening.

Thirdly, we know well how great and permanent was the debt of Luther to Occam. Now Occam is profoundly atomistic in his conception of Human Society, the State, and the Church —these complexes are all for him simply sum-totals of the self-contained individuals who compose them. And, again, he is profoundly agnostic in his theory of knowledge ; only by a leap of despair of the will, not with any activity of the intelligence, does man attain to faith, even as to the existence, the unity, and the moral character of God. The Commandments of God, which the greatest of the prophets and rabbis, which again Aquinas had magnificently propounded as expressions of God's own unalterable nature, have here become purely arbitrary enactments. Any well-informed Roman Catholic is thus bound to have some patience with the persistence of such philosophical prejudices among most of the Reformers, since such views were largely diffused in the Church during the Catholic youth of these Protestant Reformers. But the views here indicated are not the views of the Middle Ages at their best ; and this, the Golden Middle Age, was practically unknown, not only to Luther and Calvin, but even to Erasmus and Sir Thomas More. Such great Protestant scholars as the Germans von Gierke and Troeltsch, and the Englishmen F. W. Maitland and A. L. Smith, have, of recent years, worked hard and well to awaken men to the grandeur of those earlier views, and doubtless their labours will increasingly prevail.

Fourthly, the psychology of Luther, and indeed more or less of the whole specifically Protestant position, is explicable only as the work of men who were attempting to strengthen religion, and who nevertheless were, at the same time, struggling to escape from some of its abiding needs and laws, on account of certain complications and abuses which had grown around these needs and laws. Thus the point specially dear to Luther and his followers, that the act and life of faith have nothing to do, in their generation, with the senses, although, once faith is awakened, there is no harm in expressing this pure spirituality in symbols of sense, is, objectively, a doctrinaire one-sidedness. I kiss my child not only because I love it ; I kiss it also in order to love it. A religious picture not only expresses my awakened faith ; it is a help to my faith's awakening. And the whole doctrine of the Incarnation, of any and every condescension of God toward man—man so essentially body as well as mind—is against any such " pure " spirituality. Great as doubtless has been the Synagogue, yet the Temple services were not for nothing; and, great as Judaism with the Synagogue has been, Judaism with both Synagogue and Temple would have been more complete. And it is not magic, but a sheer fact traceable throughout our many-sided life, that we often grow, mentally and spiritually, almost solely by the stimulation of our senses or almost solely by the activity of other minds. Magic begins only when and where things physical are taken to effect spiritual results apart altogether from minds transmitting or receiving. It is doubtless the fear of priestly power and its intrusion into politics which has determined (from, say, Wyclif, until now) this quite unphilosophical " magic " scare among so many Protestants.

And, fifthly, there is a side of Luther, and of not a few among the various Protestant bodies, which distinctly overemphasises the simply formal side of the moral and spiritual life. Sincerity, conscientiousness, fidelity to our light, the not forcing of others beyond what they can see, and the not pretending ourselves to see more or other than we can succeed in seeing: all these are, doubtless, good and necessary things. Yet not all these things put together reach to the central religious work and problems. We have not only to remain faithful towards our own extant standards, but we have to grow adequate concerning that abundant, many-sided, rich life of nature, of other minds, and of other spirits, which lies all around us and invites us continually, not only to learn new facts, but to learn new worlds, indeed to acquire new methods for apprehending, and new systems for ordering them. And both the Stoics and Kant are here hopelessly insufficient. We all greatly require criticism, stimulation, reproof, of our most intimate and cherished convictions ; and it is our reciprocal duty, with tact and restraint, to try to serve our fellows similarly. Hegel, perhaps most probingly among all Protestant philosophers, has exposed in general this impoverishing formalism of Kant " the Philosopher of Protestantism." But I believe the true scheme, as concerns religion, to have been best developed by Cardinal Juan de Lugo, the Spanish Jesuit, who wrote in Rome under the eyes of Pope Urban VIII., at the end of the seventeenth century. De Lugo first lays down that, according to Catholic doctrine, God gives light, sufficient for its salvation, to every soul that attains to the use of reason in this life. He next asks, What is the ordinary method by which God offers and renders possible this salvation? And he answers that, though God doubtless can work moral miracles, these do not appear to be the rule, and are not in strictness necessary; that the human soul, in all times and places, has a certain natural affinity for, and need of, truth ; and again, that the various philosophical schools and religious bodies throughout mankind all contain and hand down, amid various degrees of human error and dis-tortion, *some* truth, some gleams and elements of divine truth. Now what happens as a rule is simply this : the soul that in good faith seeks God, His truth and love, concentrates its attention, under the influence of grace, upon these elements of truth, be they many or few, which are offered to it in the sacred books and religious schools and assemblies of the Church, Sect, or Philosophy in which it has been brought up. It feeds upon these elements, the others are simply passed by ; and divine grace, under cover of these elements, feeds and saves this soul. I submit that this view admirably combines a sense of man's profound need of tradition, institution, training, with full justice to the importance of the dispositions and acts of the individual soul, and, above all, with a keen sense of the need of special graces offered by God to the several souls. And such a view in no way levels down or damps the missionary ardour. Buddhism does not become equal to Mohammedanism, nor Mohammedanism to Judaism, nor Platonism to Christianity, nor Socinianism, or even Lutheranism, to Catholicism. It merely claims that everywhere there is *some* truth ; that this truth comes originally from God ; and that this truth, great or little, is usually mediated to the soul, neither by a spiritual miracle nor by the sheer efforts of individuals, but by traditions, schools and churches. We thus attain an outlook, generous, rich, elastic ; yet also graduated, positive, unitary, and truly Catholic.

10

INSTITUTIONAL CHRISTIANITY

OR

THE CHURCH, ITS NATURE AND NECESSITY [1]

WHEN, as a child and lad, I was taken, for our summer holiday and bathing, from Brussels to Ostend, I used to be impressed, ever more as the years went by, with how, the nearer we came to the sea and to its salt landward breezes, the more did the trees bend away from these blasts. These trees stood there permanently fixed in every kind of unnatural, fleeing or defiant, attitude and angle. Only after I had passed these perturbing effects and tolls of the sea, would I reach, and would I for weeks and weeks admire, this same wide sea, now found to be in itself so life-giving and so hospitable—a part of the great ocean encompassing the world. Those trees and that sea have remained with me, for over half a century, as a vivid image of the effect of the Church—be it the fact of the Church, or the fancies concerning the Church—upon large masses of modern men. In the following address I propose to follow the same order as that of my childish experiences. I will first describe the positions frequently attempted, though mostly in combinations of two or three, by those who fear the Church or the Churches, and who thus strive to find or to create operative substitutes for these despised or dreaded bodies. I will next try to define the chief causes which (apart from individual peculiarities or obvious perversities) are more or less at work in all such substitutions. I will, thirdly, indicate the still larger evidences for the abiding need, the strict irreplaceableness of the Church, notwithstanding all that *de facto* opposition, indeed even notwithstanding the understandableness, the partial justification, of that opposition. And I will

---

[1] An Address delivered in London to the Executive Committee of the British branches of the Christian Student Movement, October, 1918.

end with certain rules which I believe readily to spring from the situation as we have found it to exist by our first three investigations. Here I will only add two warnings. For one thing, I am addressing throughout only definite believers in a Personal God and a persistent Providence, and again only those who deliberately recognise in the Person, Teaching and Spirit of the earthly Jesus and the Heavenly Christ the supreme revelation of that Personal God and of man's ways to Him. And, for a second thing, I beg my hearers to be patient for a little with the ambiguity involved in the apparently synonymous or alternative use of the terms " Church " and " Churches." I believe that the sheer facts and necessary implications of the three first sets of arguments will clear up this complexity, gradually indeed but very surely, for and at the end.

I

If we take the substitutes offered to mankind for a Church in the order of their increasing extension and subtlety, we shall move through the following five positions. (In actual life the substitutes generally consist more or less of mixtures effected between some two or three of these five theoretically possible pure positions.)

There is first the substitution which will doubtless always commend itself to the half-educated man : the Individual. Religion, where such a man is at all religiously alive, is most rightly felt to be the deepest of man's experiences. But if so, what more natural, what more unanswerable conclusion can be drawn from this, readily argues this same man, than that religion, the deepest experience, is also of necessity the most private, the most entirely private, hence again the most incommunicable —the most individual—the most exclusively individual—of all things ? Besides, does not everyone know himself best ? Such a man, did he know Kant, would agree with Kant when this philosopher warns us that all attempts to influence or to mould the opinions of other men in such deepest matters are always only so much harmful interference and impertinent tyranny. The later Middle Age was already largely penetrated by this spirit. Thus the English Franciscan William of Ockham, whom Luther regarded as his "dear Master," teaches at times and generally implies that a holy individual soul can, at need, of itself alone fill the place of the Church.

Then there is another, a wider outlook, that of the Waldensians and the Quakers. Here the Family in great part supplants the Church.

Next we get a position more comprehensive still, yet one, for the most part, harsher than the second—the Sect. Montanus and that genius, his fiery follower Tertullian, are good examples of this position.

And then the substitution widens out, yet also thins down, into that of the German theologian Richard Rothe, who would deliberately oust the Church in favour of the State—doubtless a great simplification, if only it prove possible and fruitful.

And finally there is the subtlest of all the substitutions, one now again very alluring to not a few fine minds—that of Philosophy. So with the Stoics and Neoplatonists of old ; so with Hume, in so far as he retained any religion at all ; so with the Hegelians of more or less the left, as now with Dr. Bradley and Professor Bernard Bosanquet in England, and, with little or no religious sense remaining, in Benedetto Croce in Italy. Most of the followers of M. Bergson appear to be in a similar case. All these philosophical groups have some good to say of Religion —even of Institutional Religion ; but a Church is here essentially a condescension to the multitude, a largely childish symbol and *Kindergarten* for what Philosophy alone holds and teaches with a virile adequacy.

The elements of truth variously present in these five substitutions—of the Individual, the Family, the Sect, the State, Philosophy—will appear later on. Our immediate further task concerns the direct incentives for seeking after substitutes of any kind.

II

We shall never reach fairness towards these processes of substitution unless we begin with the conviction that it is impossible (in view of history at large and of the history of these

substitutions in particular) to put down these processes, simply
and generally, to the sheer perversity of human nature. Such
perversity is, indeed, very certainly more or less at work here
also, yet demonstrably, upon the whole, only as a preparatory,
or intensifying cause. This is certain because of two facts
which are simply undeniable. No institution in human history
has reaped a more enthusiastic devotion and a more boundless gratitude than the Church—and this for something like a
thousand years and amidst large masses first of Græco-Roman,
and then of Teutonic peoples, indeed also amongst the Celts
and the Slavs. And again, these enthusiastic admirers were, by
natural disposition, no better than are their descendants, nor
have these descendants acquired a congenital taint unpossessed
by those predecessors. Hence it is logically impossible to quote
the past enthusiasm as a sure proof of the Church's goodness,
and, at the same time, to take the later and present suspicion
and hostility as simply evidence of men's badness. Men have
remained throughout substantially the same, so that, if they
weigh much as witnesses when they admire, they cannot weigh
nothing as witnesses when they oppose.

The chief real causes or occasions of such frequent attempts
to evade the Church, or to supersede it by means of this or that
substitute, are, I think, four. I take them in the order of their
growing penetration.

The Church, as a Visible Institution, is, has to be, administered
by human beings. And the majority of human beings are but
average mortals who inevitably tend to work the Church, to
develop the Church, with insufficient balance, in a spirit of acute
rivalry or of worldly ambition, or at least in a *simpliste*, short-cut
manner. Yet thus to work or to develop the Church, in its multiform inevitable relations with the other God-intended activities
and God-given institutions of mankind, spells, of necessity,
more or less dangerous friction and ominous repression. And
indeed such complications can spring in part from Churchmen
truly great in other ways. Striking examples of this are the claims
of not a few of the Popes of the later Middle Age and of the
Renaissance. The Papacy had rendered priceless services to
mankind by achieving the autonomy of the Church in face of
the State—of the Church as the organ essentially of Supernature,

in face of the State as the organism essentially of Nature. And again the Papacy has been from the first, and will doubtless remain to the last, the divinely intended and divinely blessed instrument and incorporation of the Visible Unity of the Church —of the Church, as essentially but one. Yet after that great, abidingly precious victory, a certain obscuration of this permanent function could not but follow when certain Popes came, in their turn, to forget, at least in practice, the specific rights and legitimate autonomy of the State. Another striking instance of a similar oblivion is the Galileo case, where the sense has not yet sufficiently awakened or is in abeyance that Science also possesses its own specific duties, rights and powers.

Again, the Church, as a Visible Institution worked and developed, in its average manifestations, largely by distinctly average men, tends to ignore, or at least to grudge and to minimise, the degrees and kinds of truth and goodness always more or less present in such other religious bodies as may possess a long duration and ethical seriousness. A remarkable example of this is furnished even by such a God-inspired genius as St. Paul, when in his systematising and speculative mood. For when in that mood the entire Old Testament Cultus can appear, to this vehement convert to the New Revelation, as exclusively a means for bringing home to its devotees a sense of their sinfulness and of the radical inability of the Jewish Church to bring any strength whatsoever to the avoidance of the sins thus discovered.

Once more, the Church, as a Visible Institution worked and developed by average men, after conquering and winning the world " not by killing but by dying," came, some half a century after its external triumph under Constantine, to killing—to allowing, indeed to encouraging and blessing her lay children to kill in their turn, in and for matters of religious belief. The use of force in religion is, indeed, deeply embedded in the Old Testament—King Josiah's great, profoundly important and very fruitful reform was demonstrably full of it. And many of the Psalms breathe this same spirit, which indeed still appears plainly in parts of our Christian Book of Revelation.

And finally, the Church as a Visible Institution worked by average men, has shown, ever since the advent of Historical Criticism, little comprehension of, and at times an acute hostility to, disinterested scholarship, with its serious investigation and candid enunciation of the successive stages, the human occasions and the surface motives traceable in the history of the Bible and of the Church. This average attitude, on the contrary, requires a sheer identity of the successive forms, a strict sameness in even the subsidiary movements of the religious spirit. We thus find the condemnation of Richard Simon in the Roman Catholic Church, and of Bishop Colenso in the Anglican, and of William Robertson Smith and Charles Briggs in the Presbyterian Bodies.

These four checks and oppressions, especially where they appear more or less in combination, readily explain a large part of men's alienation from Institutional Christianity, even where there is not the still more decisive incentive of a decided Immanentism or even of bad living or of sheer perversity.

III

Nevertheless there lies ready for the docile mind the most varied, unforced, largely indirect and unexpected, cumulative and hence very powerful, evidence for the abiding need of the Church. If we are only sufficiently patient to persist in open-ness of mind towards the rich lessons, past and present, of the spiritual life, we shall find this evidence for the Church to be more extensive, and deeper than are the evidences against it, and indeed to be alone fully germane to the issue in question.

There is, then, first, the presumption furnished by the other levels and ranges of the multiform life of man. Thus Art, we cannot deny, is developed in and through Academies, Schools, Traditions. True, artistic genius is something more and other than is such training or than all that such training can give of itself. Yet even genius cannot dispense with at least the more indirect forms and effects of such training, if this genius is to achieve its own full power and effect. So too with Science. Science assuredly does not grow solely by means of Schools, Traditions, the succession of teachers ; yet it does, upon the whole, require such an environment and discipline. The same holds good of Philosophy, in its own manner and degree. And Ethics, to be rich and robust, requires the Family, the Guild, the State, not only as the ends of Ethics but also as its disporting ground and means. And similarly with Religion. Such maxims and habits of soul as " To be alone with the Alone " and " God is a Spirit, and they that would serve Him must serve Him in Spirit and in Truth " spring from many centuries of social philosophy and social religion. The facts of man's essentially mixed condition of sense and spirit, and of his essential sociality will always, in the long run, refute and supplant, for the masses of men, every purely individualist or purely spiritual religion or attempt at such a religion. But body and society combined spell (if thus admitted on principle as essential factors of religion) nothing less than the Visible Church.

There is, next, the actual history of Religion itself. All the great religious personalities whose antecedents, doings and effects we can trace at all securely and at all fully, sprang from religious institutions, and either deliberately continued the extant institution or founded another institution, or, at the least, very soon influenced history in such an institutional direction. This is the case with Gautama, the Buddha, in the full sense of the deliberate foundation of an Order and a Church. Still more is it so (as here springing from a long development of a religious society and a common worship, and as leading on to a great reinforcement of this social, common cultus) with the Jewish Prophets. We can here follow the interconnexion of the Social and the Individual from Elijah onwards, ever more clearly, to Jeremiah with King Josiah's centralisation of the Hebrew Worship and his organisation of a definite Church ; and then, on again to Ezechiel, duly followed by the elaborate ecclesiasticism of the Priestly Code. So too with St. John the Baptist, who, all single and original as he appears, has, in reality, a long tradition and a rich social training behind him and around him. And especially is it so with St. Paul and with the great author of the Fourth Gospel. St. Paul deliberately organises the Christian Church, liberated by him from all subjection to the Jewish Church ; and the Fourth Gospel presupposes throughout this Church character of Christianity.

Indeed also with Jesus Himself, as He appears in the Synoptic Gospels, we find such a social, institutional religion, if we but vividly bear in mind three very pregnant facts. The expectation

of His Proximate Second Coming is a fact, at least it was a
certainty for the first hearers and first recorders of the words of
Jesus ; and this fact has to be remembered, not simply as concerns this or that subject-matter of the recorded saying and doings
of Jesus, but as it concerns them all. There is no sense in using
this fact, as is now not rarely done, in explanation of the small
or no place occupied in the sayings of Jesus by the Family,
Labour, the State, Art, Philosophy, or rather of His (practically
complete) abstraction from these great duties, problems, difficulties of manifold yet closely inter-connected human life ;
and not to allow for the same fact in the question of the sayings
of Jesus concerning the Church. Again, if the precise term
" Church " was, apparently, never uttered by the earthly Jesus,
the thing itself is, in its essence, already truly present in the
most undeniable of His own words, acts and organisings. For
the parables which have for background or for centre the family
or a kingdom, an owner of a house or a vineyard, or the parables
which turn on the qualities of salt and of leaven : they all imply
a social religious organism, a hierarchy of super-ordination and
of sub-ordination as well as of co-ordination. And all this
appears as one side of the rich living paradox which, on the
other side, bids us one and all to be but the lowly servants of
each other. And the actions of Jesus entirely bear out this social,
organic, graduated—this Church conception of religion. These
acts move, emphatically, not up from the many to the few, and
on from the few to the One ; nor, again, do they proceed down
as a light of grace vouchsafed by God, independently of all other
souls, to each soul direct, so that the economy of salvation would
consist in so many parallel lines of approach, each free from
all contact or crossing by the others. No : the movement here
is down from the One invisible God, through the one visible,
audible, tangible Jesus, on to the twelve visible men formed into
a single College by Jesus Himself, and sent out by Him to preach,
to heal, to forgive sins, with solemn warnings as to the guilt
of those who may refuse to hear them. And this visible College
is given a visible Head by the visible Jesus Himself, and Jesus
deliberately changes the name of this His chief representative
to the significant appellation " Rock," in return for the recognition, by Simon alone amongst the Twelve Apostles, of Jesus

as the Messiah. And finally, if the Church exists, in such sayings
and doings as were indisputably spoken or enacted by the
earthly Jesus Himself, only in fact and in rudiment, this same
Church appears, very certainly, also in name and in all its
essential lineaments, well within the New Testament, indeed
throughout a full two-thirds of its contents.   Thus St. Paul
busily organises the Church and yet simultaneously apprehends
the Church as the very Body of Christ, and insists solemnly
upon the two great central Sacraments, Baptism and the Holy
Eucharist. We have the Johannine Gospel, penetrated from first
to last with the conception of the Beloved Community and
with these two great Sacraments, here the subject-matter of
two solemn discourses.   And indeed these Sacraments are here
summed up symbolically in the Water and the Blood which
flow from the pierced side of Jesus upon the Cross ; and the
Church is similarly symbolised by the Seamless Coat left by
Jesus, the new High Priest, to mankind—for the reality so
adumbrated is to be thus indivisible except by the sins and
schisms of men.   Indeed, the waiting of the Beloved Disciple
to let Peter pass into the empty sepulchre before himself,
although he, and not Peter, had first reached the entrance,
appears to be one more instance of the sense of order, of the
Church and of its invisible Oneness which, indeed, penetrates
the entire work.   And finally the Synoptic Gospels, in their
apparently later constituents, sum up for us majestically these
developments.   Matthew gives us the two great passages—of
the Church now solemnly proclaimed by name and to be
built upon the Rock, Cephas, Peter ; and of the sublime commission of the Risen Christ to the Apostles, sending them out
into all the world and promising to be with them to the end.
And Luke gives us the prophecy of Jesus to the disciples that
Satan would attempt to sift them as wheat ; but that He, Christ,
had prayed—not for them all, but for Simon Peter, him alone,
that his faith should never fail, and that he, Simon Peter, after
his conversion (not from infidelity but cowardice) was to confirm
them.

Our Lord died upon the Cross in A.D. 30. The two great
primitive collections of His sayings and doings, the Gospel
according to St. Mark and the *Logia*, no doubt existed in written

form already in the middle sixties. St. Paul's great Epistles cannot be more recent than A.D. 52–59. The Gospels of Matthew and of Luke (minus some later additions) belong probably, the first to A.D. 70–75, and the second to A.D. 78–85. The Fourth Gospel cannot be more recent than A.D. 110, and may well go back as far as A.D. 95. And already in A.D. 93–97 we have the First Epistle of St. Clement Bishop of Rome, a prelude to the world-wide claim and influence of Bishop Victor of Rome in the great Paschal controversy of A.D. 190, 191. In view of such facts it is not fantastic if Wernle (*Die Synoptische Frage*, 1899, p. 192) and Heinrich J. Holtzmann (*Die Synoptiker*, Ed. 1901)—these two highly competent Protestant specialists—hold as possible that Matthew xvi. 17–19, the great "Thou art Peter" passage, already expresses the Roman claims (*Selbstbewusstsein*). In any case, nothing could well be more certain than are the earli-ness, the spiritual need and fruitfulness, and the prompt emphasis, of the developments of the Church and the Sacraments. History never yields mathematical demonstration even as to the brute facts—as to their happenedness; still less can history, of itself alone, penetrate to the inner meaning of these happenednesses; hence we can, if we will, stiffen and close our minds against all these developments, we can, at least, treat them as artificial accretions. But the moral certainty special to history will then raise great difficulties against us in view of the earliness of the developments concerned, and Christianity will then be forced to appear as having fraudulently, or at least quite externally, acquired the hands and the feet, the food and the heart with which it worked, moved, sustained itself, loved and struggled against an acutely hostile world and with which it eagerly and increasingly conquered that world during those early decades and the subsequent three centuries of Catacombs. One thing in any case even the simplest logic forbids us to do. We are not free—though how often this is done !—we are not free to accept certain formulations of doctrine, which appear clear and definite only in the middle and later New Testament, as accurate enunciations of the facts and beliefs implicitly present from the first ; and to evade or to explain away other, parallel develop-ments, because we do not like their content. " God so loved the world," this great passage may appeal to us more than " Thou

art Peter ": yet only both, and not one only, can, for a large
and logical outlook, represent the genius of Christianity, com-
paratively late as may be both these articulations of it.

And there is finally a third group of proofs for the need of
the Church—evidence, largely delicate and difficult to trace in
detail, yet very real and impressively spontaneous and convergent.
We here get evidence both of the impoverishment which follows
upon conscious rejection of the Social, Institutional element of
religion, and of the unconscious indebtedness of the individualist,
to such social and institutional religion, for much of such
adequacy as he may retain.   And there is, contrariwise, the
evidence of the heightened good which springs from deliberate
persistent acceptance of the Church as such.   Here we cannot
do more than give some specimens from the very large mass of
facts. Thus, as to the impoverishment in the lives of Churchless
religionists, we can trace a certain incompleteness in a man's
humility, so long as it consists of humiliation before God alone,
and as it claims to derive all its religious help without any
mediation of the senses and of society—purely spiritually from
the Infinite Pure Spirit alone. Complete humility imperatively
demands my continuous recognition of my own multiform need
of my fellow-creatures, especially of those wiser and better than
myself, and of my life-long need of training, discipline, incorporation ; full humility requires filial obedience and docility towards
men and institutions, as well as fraternal give and take, and
paternal authority and superintendence.   All this, as against
the first of the substitutes for the Church, Individualism.   The
second and fourth substitutes, the Family and the State (when
taken thus not in addition to, but in lieu of, the Church), tend,
the first, rather to a sentimental moralism, a mutual admiration
society ; and the second, to a morality and inchoate religion of
a natural, a Golden Rule type, as in the cases of Confucius and
of Bentham.   The third substitution, that of the Sect, is rather
a one-sidedness than a sheer error, and will be considered later
on.   But the fifth, the last substitution, that of Philosophy, is
probably, for men of education, the most inflating error amongst
all these substitutions.   There can be no doubt that where such
patronage of the toiling moiling Church folk by " superior "
philosophical insight does not induce pride and complacency,

this can only spring from certain rare qualities in the character concerned. In any case such a soul lacks the very definite training in the *creaturely* mind, so richly furnished by Church appurtenance.

But again. The men who practise these several substitutions draw such good as is often largely present within them, for the most part from the work and effect across the centuries, and from the still persistent influence, however much ignored, of the Church and of the spirit of the Church. Thus the Individualist derives his frequent sense of the sacredness which attaches to each single soul, not from his Individualism as such, but from the long, slow elaboration by the Christian Community of the value of its several constituents—the various, all more or less unique and different, members of the Mystical Body of Christ. The man who substitutes the Family, similarly takes the said Family as it has been slowly, most costingly elaborated by means of religious ideals, especially now for well-nigh nineteen centuries by Christian ideals. It was the doctrines, the religious facts, of the Holy Trinity, of the Fatherhood of God, of Christ's Mother, of God's Children, and of the Church as an organism of inter-dependent, mutually supplementary, variously related members : it was these spiritual forces which, at their best, ended by pro-ducing something like ideal Families amongst men at large. Again, the man who substitutes the State for the Church very largely finds such sufficient nobility in the State as he may acquire and reveal, through the mirage thrown on to his image of the State by the ages-long and world-wide work of the Church at its noblest. And finally the man who substitutes Philosophy retains or reaches some depth and delicacy of outlook, largely because the tenets or temper of mind thus adopted by him spring from philosophies which are themselves more or less penetrated by genuine religious instincts, such as Platonism, or Stoicism, or (especially) Neoplatonism, or which have been considerably influenced by the Jewish or Christian Churches, as with Philonism and the outlooks of Leibniz and Locke, Kant and Hegel. The advantages of a direct, deliberate acceptance of, and of a life-long submission to, the Church, will be best indicated in conjunction with the suggestions for the most fruitful working of such acceptance and submission.

IV

How then are we, scholars or scientists, to work or to develop
our extant or incipient Churchmanship in the borderlands and
mixed territories created for us by the very fact of our earnest
scholarship and fervent Churchmanship ? What, as we grow to
scholarly and to spiritual maturity, is to be our final conception
of the nature and function of the Church for and within this our
mixed and multilevelled life ? Or rather, which are the extant
currents of Christian and Catholic thought and work, which are
the personalities of the past and present of the Church, that
furnish us with the amplest and most appropriate dispositions
and insights for our own further application and development ?
I believe that seven sets of insight and action, of suffering and
temperament are involved and required in the fullest and most
fruitful functioning of Churchmanship in these difficult and
delicate subject-matters. Each of these sets of dispositions and
actions, even if taken alone, remains more or less an unrealised
ideal for each and all of us single souls, indeed even for each
and all of the entire religious bodies. But then " Ideal " does
not mean " Utopian." Each of these ideals exists largely realised
in quite a considerable number of doers and thinkers, strivers
and sufferers ; and the inception, or the fostering, or at least
the occasion, of all these ideals sprang from, and continues in,
this or that religious body or (in different degrees and ways)
within them all.

1. The deliberate recognition and the daily acceptance of
limitations and sacrifices imposed upon the single soul's direct
individual claims, as inevitable consequences and costs of this
soul's appurtenance to any Community—to any Church extant
in our earthly life. This, even where the individual claims are
not, in themselves, bad or unreasonable ; or, again, where the
requirements of the Church officials or the temper of the Church
majority are not, in themselves, wrong or unwise. The greater
number of such cases of apparently useless friction or depressing
isolation will, indeed, spring from no definite badness or wrong-
headedness on either side, but simply from the twin facts that
we ourselves are rarely free from unreasonable fastidiousnesses

or from the unmanly desire to get without cost, and that also our Church superiors, equals and inferiors are men and not angels, as indeed human superiors, equals and inferiors are in every conceivable earthly community, religious or political. The majority of men, as indeed the majority of our own impulses, thoughts and doings, are, upon the whole, very ordinary, unimaginative, mechanical; and indeed both these our fellow-men and we ourselves can and do mix more or less of positive badness with this our prevalent ordinariness. We undoubtedly possess the right, indeed, the duty, to do what we can to raise the average level; we may not commit sin—what we clearly know to be wrong or false—let who will command it; indeed we may be required by our conscience to hold our own quite openly and to speak out frankly. Assuredly not all the schisms and separations, past or still present amongst men, were originally only the fault, or even much the fault, of the seceders, and little or in nowise the fault of the bodies which the seceders left, sometimes more or less unwillingly. Yet it remains true that there can be no Church for us on earth, if we will not or cannot put up with faulty Church officials and faulty Church members; and again, that we shall never put up with such faultiness sufficiently unless we possess or acquire so strong a sense of all we have to gain from Church membership as to counterbalance the repulsiveness of such faults. This our sense of need has to be thus strong, since the faults of Church people are not simply the same, in kind and degree, as the faults of ecclesiastically unattached mankind. No: these faults are largely *sui generis*, and would, in great part, disappear with the disappearance of the Church. A large illustration of this, our whole first, difficulty and need is furnished by the very careful *Life and Letters of John Henry Cardinal Newman* by Mr. Wilfrid Ward, 1912.

2. The deliberate recognition that a Church, worthy of the name, can never itself be a society for the promotion of research, for the quest of an as yet unfound good. A Church cannot exist without certain credal affirmations, with their inevitable delimitations. It must be a vessel and channel of already extant, positive religious experience and conviction, with at least a rudimentary psychology and philosophy of its own. It has

continuously to risk excessive detail and over-precision ; it simply cannot find room within itself for any and every negation. The Congregationalist Dr. P. T. Forsyth has brought this out with rare force in his most striking book, *Theology in Church and State*, 1915.

3. Discrimination between facts and principles which rightly claim our absolute interior assent, and deductions and details environing these facts and principles which call only for our conditional belief and practical conformity. The absolute assent goes to the great " Necessary " Realities of religion and to a nucleus of Contingent Historical Happenings—self-revelations and incarnations of those Realities within our earthly human life of time and space. The interpretation of those " Necessary " Realities and of the Church's faith in them undergoes some modification, slowly across the centuries, by the Church's theologians, as these theologians are tested and assimilated by the Church authority itself. Hence there exists a certain legitimate distinction between, on the one hand, these Realities themselves and the faith of the Faithful concerning them, and, on the other hand, the analysis and theory of Theologians concerning this faith. There exists indeed a very real relation between Facts, Faith and Theology, but the relation is not one of sheer identity. The Realities themselves change not ; the Faith, the Life in them change not : only our understanding, our articulation of the Facts and of the Faith grow and indeed adapt themselves more and more to this abiding Faith and to these persistent Facts, yet they do so in and through categories of thought which more or less vary across the centuries. And again the precise extent possessed by the nucleus of fully Historical Happenednesses essential to the Christian faith is also a subject-matter demanding a certain conditionalness of belief. For the evidence as to this or that historical happenedness has, of necessity, to be of an historical, critical, documentary kind. Yet also in this entire range of happenednesses there are two fundamental points which demand our absolute assent : that a certain nucleus of historical happenednesses is absolutely essential for the Christian faith, and that God has seen to it, and will continue to the end of time to see to it, that sufficient historical evidence for such a sufficient nucleus will remain at men's disposal on

and on. All genuine religion, especially Christianity, is revelational, evidential, factual—this also within the range of sense-
and-spirit, and can never become a system of pure ideas or of
entirely extra-historical realities. On the other hand, the precise
amount, the full list of historical happenednesses cannot, *qua*
so much happenedness, be kept entirely outside all examination,
testing and delimitation by sober and reverent historical criticism.
The ultimate, alone fully adequate, guarantee that the nucleus
will persist sufficient for the Church's faith to the end is thus,
in strictness, not the Church but God ; and, more precisely
still, not the God of Revelation and Supernature, but the God
of Reason and of Right Nature, or rather, God as the Divine,
unshakable Foundation both of Revelation and of Reason, and
both. The most continuous perception of this now increasingly
important point has, I think, been attained by Professor Ernest
Troeltsch, in his later books and papers.

4. Recognition, persistent, frank and full, of elements of real
truth and goodness, as more or less present and operative within
all the fairly mature and ethical forms and stages of religion
throughout history and the world. These elements indeed all
come from God and are all intended to lead to God, the One
God of all truth and of all creation. Yet this recognition requires,
as its constant companion, an equally definite conviction as to
the unequal richness in such elements as they are furnished even
by the greater religions or indeed the world-religions. Buddhism
is poorer in such elements than is Hindooism ; Hindooism is
in general considerably less true than Mohammedanism ;
Judaism is much more tender, rich and spiritual than Mohammedanism ; and finally Christianity markedly exceeds Judaism
in its range, depth and elasticity of religious insight and life.
And religion is so truly the deepest and the most delicate level
of man's life that any and every, even seemingly slight, difference
in such degrees and kinds of truth and goodness is of profound
importance. The Scotch Nonconformist Missionary in India,
Dr. J. N. Farquhar, has admirably applied such balanced justice
to an immense mass of detailed facts in his fine *Crown of
Hindooism*, 1915.

5. Recognition, as regards Christianity, of a large element of
truth in what can roughly be called the Sect-type, yet also of

K

a genuine injustice in this same Sect-type in so far as it may be
irreconcilably hostile to the Church-type. The Sect-type, like
the world-fleeing elements in Neoplatonism and Buddhism,
and like the similar temper in Christian Monasticism, is profoundly right in its sense that Other-worldliness, Detachment
and Poverty, in a word the ascetical and transcendental temper,
are essential to all virile religion. Thus such protests as those
of Tertullian, of Valdes, and of Kierkegaard are, so far, true.
They are true, not only against such immorality or scandalous
worldliness as may have actually defiled the Church of their
day or country ; they remain still more precious, because thus
useful for all times and places, as bitterly tonic warnings against
any Church life and Church ideal which does not fully embrace
and cherish also this negative, ascetical movement, and which
would admit This-worldliness, provided only it be sufficiently
refined and sufficiently moral, as more or less complete. Yet
we must, at the same time, recognise the complementary truth
that Detachment, that World-flight alone, that all Universal
Monasticism are, or would be, ideals of an erroneousness equal,
even though opposite, to the error of sheer This-worldliness.
Only the two movements of World-flight and of World-seeking,
of the Civilising of Spirituality, and of the Spiritualising of
Civilisation : only This world and That world, each stimulating
the other, although in different ways, from different sources and
with different ends : only these two movements together form
man's complete supernaturalised spiritual life. But if so, then
the Church's large and leisurely occupation with Art, Philosophy,
the State was not and is not, in itself, a corruption, but a normal
expansion of one of the two necessary halves of the Church's
own complete nature and end. And this again means that the
Sect-type in fact represents, at its best, one half of the whole
truth, whereas the Church, at its best, represents both halves
of the same whole truth—this, however, only because and where
the Church manages to incorporate within itself the Sect—what
was the Sect, now sectarian no longer, since no more claiming
to be the whole. Here again, it is Professor Troeltsch who has,
I think, most persistently traced out this great twin truth along
the widest tracts of history.

6. A sensitively historical, a penetratingly philosophical, above

all a delicately spiritual apprehension concerning the humble-
ness of the apparent beginnings, the slow, or intermittent, or
bafflingly sudden manifestation of the implications and requirements of the Jewish and Christian religions ; and a similar apprehension of the varying, more or less imperfect methods and
impatient analyses which so largely accompanied developments
essentially faithful to the immanental logic of these religions.
We shall have to become vividly aware, in these respects, of three
groups of habits, dispositions and acts as having frequently
accompanied the teachings and work even of great inspired
Saints and heroes, legislators, rulers and writers, in the past—
in the Bible as really as in the Church. There is the frequent
pseudonymity of the writings. This was not " a lie " ; this, on
the contrary, was deeply admired, in Hellenistic times, amongst
cultivated men in general. Thus the Neo-Pythagorean school
produced an immense pseudonymous literature—writings of
" Homer," " Pythagoras," " Plato," etc. These writings not
only bore these great names from a mighty past, but they were
deliberately composed in a form as like as possible to the actual
or presumable writings of those far-distant worthies. And yet
Iamblichus, in his life of Pythagoras, singles out such pseudonymous authors for special praise precisely because they thus
revealed themselves more aware of their actual position of
debtors to, and transmitters of, past wisdom, than did the writers
of other schools who resorted less to this literary device. Some
of the books, or parts of the books, of the Old and even of the
New Testament (whilst, in their content, truly parts of the
tradition which they claim to represent) were more or less certainly composed, as regards their form, in a similar literary
temper of mind. Thus we cannot press the ascription of the
actual texts of Deuteronomy or of the Priestly Code to Moses
as their writer, nor of the Book of Wisdom to King Solomon.
The same appears to hold good of the Epistles of Jude and of the
Second Peter. Indeed it has become more and more difficult to
accept literally the apparent claim of the grand Fourth Gospel
itself to be the sheer record of the writer's own ocular and aural
experiences. It is certain that, in all these cases, the gain to the
comprehension of the great facts and truths enshrined in these
writings which results from the recognition of this ancient

literary method is, in the long run, amply worth the cost of the complication thus introduced for us into their vehicles. This applies also, *mutatis mutandis,* to more or less similar pseudo-nymities traceable in later Christian writings.

There is next, the throwing back into the past (even further and further back, and ever with greater precision as to sup-posed exact times, places, and other particulars) of the religious experiences, analyses, habits, institutions of the present, as these are found or experienced by the writer within himself and around him. And there is the corresponding projection into the future, with a similar minute identification, of facts or theories of the present. Hence the Dominican Père Lagrange could well point out that the detailed instructions to Moses concerning the *minutiæ* of the Jewish Cultus which we find in the *Priestly Code* cannot be pressed as so many downright hap-penings ; and so also we cannot press the details in the equally precise prophecy of Ezekiel concerning the future reoccupa-tion of Palestine by the Twelve Tribes, as so many future sure and sheer happenings. A somewhat similar, though much slighter, overleaping of time and of its work, can be traced in the scenes and discourses of the Fourth Gospel, where the articulations achieved in the Christian Church's experience of some six decades appear already fully expressed in Our Lord's very words and acts.

And finally there is Persecution—the use of physical force and the spirit of revenge and of unqualified condemnation. We thus get, in the Old Testament, the extermination of entire Canaanitish tribes, and again the execution of numerous priests of the high places, presented to us as solemnly required by God Himself and as solemnly blessed by Him ; indeed the central step forward achieved in the Jewish religion by the reform of King Josiah is closely bound up with these executions. As to the spirit of revenge, it penetrates not only many a Psalm but it still colours the New Testament Book of Revelation. And as to utter condemnation, there are sayings in the Fourth Gospel of a stringency which definitely surpasses the tone transmitted to us by the Synoptic Gospels.

I submit that all men of education will have henceforth to learn the difficult lesson of patience and fairness with regard to all these three points. We will not deny the reality of such facts nor their imperfection, even though we find them thus in the Bible itself, as part of the means or accompaniments, in those times, of genuine growths in the light from God ; nor will we, when we find them in the Church, straight away reject as essentially untrue or evil what may indeed be more or less obscured or stained by the same defects. We will, on the contrary, discriminate, both in the Bible and in the Church, between a substance which, at the least, may be good and divinely intended, and the accidents, which are human imperfections divinely permitted. We must courageously admit that even persecution has had its share, very certainly in Old Testament times and apparently even in some Christian times, in consolidating and purifying, and in giving independence to, the Jewish and Christian Churches. And as to the pseudonyms and the tendency to ignore history, it will be assuredly deeply unfair to persist in two, mutually incompatible, old habits of mind—to ignore such pseudonymity and overleaping of history in the Bible and (in so far rightly) to accept there such pseudonymous works as nevertheless most precious spiritual guides and as substantially true and valuable even as historical documents : yet instantly to stamp as "fraud," "deceit," " tyranny," " mere works of men " such instances, upon the whole lesser instances, of the same two processes as may appear within the development of the Christian doctrine, order and discipline. Certainly, the three, closely parallel, developments of the powers and functions of Priest, Bishop, Pope cannot be treated as legitimate or as spurious, merely according to the absence or the presence of these two processes alone. These developments may well be in substantial accord with the deepest implications and acts of Jesus, Paul and the early centuries, and with the immanental necessities of a Church called upon to endure and to spread throughout our earth's time and space, and may yet show, in the details of their evolution, unhistorical imagination, pseudonymous documents, even now and then *some* dishonesty. It is really time that such discriminations became the common property of all serious scholars whatever their religious allegiance. But indeed already such men as the late Professor F. W. Maitland, an avowed Agnostic, have been admirably full of such

discriminations. Such men are too historically minded not
vividly to perceive how honest, and even how substantially true,
can be men unpossessed of historical imagination.

7. All the preceding positions involve the apprehension, and
press forward to the full profession, that it is but One God who
operates throughout the various stages and ranges of multiform
reality and throughout the correspondingly various responses
of mankind. The One God thus operates, in the most diverse,
astonishingly delicate, interrelated ways, aiming throughout at
a rich unity in diversity—a unity the closer and the more all-
penetrating, the more ultimate is the level and the range concerned. If so, then the Family, Science, Philosophy, Art, the
Handicrafts, the State are all intended to possess their several
unities and autonomies. And is Religion, especially the Christian
religion, and in this again the Christian Church, to be an exception, indeed thus to stand at a lower level, as to unity ? Surely,
the only exception here legitimately conceivable is that the unity
here should be exceptionally great. There is nothing whatsoever to show that Jesus implied, or would desire, a multiplicity
of Churches ; and St. Paul, the Fourth Gospel, and the great
Church passages in the Synoptists, teach, with full emphasis
and deep emotion, the Sacred Oneness of the Church, and
picture Jesus as solemnly founding this One Church for all
ages and races.

Philosophers such as Sir Henry Jones are now coming to
analyse the consciousness of the human infant as composed,
from the first, of the direct experience of object and subject,
the two in their mutual interaction thus constituting, from the
first, man's single world of consciousness and knowledge. Man
articulates these rich contents of his mind, which at first are
throughout vague and confused, only gradually and never
exhaustively ; yet, from first to last, *there* he has his one world
given to him. Investigators of the Social Life and of the State
and of their conceptions, such as Frederick William Maitland,
are now reaching out to the discovery that man, from the first,
possessed, however dimly, the sense both of the Individual and
of the Community ; so that man but clarified, slowly as the time
went on, both these conceptions each through and with the
other. Man thus, did not, in spite of appearances, jump out of

Individualism into Communism, or out of Communism into Individualism. But he possessed, however inchoately, from the first, the One life, itself both individual and common from the start. Somewhat similarly, though here driven, not only by a vivid historical imagination but still more by a tenacious spiritual sense, Professor Rudolf Sohm finds the primitive Christian consciousness never to have been other than essentially Catholic —always to have felt the sacredness, the rights, the duties, and the powers of the domestic and otherwise local " Churches " to proceed entirely from their expressing, here and now, the powers and sacrednesses vested in the One Catholic Church spread throughout the world. Here also the whole is, if not before the parts, yet coeval with the parts, and from the first constitutes the parts as parts.[1] If this be true, the late Dr. Edwin Hatch and Professor Adolph von Harnack have been misled by appearances when they have taken the Church at large to have been, really and literally, upbuilt out of originally independent congregations. Then too we have had a very wide and very independent, and in no wise ecclesiastically trained thinker, the American Professor Josiah Royce, whose last course of lectures, " The Problem of Christianity," found this problem to centre in the reality, indeed the necessity, of a " Beloved Community " and of loyalty to it as the great means of spiritual growth in the individual. A pity only that—in many other similar present-day gropings after religious community and unity—the position remains vague and weak, because adopted without its original concrete, historical root and without a distinct Christ and a distinct God.

It is Adolf von Harnack who, perhaps best amidst latter-day non-Roman Catholic writers, has, with exemplary candour and courage, pointed out how closely Catholic and Roman are inter-twined in actual history—how it was in and through Rome that Christianity definitely awoke to the character of Oneness as inherent in itself, a Oneness not simply of the Invisible Com-munity formed by all true believers, known as such in strictness to God alone, but the Oneness of a Visible Organisation possessed

[1] Henry Jones : *A Critical Account of the Philosophy of Lotze,* 1895, pp. 102–18; F. W. Maitland, *Collected Papers,* 1911, vol. ii., p. 363 ; Rudolf Sohm, *Wesen und Ursprung des Katholizismus,* 1909, *passim.*

of various officially superior, equal, and inferior members. Surely such a conception, such a fact, alone fully accords with man's nature, so essentially a sense and spirit composite ; with the life and work of Jesus, real spirit working in and with real senses ; and with the central genius of His religion, the manifestation of the Spirit, God, in terms of sense as well as of spirit, and the call of man, sense and spirit, through sense to sense's spiritualisation.

It is well that von Gierke, F. W. Maitland, A. L. Smith, J. N. Figgis and P. T. Forsyth—Lutheran, Agnostics, Anglican, Congregationalist—should, during these last three decades, have been busy (more fruitfully than with sheer abuse, or even than with discreet silence), with the immense, unique services of Rome, precisely also in this matter of Unity. For myself I do not doubt that the day may—the day will—come when Rome (what is true in the Protestant instincts even more than in the Protestant objections having been fully satisfied) will again unite and head Christians generally, and this in a temper and with applications more elastic than those of the later Middle Ages and especially than those of post-Reformation times. The Visibility of the Unity is doubtless here the central difficulty ; yet nothing which falls deliberately short of Visible Unity can or should be the goal. Nevertheless, in a certain very real sense, such thinkers as Josiah Royce are more ecclesiastical than ever will be the Church itself. For a Catholic the full end and the deepest centre of the Church can never be simply the Church, still less the simply human social virtues taken as such, virtues which, by abstraction from much else, we can more or less segregate from out of the Church's total fruits. For the Catholic, the Church essentially possesses, seeks, finds and leads to God, Who alone can and does constitute the fully adequate home of the supernaturally awakened soul. The Church is doubtless, historically speaking, rather the substitute for, than the expansion of, the Kingdom of God. But whether this Kingdom of God, for which the Church waits and for which she prepares, is to come suddenly or slowly, in this world or in the next, or a little here and fully hereafter : in any and every case the Kingdom of Heaven will, for the human soul, doubtless include the society of this soul's fellow-creatures, each contributing to the joy of all the others. Nevertheless : the root, the centre and the crown of all this social joy will be God—God apprehended as more and other than all men, than all possible finite beings put together —indeed as more and other than are His life and love in and for all His creatures. The Church, the Catholic Church in its fullness, the Roman Catholic Church, here again has fathomed the needs and implications of religion : the doctrine of the Holy Trinity, even the seemingly Pantheistic insistence upon Substance in the Trinity and upon Things in the Sacraments are, at their best, grand preservatives against all sentimental humanism —against everything that would make God into but a mirror, or into a mere purveyor, of men's wants. Man's deepest want is, in reality, for a God infinitely more than such a mere assuager of even all man's wants. Especially also is He more than the awakener of all, even of our noblest, national aspirations. And thus again we persistently require One great international, supernational Church which, by its very form, will continuously warn us of the essentially more than national character of all fully awake Christianity.

A sense and spirit religion and a single world-wide Church : God thus becomes, not only the sole possible originator, preserver and renovator of such a Church, but also the central end and attainment of such a Church. We shall thus in the One Church, through the One Christ, reach, most fully and firmly, the infinitely rich One God.

11

CHRISTIANITY AND THE SUPERNATURAL [1]

LARGE nets in the deep sea are useless there unless we buoy them up—heavy as they are on land, heavier still in the water—with light cork floats here and there. So now I will strive to keep our present conference, busy as it is with the profoundest facts and experiences, afloat by here and there a homely little simile or a harmless little jest.

Have you ever kept tree frogs? If not, do! How amusing they are with their intermittently voracious appetite! Especially the young frogs: they will jump at and seize a blue-bottle nearly as large as themselves, and will laboriously push it down their maws with their funny little front feet. But feed them with crickets from the kitchen and watch their procedure. The frog will seize a cricket, hard, long, and thin, and will push this struggling down its throat. The cricket insists upon dying within the frog cross-wise, but the frog pats his white abdomen from each side, till he gets the cricket, now at last killed by the gastric juice, into proper conformity with the inside of the frog himself. I am now asking you to leap forth to seize and to assimilate, as well as you can, a mass of spiritual food which may well at first lie uncomfortably athwart your minds. Be patient; before the end, I hope greatly to relieve the situation—we shall then *pat* our minds; and the food, so unwieldy at first, will, I trust, find its proper place and will really feed us. No food can feed us properly without considerable friction generated and overcome.

Let me now introduce the subject seriously by dwelling for some moments upon four discriminations, which will, I think, help us much to concentrate and to clarify our investigation.

[1] An Address delivered to Junior Members of the University of Oxford in May, 1920. Reprinted from *The Modern Churchman*, June, 1920.

First of all, then, we are busy here, not with the Miraculous, but with the Supernatural. When Bossuet and Fénelon had their celebrated controversy concerning the spiritual life, Fénelon, towards the end, insisted against Bossuet (who found downright miracle in the more advanced states of prayer and of self-surrender) that the entire spiritual life, from its rudimentary beginnings up to its very highest grades and developments, was for him, Fénelon, essentially and increasingly supernatural, but at no point essentially miraculous. Thus Fénelon found the human soul, at every stage of its spiritual career, to remain still within the characteristically human kind of freedom, our poor little liberty of choice ; whereas Bossuet considered the soul, in its fullest supernaturalisation, to be, even in this life, literally established in grace, and to get beyond the imperfect liberty of choice. So too, as to the operations of the mind : according to Fénelon the human mind, at least in this life, remains throughout more or less successive and discursive in its operations ; } *epist.* with Bossuet, in the highest state, the mind becomes entirely intuitive and simultaneous in its action. I believe Bossuet, in this matter, to have been wrong, and Fénelon to be right. With Fénelon we will not deny the possibility, or even the actual occurrence, of miracle, in the sense just indicated, within the spiritual life. Still less will we deny historically attested miracles in the Bible and elsewhere. But we will simply hold with Fénelon that the spiritual life of Prayer, of Love, and of Devotedness is, even in its fullest Christian developments, essentially not miraculous but supernatural. Hence we can in the spiritual life more or less foretell its future operations, and we can very largely discover certain great laws and characteristics within its past operations, the limits arising here, not from anything really sporadic in the subject-matter, but simply from the difficulty, patent in every kind of human science, of bringing the analysis and theory of very certain, richly experienced facts, to a clearness at all equal to the vividness of the experiences ; and again from the great need for the observing soul to be very pure from distracting or distorting passions and very docile to the delicate facts and their manifold implications.

Again, what concerns us here is not the Supernatural in its contrast and conflict with sin and sinful human nature ; but the Supernatural as distinct from healthy Nature, and the inter-aid and yet tension at work between them. It certainly looks at first sight as though the dread battle between the simply Bad and the Good of whatsoever kind were the more promising mental problem for us, just as this battle is the more pressing practical concern of us all, especially in our earlier years. Yet I have come to the conclusion, with many another recent or still living thinker belonging to the most various religious groups, races, avocations and temperaments,—that a certain monotony, dullness, oppression, besets much of the spiritual practice and principles of many religious persons ; that these qualities are fatal to the charm, freshness and freedom essential to religion at its best ; and that, not the contrast between sin and virtue, but the difference between Nature and Supernature can furnish a solid starting-point for the recovery, the resuscitation of religion, as by far the richest, the most romantic, the most entrancing and emancipating fact and life extant or possible anywhere for man.

And thirdly we have to do, in the body of this address, not with the implications, however real—indeed, necessary—of super-natural dispositions, forces, acts, effects, but with these same realities as they appear at first sight, as they feel (at the possible minimum of awareness and analysis of what the soul is achieving or experiencing) to the agent or patient himself. It was Dr. W. G. Ward, " Ideal " Ward, that brilliant Balliol lecturer, and later fervent, indeed partly extravagant, Roman Catholic—a great supernaturalist—who first taught me that the Super-natural should not be directly identified and measured by the amount of its conscious, explicit references to Christ or even simply to God, but by certain qualities which we shall attempt to trace later on, and of which heroism, with a keen sense of givenness and of " I could not do otherwise," appear to be the chief. Thus a man may perform a truly supernatural act, or be in a genuinely supernatural condition of soul, and yet may possess, at the time or even generally, only the most dim and confused—a quite inadequate—theology.

And finally my examples and my analysis will mainly be derived from what I know best and love very dearly, from what made me into the little of spiritual worth that I may be—the devotedness and faith at work within the Roman Catholic Church. But this does not mean that noble, truly supernatural devotedness does not occur elsewhere in other Christian bodies, indeed also amongst Jews and Mohammedans, or amongst Parsees, Hindoos and Buddhists, even amongst that apparently increasing mass of men who would be puzzled to say where they stand theologically at all. Yet my insistence upon Roman Catholic cases not only means that I am obliged, if I am to speak at all effectively, to speak of what I know much the best, but it also expresses my very deliberate, now long tested, conviction that, be the sins of commission or of omission chargeable against the Roman Catholic authorities or people what they may, in that faith and practice is to be found a massiveness of the Supernatural, a sense of the World Invisible, of God as the soul's true home, such as exists elsewhere more in fragments and approximations and more intermittently. Many, perhaps most, of you young men must, in this great war, have come across not a few supernatural acts and dispositions : happy you! By all means dwell, as I speak on to you, upon your own recollection rather than upon my own. My own examples are given merely to illustrate certain recurrent realities and traceable laws, and thus to give us greater acuteness and accuracy of perception when we come to conclude as to Christianity and the Supernatural.

Now, for the purpose of bringing out into full relief the Supernatural as it is necessarily experienced prior to any full analysis of its content, we will, for the body of this address, consider two sets of facts : the difference between the Natural and the Supernatural, in their respective illumination, power and goodness; and the Supernatural in actual operation within the great virtues constitutive of the spiritual-moral life.

I

With the decay of the Middle Ages, from about A.D. 1300 to 1450, and then on into the (first Christian then Pagan) Renaissance and the Protestant Reformation, men largely grew weary of the monastic ideal; and, influenced as much by the atomistic and sceptical late mediæval philosophy as by the many complications brought in the course of the ages by the exempted position of the great monastic corporations, they at last determined to dig up the very roots of all and any monasticism. One half of Europe paid a heavy price for this apparently quite simple return to the supposed utter uniformity of call for all men as described in the Gospels. For the price paid was not so much the suppression, alongside of the dissolute houses, of monasteries that were still centres of the most beneficent devotedness ; nor even so much an unlovely subtlety of interpretation of those Gospel records which, when taken quite unsophisticatedly, tell a very different tale. The heaviest price paid was the eradication, as thorough as the new zeal could make it, from men's minds henceforwards, of a very noble and enriching, a difficult and delicate discrimination and instinct, operative up to then within the Christian consciousness. The distinction here meant was all-pervasive during the Golden Middle Ages—say from A.D. 1050 to 1270—especially in Aquinas and in Dante : the distinction, not only between Good and Evil, but between Good and Good, between Natural Good and Supernatural Good. Thus bodily cleanliness, honesty in buying and selling, submission to the police and due tax-paying to the State, a fair amount of courage, too, in war—this and the like, with a dim sense of God—the God of Honesty—in the background, all this was held to be indeed from God, to be necessary, to be good. But it was (or would be, did it anywhere exist thus, quite unmixed with Supernature) only Natural Good. And such a simply Natural Goodness would, for survival beyond death, merely conceive or desire this Natural Goodness, with the dim background of God, to continue for ever, less suffering, offences against this rational code, and death. We have here, for a spiritual landscape, a parallel to a great plain—say that of Lombardy—with its corn ; we could now add its potatoes. Bentham amongst recent Englishmen, and Confucius amongst the great ancient and non-European moral and religious leaders, represent this sane and sensible, but dry and shallow outlook.

Now the natural virtues and the natural outlook and hopes, all more or less dominated by the Body and its requirements (its most legitimate requirements), remain, in various degrees, as regards their materials and even their immediate occasions

and proximate motives, a strict necessity and full duty for us all.
Even the loftiest sanctity finds here the substratum, the subject-
matters, the occasions for its own supernatural life. But man's
life—so this same rich doctrine proceeds—has not, as a
matter of fact, been left by God as He might have left it, at a
purely natural level of activity and happiness either in this life
or in the next. Man possesses indeed by Nature both an actual
and a possible thirst for God. But, unless supernaturally stimulated, this thirst requires no more than a certain unity in man's
activity and outlook and a certain harmony between both, with
God as the ultimate invisible reference of the whole. This
natural capacity for the God of Nature and for all the natural
virtues has, however, through God's sheer bounty, been stimulated to beyond its natural awakeness by His own condescensions towards us—His Incarnation in the life and work of Jesus
Christ constituting the centre and fullness of all this ceaseless
movement from God to man. Thus God, so to speak, has put
salt into our mouths, and we now thirst for what we have experienced. We now long for Supernatural Good, Supernatural
Beatitude. Now acts and dispositions become possible, attractive,
even actual within us and by us, which no State, no Guild, can
ever presuppose or require. Now decency is carried up into
devotedness, and homeliness into heroism. Here the activities are
primarily concerned with the Soul. Simple justice and average
fairness are transfigured into genial generosity and overflowing
self-devotion. Competition is replaced by co-operation, indeed
even by vicarious work and suffering. And now the desire for a
simple survival of the natural activities and of the natural happiness, and of a dim and discursive sense of God, is replaced by
thirst for the full expansion and the final establishment of the
human personality in an endless life of such self-devotion and
of a vivid, intuitive vision of God, supreme Author and End of all
Nature and Supernature. The State is fanatical the moment it
attempts to require or to supply such motives, virtues and con-
summations ; and the Church is an irritating superfluity, a
feeble ditto of the State the moment it forgets that this precisely
forms its specific work and call : the awakening, the training, the
bringing into full life and fruitfulness of the Supernatural Life.
   But pray note : this outlook, if the truer, is, where at all

complete, by far the costlier—costlier even as a theory, still more costly in practical execution. For it means high heroism, yet also hospitable homeliness, it means the Alpine Uplands—the edelweiss and the alpenrose—as well as the Lombard Plains with their corn and their potatoes ; it means poetry and prose, a mighty harmony and a little melody, or rather it means, taken as a complete whole, a great organ recital, with the *grand jeu* stop of Supernature drawn out full and all the pipes of Nature responding in tones each necessary in its proper place, yet each sweeter and richer than its own simply natural self.

And again note that the material of the Supernatural is not only the heroic, but also, indeed mostly, the homely ; just as the material of the Natural can, contrariwise, be not homely but heroic. St. Paul tells us that whenever we eat or we drink, we should do it, and all our other homely natural duties, for the glory of God. And, contrariwise, St. Paul declares that a man may perform acts materially as heroic as is the giving his body to be burnt or his distributing all his possessions amongst the poor, and yet these acts may remain at the natural level, indeed may become " splendid " vices, owing to the absence of the supernatural motive or to the presence, central and determining, of motives of vanity and pride.

Yet, although the Supernatural is thus more frequently at work in the homely form, this supernatural homeliness always possesses some, and at times much and very much, real heroism ; and again, the Supernatural is more striking, more easily seized in its massively heroic form. Hence, in the instances of the Supernatural now to be given, the massively heroic will be represented in a proportion considerably greater than it obtains in real life.

II

I will group my examples under seven heads, seven great virtues, here at their supernatural level, which together, like the seven prismatic colours, form a rainbow of thrilling, ceaselessly rejuvenating, reconciling beauty, truth and goodness, thrown in splendour over the swampy tracts and murky atmosphere of poor, average and less than average human ugliness, insincerity and mediocrity of all kinds and degrees. I deliberately make the selection as wide as possible, within the range of my vivid knowledge, in order to bring out clearly the unlimited generosity of God and of man, in these their great call and response.

First, let us take Courage—the virtue which always expresses or confers youthfulness unfading. There is the Jewish Rabbi of Lyons, chaplain in the late war, holding up, at a dying Catholic soldier's request, this soldier's crucifix before his eyes, and this amidst a hail of bullets and shrapnel flying all around them. The Rabbi was killed, not indeed at that moment, but soon after his touching heroism. And then there is that instance of most painfully difficult moral courage, a virtue at all times so costly and so especially manly, of Walter Bagehot at sixteen. We have here a youth already possessed of the sensitiveness of genius, full of love of wholesome popularity, and averse to all disloyalty and eccentricity, faced with the ordeal of choosing between the possibly life-long reputation of a sneak or the deliberate toleration of a grave immorality, accidentally witnessed by himself, an immorality which would be spread right and left throughout the school by a fellow-scholar, the son of particularly powerful patrons of the institution. The decision evidently cost Bagehot a very agony of suffering; and it took years before he could recover the trust of some of his contemporaries. But who can seriously doubt that he did right to face all that obloquy, that his act, incapable though it be of direct appeal to any generous-hearted lad, takes rank amidst the rarest heroisms?

Let us next take Purity—that immensely virile virtue, always treated as impossible by those senile children, the cynics, everywhere. Here I will take, not instances of much tried yet complete fidelity in unhappy marriages, although there too the Supernatural shines forth magnificently, but two cases, watched most closely by myself, of full voluntary celibacy. Some of you will know what Schopenhauer, assuredly no Christian of any kind, still less a Roman Catholic, says about such celibacy—how he considers it to be the culminating manifestation of the Supernatural and how its rejection, by the Protestant Reformers, meant nothing less than the dethronement of the Supernatural. Doubtless, this or that phase, this or that disciplinary rule, of celibacy is open to severe criticism as excessive or harmful, and anything that really belittles marriage, the divine call at all times for the large majority of the human race, is assuredly to be rejected. But to taboo all celibacy, or even simply not to assign to it, at its best, a definite, very high and wide place, function and honour within the Christian life and Church, is to fail to seize one of the two movements of this very life and Church— the movement so classically exemplified in the persons of the Precursor, the Founder, and the greatest of the Apostles, and again by such world-renewing figures as St. Augustine, St. Benedict, and St. Francis. Certainly I know, beyond the possibility of doubt, that I myself could never have been regained by any but a celibate cleric to purity and to God—however much, since I was thus costingly regained, I may appreciate the beneficence of a married clergy, and however clearly I may perceive the dangers and drawbacks of too large an extension of obligatory celibacy. Instances of thoroughly happy, and in such cases always specially fruitful, Christian celibacy are fortunately not rare in the Roman Catholic Church. But I have constantly before my mind two men to whom, precisely as such specifically Christian celibates, I owe infinitely much. The one was a Dutch Dominican Friar, a man of gentle birth and of great religious experience, who first trained me in the spiritual life in Vienna —fifty years ago. What a whole man that was! One with all the instincts of a man, yet all of them mastered and penetrated through and through by the love of Christ and of souls. And the other was a French Secular Priest, a man of vehement, seething passions, and of rare forces of mind, whose will of iron, by long heroic submission to grace, had attained to a splendid tonic tenderness. I owe more to this Frenchman than to any man I have ever known in the flesh. Now both these men would have remained incredibly smaller had they listened to the subtle explainers away of the renunciation, visible as well as invisible, preached and practised broadcast by the central figures of the Synoptic Gospels, and if they had settled comfortably into a married life. Like their great predecessors, Aquinas and St. Francis, they required the height of celibacy from which to

shine and to rain down upon the just and the unjust amidst
their dearly loved fellow-men.

Let us take as our third virtue, Unlimited Compassion and
love even of enemies. Courage and Purity unfeigned, gained
by close intercourse with God, will readily lead to some such
heights. The French cleric just referred to was profoundly
convinced of the irreplaceable fruitfulness of celibacy in lives
devoted to specially difficult reform work ; hence he was
most sensitively insistent that any one who felt himself called
to labour for such reforms should himself practise at least as
much as was the actual practice amidst those whom he desired
to gain to his views. Thus when the Carmelite Père Hyacinthe
Loyson abandoned the cowl and married, and nevertheless
continued to act as a still possible reforming Catholic priest,
the Abbé felt, and never ceased to feel, keenly, the sterilising
shallowness of such a combination. Yet when, many years later
Mme. Loyson died, the Abbé, as he told me himself, flew at
once to the bereaved old man and poured out all his treasures
of consolation and of communicative strength. No easy-going
indifference could here achieve so much ; the sympathy of such
an one would, in a sense, be too easy for it to be operative, as in
this case, through its very costliness. The other instance is that
of a young Anglican officer and of his bearing towards a malignant
personal enemy. Captain Horace de Vere, as was told me by his
cousin who had been in close touch with the events to be described, had recovered from his wounds in the Crimean War,
and was back in England in full health, a most happily married
man, and the father of two little girls. He continued his military
profession and deep interest in his men. He had instituted a
small fund from which the troopers of his company were to
receive a little extra pay for any week throughout which they
had remained sober. One of these troopers nursed feelings of revenge against the Captain, since this officer could not honestly do
otherwise than pass the man over for many weeks in succession.
At last, on parade one day, the trooper shot the Captain through
the back and lungs ; but the doomed officer lingered on for a
fortnight. Even now the trooper's vindictiveness was not
assuaged, and, although he knew well that execution awaited him
if the Captain died, he nevertheless persisted in open expressions

of hope that his officer would die. But de Vere, after providing for his young wife and little girls, concentrated all the strength that remained to him to win his murderer's forgiveness, and to soften that poor hate-blinded heart. And he succeeded : the Captain died fully resigning into God's hands the wife and the children and his own life, still well on the upward grade. He lost his bodily life, but he gained a soul : he went to God assuredly a saint, the meek, self-less victor in a struggle between malignant hate and perfect love.

Let us take for our fourth Supernatural virtue Humility, which, though it is rightly appraised as the true foundation of all the other virtues, I put thus far on in our series, since it is hardly in reality a virtue for the young—conceit is so pardonable before thirty and becomes fully ridiculous only when the accumulating years bring no self-knowledge and lowliness of mind. Perhaps the least inadequate instances of Supernatural Humility alive within my own mind are furnished by the unflinching welcome given, by certain Jesuit novices, to humiliations with regard to their own knowledge and its importance for others, and by their eager utilisation of these humiliations for purposes of interior growth. There indeed stand before me other, more genial and more mellow instances of Humility, but these other instances concern Humility of the Natural and homely, and not of the Supernatural and heroic kind.

Then for our fifth virtue let us take Truthfulness, where it reaches an heroic depth and delicacy. I put it thus quite late in the series, since such Truthfulness presupposes especially Humility, Purity and Courage, yet also generous abandonment of all grievances and bitter feelings against any man. Also because, especially since the Renaissance, perfect truthfulness, in view of the new exigencies in matters of history and of sensitive interest in subject-matters of no direct religious significance, is, I believe, the most delicately difficult of all the virtues for the average institutional religionist. Such an one finds it all but impossible not to tidy up reality of all kinds into what he thinks such reality, as God's will or permission, ought actually to be. For heroic Truthfulness in matters of history I have then, before me, the great French Benedictine historical discoverer and critic, Jean Mabillon, who, after a long life spent in the most candid research amidst considerable opposition, died grandly insisting to his disciples upon Truth, and Truth again, in all their work. And as to heroic watchfulness and accuracy with regard to natural facts apparently of no religious import whatsoever, there is the impressive death of the Jesuit astronomer, Father Perry, sent by the British Government, as head of one of the expeditions to the South Seas, for the observation of the transit of Venus. Perry, shortly before the transit, was seized by a fever which would surely promptly kill him. He thereupon quietly made his preparations for death and received the last Sacraments, and then absorbed himself, as though in perfect health, in the transit. From the first moment to the last he took and registered all the manifold delicate observations with flawless accuracy. And then, immediately the little planet had ceased all junction with the great resplendent sun, the hero astronomer gently fell back into unconsciousness and death.

Then as our sixth, penultimate, virtue comes entire Self-Abandonment in the hands of God, a disposition so great as to seem indeed the very culmination of all devotedness, and so richly inclusive as to render its agents easily classable under several other virtues. Two vivid memories are here before me. There is an Irish Roman Catholic washerwoman with whom I had the honour of worshipping some thirty years ago in our English Midlands. She had twelve children, whom she managed to bring up most carefully, and a drunkard husband, an Englishman of no religion, openly unfaithful to herself. The constant standing of many years at last brought on some grave internal complications : a most delicate operation would alone save her life. Whilst resting in hospital against the coming ordeal, with the experts thoroughly hopeful of success, a visiting surgeon came round, really the worse for drink, and insisted with trembling hands upon an examination then and there. This doomed the patient to a certain death, which duly came a week later. Yet from the first moment of the fatal change to the last instant of her consciousness (so the priest who attended her throughout declared to me after all was over) she was absorbed in seeking to respond, with all she was, to this great grace of God, this opportunity of utter self-abandonment to Him, and this although she dearly loved her children, and although she knew well that her eyes would hardly be closed before their father would marry a bad woman and give her full authority over this, their mother's darling little flock. All possible plans were made by the dying woman for each of the children, and from the first moment she spontaneously exacted from the priest a promise to prevent any prosecution of the fuddled surgeon—she never stopped to consider his offence even to forgive it ; it was God, and the utter trust in Him, and in the wisdom, the love of His Will, that swallowed up all the pain, physical and mental, and all possible conflicts and perplexities.   And the second memory is of one of the Carmelite Fathers, whom we knew familiarly as one of the ministers of our Church on Campden Hill. Not an interiorly harmonious, not a directly attractive, man was Simon Knapp in ordinary circumstances. A tall, gaunt, though utterly gentle-manly figure, a vehement over-straining nature ; an adviser prone to demand too much. Apparently a non-fit, a rolling stone. But the great War came, and though past fifty, he succeeded with his Order and with the War Office in securing, as in the Boer War, once more his darling wish to go and to serve with all he was, in the very midst of the acutest dangers, and, if God would deign, to die with and for others. This time he had his life's desire to the full. My daughter listened to a young officer, a man apparently of no religion, who described how he had himself seen Knapp, without weapons of any kind, offensive or defensive, standing in the midst of a very hurricane of bullets and shrapnel, utterly oblivious of death imminent at every moment, indeed radiant with happiness as he bent over, supported and comforted, the wounded and the dying. This man had found his true element, his full expression and joy at last ; a grand example of the reality and the character of the Supernatural.

You may well ask where can we find any further heroism, our seventh and last virtue ? Did not even our Lord's own life here below end with utter self-abandonment, indeed with the great cry of desolation upon the Cross ? But the answer is already more or less given in our last example, although the point is, I believe, so crucial for the full elucidation of the Christian Spirit and outlook at their completest, as to deserve, indeed require, a separate final class of virtue to itself.

Spiritual Joy, Beatitude, does not, indeed, always accompany

or crown in this life even high heroism, although I believe this
non-flowering of heroism to be always caused by some inhibitory
influence distinct from the heroism as such. Yet Spiritual Joy,
Beatitude, does appear in the very greatest, the most supernatural,
acts and lives. Thus with our Lord Himself, we have the great
rejoicing in the spirit during the Galilean ministry ; and if the
last act of His Life appear to be the cry upon the Cross, we have
to remember that the specifically Christian conception of Jesus
Christ absolutely requires, not only the sufferings of the Passion,
but also the Beatitude of the Risen Life ; neither alone, but only
the two, the bitter-sweet together, form here the adequate object
of our Christian faith. Perhaps for this crowning virtue, which
alone differentiates quite fully the ultimate Christian outlook
from all Stoicisms and categorical-imperative schemes, two great
historical figures can be best cited, although I have myself been
set upon my feet, for now wellnigh thirty years, by one who,
himself of most melancholy natural temperament and full of
mental and physical suffering, radiated this tonic joy from his
darkened room and couch into how many deeply tried souls !
It was this my later trainer who finally removed all doubt from
my mind as to the full reality of the joy reported to have streamed
forth from the greatest of the saints. Especially two such great
ones are ever with me—Catherine Fiesca Adorna, that unhappily
married, immensely sensitive, naturally melancholy and self-
absorbed woman, who ended, as the Saint of Genoa, on the note
of joy and of overwhelming joy ; and, above all, the Poverello,
St. Francis of Assisi, who, next to Our Lord Himself, appears,
amidst all the Saints we know of, to have most completely
brought out the marvellous paradox of Christianity—utter self-
donation with entire spontaneity, a heroism quite unrigorist, a
devotedness of supreme expansiveness and joy.

Let us now conclude all by attempting to draw out the implications which, doubtless in most cases, are in part but dimly
perceived by the heroic agent himself. I believe these characteristic implications of the Supernatural everywhere to be
five, and that Christianity at its best, more fully and persistently
than any other religion, possesses these same characteristics
with an explicitness and vividness which answer to and develop

and complete, most powerfully, those five great implications of the Supernatural everywhere.

First, then, the Supernatural experience, act or state, appears always, for us human beings, on occasion of, in contact with, and as the transfiguration of, Natural conditions, acts, states. Indeed, the Spiritual generally, whether natural or even supernatural, is always preceded or occasioned, accompanied or followed, by the Sensible—the soul by the body. The highest realities and deepest responses are experienced by us within, or in contact with, the lower and the lowliest; only in the moments of deepest spiritual experience do these humbler precedents and concomitants disappear from the direct, or at least from the more vivid, consciousness, and does the Natural substratum seem to be entirely submerged by the sheer Supernatural. Hence the genuine Supernatural always brings with it a keen sense of the recipient's littleness—he is so hemmed in by, and indeed so largely bound up with, his small human capacities as they front the immensity of the divine life. Even in the Beyond, sound doctrine tells him, limitations, and consciousness of limitations, will not entirely cease. There, too, there will be a body, even though a glorified body; there too succession, not simultaneity, will more or less obtain; and the Vision of God, although centrally apprehended by intuition, will be exhaustive only of our own, even there still limited, capacity, and will never be co-extensive with the infinite God Himself.

Now in such statements we have already expressed great insistences of Christianity as it develops and articulates the general supernatural experience. And especially does Christianity carry out and give the deepest practical effect to the groping, involved in that experience, towards History, towards that mysterious paradox of the Here and Now as the necessary occasions and vehicle of the deepest sense of God, the Reality above Space and Time. And Christianity further carries out and gives deep practical effect to the groping, also involved in that supernatural experience, after contact, not only of spirit with spirit, but of spirit with sense—the visible, audible, tactual Sacraments arousing, articulating, transmitting, through human spirits to other human spirits, super-sensible Grace and Strength.

I submit that in this matter, neither the Quaker position (which refuses the Sensible both as antecedent help and as consequent expression of the Super-sensible) nor even Lutheranism (which, where most fully itself, refuses the antecedent Sensible, but readily accepts the consequent) : I submit that both, in different degrees, are inadequate in face of the intimations of the supernatural experience, where Sense as readily precedes Spirit as Spirit is succeeded by Sense.

Secondly, the Supernatural experience, act or state, is never quite solitary, but, even in the penumbra of consciousness of the experiencing soul, and still more in unanalysed ways, it is profoundly social as well. Lucretius gives us the noble image of the successive generations of mankind as runners in the torch race, where each generation, as it sinks in death, hands on the torch of human knowledge and experience to the next generation, to the younger runners who have come up to the old ones and who are fresh for further running. But the succession of spiritual example and training is, if less obvious, far deeper and more entrancing still. Here it is literally true that behind every saint stands another saint, at least as he lives on in writings by himself or about him. In vain do all mystics, as such, vividly feel their experience to be utterly without human antecedent connection. Behind St. Paul stands the Jewish synagogue and the earthly Jesus ; and behind George Fox stands the entire New Testament. Here is the abiding right and need of the Church, as the fellowship and training school of believers. And indeed the mystics, in so far as they remain Christian, have moments of the noblest perception, not indeed of Sacraments and the Visible institutional Church, but of the Invisible Church—a great reality for us all. Thus I know of no more moving account of the one Catholic Invisible Church than is that of the Lutheran Rudolf Sohm, the life-long impugner of all Institutionalism.

Thirdly, the Supernatural experience, act or disposition always bears an evidential, metaphysical, more than human and other than human implication and character ; and yet, whilst thus affirming Presence, Reality or Otherness, it also always affirms or implies the incompleteness (even within the range of finite capacities) of this genuine experience of Ultimate Reality. God is here, but not God exhaustively, not in the fullness which

[margin note: diff. degree of human insight into God]

He is and which He Himself knows ; not even in the fullness
with which He may be known by other larger and more devoted
human souls. This vivid sense of the unequal distribution of
God's light and of man's insight, implicit in all the Supernatural
experiences before they have been flattened out by all-levelling
Pantheisms, is met and fully articulated by the Christian conception of Jesus ; here, in this genuinely human mind and will,
the series of all possible Supernatural experience by man (each
experiencing soul well aware that other souls could know, love,
will God and His creatures far more and better than itself)
reaches its implied goal and centre. For Jesus is conceived by
the Christian Church as Christ in a sense far transcending
that of the Jewish Messiah. Jesus here is declared to hold
in His human mind and will as much of God, of God pure, as
human nature, at its best and when most completely supernaturalised, can be made by God to hold, whilst remaining
genuine human nature still. And yet this same Jesus (though
He is the Christ in this supremely heightened sense) remains
thus still also truly Jesus—that is, a human mind and
human will bound to a human body, to sense stimulation, to
history and institutions, to succession, time and space. He
can thus be our Master and our Model, our Refuge and our
Rest.

[margin note: 4) suffering]

Fourthly, the genuinely Supernatural experience, act or disposition is always more or less accompanied by Suffering in
Serenity, by Pain in Bliss. The very mixedness of the position
and powers of the human soul cannot fail to produce some such
effects, where this soul is raised to its highest possible recipiency
and work. The Suffering and the Serenity are, indeed, so inter-
locked that the supernaturally advanced soul ends, without a
touch of morbidness or unreality, by ignoring, or even by desiring,
the suffering, not of course for itself—what folly that would be !
—but as the price and signal of its own growth in solid joy. I
doubt not that an equivalent for such noble, freely willed suffering
will exist in Heaven itself. Now here again, here especially,
Christianity meets, indeed alone efficaciously unravels, develops
and satisfies this, the soul's deep longing. For it is literally true
that only Christianity deliberately trains its disciples to escape,
on the one hand, the harshness and unreality of Stoicism,

and, on the other hand, the shallowness and shiftiness of Hedonism. Christianity teaches that suffering is most real and in itself everywhere an evil ; yet it does not, because of this, either fall into any ultimate pessimism, or drown care in fleeting pleasure. Sin, for Christianity, always remains a greater evil than any suffering whatsoever. Suffering here is grappled with ; and (whether as atonement for sin, or as transfiguration of Nature to a Supernatural level) Suffering and Pain here powerfully aid the acquisition of Serenity and Peace. And Christianity teaches all this once more, not as a thin theory, but by the supreme concrete example of Jesus, the Christ—a life overflowingly rich in loneliness, failure, pain even unto agony ; yet, in and through all this suffering, a perennial source of world-embracing joy.

And fifthly, the Supernatural experience always involves (though in this its deepest content often especially obscurely) the reality, indeed some dim sense of God. Qualities, such as reality, transcendence, presence, existence—these are not apprehended as abstractions floating in the air, or fancied in the mind ; such qualities, or the impressions of such qualities are, however confusedly, however unuttered even to itself by the apprehending mind, felt and loved as effects and constituents of a Reality distinct from the apprehender, and yet a Reality sufficiently like the human spirit, when thus supernaturally sustained and sublimated, to be recognised by this human spirit with rapt, joyous adoration as its living source, support and end. True, Judaism and indeed also Mohammedanism meet this experience by a doctrine truly appropriate. We are now coming clearly to discern traces of such a faith also in the earlier Parseeism and in primitive Hinduism. Yet it remains a fact that, given the truth of Theism, Christianity brings to this truth a depth of roots, a breadth of inclusions and utilisations, and a penetrative delicacy of applications matched only very partially and sporadically elsewhere. For in Christianity its faith in God is the culmination and resolution of the other four convictions and tensions—of the belief in the natural-supernatural character of human experience as a whole ; of the insight into the social-solitary quality of all religion ; of the apprehension that the supernatural endowment is very unequal amongst men, and that there exists one supremely rich, uniquely intimate union with God, in one particular human mind and will; and of the experience that an element of Suffering enters into every Serenity. Thus everything beautiful, true and good, of whatever degree or kind, is indeed included within Christian Theism, but it is included therein according to certain very definite principles; the whole is thus not a guess or a jumble, a fog or a quicksand; it is a certainty as rock-firm as it is rich and elastic, a certainty groped after and confirmed by all that is virile, pure, humble, truthful, tender, self-immolating and deeply joyous in the depths of man's longings and attempts. Perhaps the most exquisite of all the sceptical minds I have personally known was wont, in his deeper moods, always to end by admitting with me the substantial unanswerableness of the argument that, if man did not somehow have a real experience of objective reality and truth, he—a creature apparently so contingent and subjective through and through—could never, as man actually does in precise proportion to the nobility of his mind, suffer so much from the very suspicion of a complete imprisonment within purely human apprehensions and values. It is precisely this ineradicable sense of and thirst after Reality which, already deeply met by any and every supernatural act or disposition, is developed to the utmost by Christianity with its immense richness of subjective moods and needs, all taken as effects of realities great or little, as helps from the real God, or as, because out of harmony with the reality of things, obstacles to union with the same Divine Reality.

I take the above five intimations to complete the direct content of the Supernatural, as generally experienced by man here below. Nevertheless, any considerable experience of this content, as analysed even apart from any definite Christianity, readily leads to, and furnishes most solid grounds for, belief in Personal Immortality. Such belief is unchangeably part and parcel of all fully-developed Theism and especially of Christianity. Yet the fully wholesome foundation for my belief in my survival is God and my need of a future life as the alone adequate environment and condition for the full and habitual exercise of that Supernatural life which here below I can live only amidst so much that hampers it, and which nevertheless, even already here and now, alone gives true worth and significance to whatever is nobly human either in others or in myself.

Two little anecdotes and I have done. When Frederick William Faber, the Roman Catholic hymn writer and spiritual teacher, was lingering on in a tedious last illness, he asked whether he might receive the Last Sacraments once again. But the doctor declared that this was really the same illness as that in which he had already received them, hence the Superior had to refuse the sick man's request. " Well, if I cannot have the Last Sacraments, give me Pickwick ! " exclaimed Faber. A good homely example of the Supernatural and the Natural, and of how well they can co-exist in the same, in a thoroughly fervent, soul.

When my eldest daughter, some eight months before her own death, succeeding in reaching from Rome the centre of the terrible devastation just then caused (December, 1914) by a specially violent earthquake in the Roman Campagna, she promptly had her observation riveted by a most striking contrast. There lay before her the wreckage and the ruin, the apparently blind and stupid carnage inflicted upon sentient, homely mortals by sheer physical forces, gas and fire ; and terrified villagers merely added to the cruel confusion. And in the midst of all this death and destruction moved about, completely absorbed in the fate of these lowly peasants, Don Orione, a Secular Priest, a man looked upon by many as already a saint from and for the humble and the poor. He was carrying two infants, one in each arm, and wheresoever he moved he brought order and hope and faith into all that confusion and despair. She told me that it made them all feel that somehow Love was at the ultimate bottom of all things, a Love which was, just then and there, expressing itself through the utterly self-oblivious tenderness of this lowly priest. I dwell upon this cleric because, in his long and large labours amidst young people in Rome, he was never happy, as he himself told my daughter, until (in, say, nine cases out of ten) the young man was honourably in love with a pure young woman and until the young woman was honourably engaged to a steady young man. Here again, then, we have the union of the heroic with the homely, the genial loftiness of Christ—Asceticism without Rigorism and Love without Sentimentality. The Supernatural thus proves richly hospitable ; there is indeed no expansion, no leisurely happiness, no joy comparable to that of a life completely docile to the God of Nature and of Super-nature. The comfortableness I hoped to find for you has thus, I believe, been really found.

INDEX

I.—OF PERSONS, PLACES AND DOCUMENTS

L

Ward, James :
  on Concrete and Abstract Time, 69, 70;
  on Analytic and Genetic Method of
    Research, 140, 141
Ward, Wilfrid, *Life and Letters of
  Cardinal Newman* (1912), 267
Ward, William George, " Ideal " :
  his excessive expressions, 172 ;
  distinguishes, in Supernatural Acts,
    between their implications and their
    express references, 280
Webb, Clement C. J., on Revelation,
  55, 56

Wellhausen, Julius :
  on Moses, 73 ;
  on Elijah, 74 ;
  on the Prophets, as " storm-birds," 74
Wernle, Paul, *Die Synoptische Frage*
  (1899), 263
Wette, W. M. L. de, 151
White, Andrew, *History of the Warfare
  of Science and Theology* (1903), 59
Windelband, Wilhelm, on Transsubjective Worlds of Æsthetics, Diano-
  ëtics and Ethics, 53
Wyclif, 251

II.—OF SUBJECT MATTERS

ABERRATIONS, three :
  below level of Natural Human Acts,
    9, 11 ;
  and three, above this level, 11
Abiding Consequences :
  indissolubly part of teaching of Jesus,
    xi. ; 210, 211 ;
  absent in every Pantheism, 220
Abraham's Bosom, 136, 137
Abstract Ideas, alone quite clear and
  readily transferable, 100, 101
Accessions, the Religious, 94, 95
Adoration, essential to Religion, 90, 91
Affirmations :
  the four great, of Religion :
    Revelation and Miracle, Creation
      and Personality, 42, 48 ;
    Creation, 48, 49 ;
    Personality, 49, 50 ;
    Revelation, 55-57 ;
    Miracle, 57, 58 ;
  of real existence, the appropriate tests
    for, 100-5
Agnosticism, Philosophical, an artificial
  system, 71, 72
Analytic and Genetic Methods of Research contrasted, 140-42
Anthropocentrism, costliness of change
  from, to Theocentrism, 12, 13
Anthropomorphisms, Religion well
  aware of its, 38-41

BAPTISM, difficulty as to Infant, how
  wisely met, 203, 204
" Beloved Community," the, 275
Buddhism :
  the Wheel of Life and *Nirvana*,
    together, the substance of, 89 ;
  in contrast with Christianity, 213

CATACLYSMS, the three, foretold by
  Jesus, 122
Catholic, the Christian consciousness
  from first essentially, according to
  Rudolf Sohm, 274, 275

Catholicism :
  concerning Essentials of, 227-41 ;
  the three elements of, which make
    for inclusiveness, 233-35 ;
  the three qualities specially needed
    in, at present day, 238-41 ;
  and Protestantism, the Convictions
    Common to, 246-48 ;
  further convictions in process of be-
    coming common to, and Protes-
    tantism, 248-53 ;
  duty of, to welcome every religious
    light and grace manifesting itself
    outside its visible bounds, 233 ;
  the eight great successive develop-
    ments of, 244, 245 ;
  in New Testament, 262-64 ;
  and Roman claims, 262-65, 275,
    276 ;
  and Extreme Curialism, 228-32
Catholicism, Mediæval :
  Troeltsch on, 174-77 ;
  contrast between Ancient Christian
    positions and, 175-77
Celibacy of the Clergy, 232 ;
  at its best, profoundly efficacious,
    285-87 ;
  Schopenhauer upon its abolition by
    Protestant Reformers, 285, 286 ;
  the Central Christian Figures, Volun-
    tary Celibates, 286, 287
Children, education of, what matters
  supremely in, 106-8
Choice, the Liberty of, an imperfect
  kind of Liberty, 17
Christian Religion, sketch of its history,
  80-89
Christocentrism, excessive, caricatures
  the true temper of Jesus, 135, 136
Church :
  abiding need of, three great groups
    of proofs for, 259-65 ;
  fact and name of, in New Testament,
    260-62 ;

INDEX

Good faith present and absent in souls, contrary to all human expectation or appearance, 3–5

HELL :
the prevalent rejection of every kind of, 205, 206 ;
yet some doctrine of Abiding Consequences essential to the deepest, the Christian, outlook, 206–13 ;
two excesses to be guarded against, 213–15 ;
Synoptic Gospels on, 209–11 ;
St. Paul and Final Restitution of All Things, 211, 212 ;
Origen does not deny, 206, 211 ;
essence of, lies, above all, in its Unendingness, 221
Heroic, the, and the Homely, both furnish occasions and materials for either Natural or Supernatural Acts and States, 284
Historical Religions, their " mere details," 92
History, sense of, its recentness and importance, and affinity between Christianity and, xvi., 270–74
Human acts and lives :
the three instincts which lie below level of specifically, 8, 9 ;
and the instincts which lie above same level, 11, 12
Humility, examples of Supernatural, 288

IMMANENTISM, its present prevalence and abiding insufficiency, 90, 91
Immortality :
Religion cares only for, of a certain kind, 196 ;
religiously valuable belief in, proceeded from faith in God, 197 ;
personal, not directly intimated by Supernatural Acts and States, 296, 297
Impartiality, not Neutrality, wanted in study of the Religions, 7
Importance of more or of less of insight, apart from all questions of responsibility, 5–7
Incarnation, the, involved Incarnation in some particular human nature, 125, 126
Inclusiveness, need of practice of, by religious men, 63
Instincts, transformation of predominantly animal, into moral and spiritual energisings and habits, 154
Institutional Christianity, 254–77 ;
the five substitutes attempted for it, purely or in combinations, 255, 256 ;

how it has lost its immense popularity, 256–59
Institutional Element of Religion :
its presence and importance in every religious life, 13–16, 92, 93 ;
in Our Lord, St. Paul, St. Francis, William Law, 14 ;
in George Fox and other Quakers, 14, 15 ;
difficulty of, 59–61 ;
requires careful, costly cultivation, 15, 16
Invincible Ignorance, range of, 3, 4 ; 221–23
Israelitish-Jewish Religion, sketch of its history, 72–80

JOY :
Perfect Religion involves,18 ; 290,291 ;
no formal Roman canonisation in absence of, 18 ;
examples of Supernatural, 290, 291

KINGDOM of Heaven, the :
original doctrine of, was permeated with *Parousia* expectations, 127–29 ;
what it is in preaching of Jesus, 158 ;
and the Church, 260–64

LAYMEN in Church, large place assigned by Providence to, 233
Liberty, Perfect and Imperfect, their difference, 16, 17, 221
Limbo—a state of Natural Happiness in the Beyond, 203–5

MAGIC, excessive fear of, amongst Protestants ; where Magic begins, 251
Man :
his double constitution, 169 ;
always stands after God, in teaching of Jesus, 157, 158
Manichæism :
in Augustine's life, 86 ;
how to avoid, in doctrine of Abiding Consequences, 214
Middle Age, the Golden :
its characteristic outlook, 174–76 ;
practically unknown to Protestant Reformers and their Renaissance Catholic Contemporaries, 250 ;
its difference from Late Middle Age, 282
Millennarianism :
its various forms, 136, 137 ;
its tough vitality but serious inadequacy, 136–40
Miracle :
its essence, 57, 58 ;
and the Supernatural, 279
Mohammedanism, 89, 90
Monolatry, 73, 74